USING THE TYPEFINDER

Method 1: By Category

1. Choose the main category of typeface.
2. Using the thumb index (see right) turn to the beginning of your category.
3. From the characteristics list at the beginning of the category, select the specific group within your category or browse the entire category.
4. Turn to the specimen numbers listed, and select the style that best suits the work.

Method 2: By Earmark

1. In trying to either match or choose a typeface based on the style of particular characters, consult the recommended order for selecting letters (see p. 97 bottom right). Then select the letters you wish to consider.
2. Look through the *Common Earmark Tables* (see p. 98–106) to see if the letters chosen have 'common earmarks.' If they have, choose other letters.
3. Find the letter in the *Special Earmark Tables*.
4. Look through the illustrated specimen letters and match your typeface with the 'earmarks' or choose a typeface which has the earmarks, i.e. style, you desire.
5. When a match or selection has been made on one or more letters, look up the typeface specimen from the numbers listed just below the letter.

Method 3: By Index

1. With the typeface name, look up the name in the index (see p. 276).
2. Refer to the typeface specimen line listed. The book has specimens for 700 typefaces, but there may be more than one name for the same face. The index has cross-referenced almost 2000 typefaces. For typefaces which have no specimen line number, you must look to the cross-referenced faces for a specimen line number listing.
3. If the typeface is not listed, use the 'earmark method' if you have a sample of the typeface. Since the advent of PCs and DTP, the proliferation of typefaces has been geometric.

SLOPING E-BAR
(VENETIAN SERIF)
e
ANGLED STRESS
OBLIQUE SERIFS
(OLD STYLE SERIF)
od
VERTICAL STRESS
OBLIQUE SERIFS
(TRANSITIONAL SERIF)
od
VERTICAL STRESS
STRAIGHT SERIFS
(NEW TRANSITIONAL)
od
ABRUPT CONTRAST
STRAIGHT SERIFS
(MODERN SERIF)
od
SLAB SERIF
II
WEDGE SERIF
(HYBRID SERIF)
II
SANS SERIF
GG

FLOWING
SCRIPTS
Scr
NON-FLOWING
SCRIPTS
(INCLUDING
BLACKLETTER & UNCIAL)
Scr
UNMODIFIED
(FORMAL TEXT SHAPE)
UN
FAT FACE
& THIN FACE
(UNMODIFIED & MODIFIED)
FT
ORNAMENTAL
OR
MODIFIED
SERIF
MS
MODIFIED
SANS SERIF
MSS
MODIFIED
OUTRAGEOUS
MO

Rookledge's International TYPE *finder.*

The Essential Handbook of Typeface Recognition and Selection

by Christopher Perfect and Gordon Rookledge

Revised Edition with a Preface by Adrian Frutiger and Biographical Notes on Leading Type Designers.

MOYER BELL LIMITED

Mount Kisco, New York & London

Imprint

Published by Moyer Bell Limited

Original design and artwork by the Perfect Design Company Limited, London. New designs by Phil Baines, artwork by Gavin Martin Limited. Biographical notes by Sarah Rookledge. Historical introductions and new typefaces compilation by Phil Baines. New typesetting by FMT Graphics Ltd., London and Capital City Press, Montpelier, VT. New typeface specimens supplied by Linotype-Paul Limited and The Monotype Corporation. The cover design is by Suzanne Lobel of the Madkat Studio, New York, NY.

**LIBRARY OF CONGRESS
CATALOGING-IN-PUBLICATION DATA**

Perfect, Christopher.
Rookledge's international typefinder : the essential handbook of typeface recognition and selection / Christopher Perfect and Gordon Rookledge—New Edition

p. cm.

Includes index and bibliographic references ISBN 1-55921-052-4 (pbk.)
1. Printing—Specimens—Handbooks, manuals, etc. 2. Type and type-founding—Handbooks, manuals, etc. I. Rookledge, Gordon. II. Title.

Z250.P42 1991
686.2'24—dc20 90-22983
CIP

Printed in the United States of America
Distributed by Rizzoli International Publications

Acknowledgments to the first edition

We are indebted to the principal collaborators who helped formulate the content of this book: Eiichi Kono MA (RCA) MSTD and Alfred Lubran FRSA. Without their considerable efforts and skill its publication would not have been possible.

Our thanks are also due to the staff of The Perfect Design Company Limited, especially Fiona Barton and Matthew Kirby, as well as Leslie Carvalho and Andrew Bennett for their painstaking skills in the preparation of the artwork; to the staff of Gavin Martin Limited and Brian Thompson for print production; to Mel Hobbs and his staff at Text Filmsetters for supplying a large percentage of the typeface specimens and for getting the most out of a Linotron 202 typesetting machine.

Also to the following companies and individuals who supplied typeface specimens and information: Alphabet Limited, Apex Typesetting Limited, Apex Photosetting Limited, H. Berthold AG, Character Photosetting Limited, Diagraphic Typesetters Limited, Face Ronchetti Limited, Filmcomposition, Linotype-Paul Limited, Margaret Calvert, The Monotype Corporation, Pinnacle Phototype Limited and Stempel Haas.

Christopher Perfect
Gordon Rookledge
1983

To Jennie, Sarah, Gavin and Emma for all their patience and understanding over the years. (G.R.)

For my wife, Tessa. (C.P.)

CONTENTS

Preface to the first edition by Herbert Spencer RDI Dr RCA

As with other inspired innovations – such as the safety pin, the paper clip, the zip-fastener, and the ball-point pen – now that *Rookledge's International Typefinder* is here one wonders how it was possible to function for so long without it. Though it may lack the universal significance of some of the other innovations I mentioned, for the graphic designer and typographer this publication is without doubt a real milestone.

Fundamental changes in printing technology and the rapid development of alternative media for distributing ideas and information during the past twenty-five years have released a torrent of new type designs – some good, a few excellent, and, inevitably, many bad.

This book will be used, first, as an invaluable working tool enabling the designer quickly to identify and to select particular typefaces for his immediate purposes. However, for the student this publication will serve another – and, in the long term, perhaps an even more important – function: by highlighting and indicating the essential characteristics of each typeface shown it will *educate* the user to distinguish between good and bad designs, between sound and sloppy solutions, between the imaginative and the merely perverse – in fact, to separate the grain from the chaff. And for that the publisher and editor will deserve the gratitude of all readers as well as of all designers.

This typefinder, then, is a publication of major importance. The task of assembling and arranging the enormous number of specimens it contains must have been a daunting one. It was Gordon Rookledge who recognised the need for such a book and it is due to his enthusiasm, persistence and tenacity that the idea has become a reality. Christopher Perfect has worked with exceptional editorial dedication and design skill to define and evolve the original concept for this book, and, in collaboration with Eiichi Kono, to bring the project to fruition. Both of them, publisher and editor, are to be congratulated on having fashioned not just a tool but a powerful weapon in the fight for better, more effective, typography.

Introduction to the first edition

The recognition and selection of typefaces is a regular everyday task for the practising graphic designer and typographer. Yet, up until now, no single reference source has been available to assist in these processes. This book has been produced especially to fill this gap, serving as an invaluable working tool for everyone who works with type.

It is the editor's experience that other than expert or highly-experienced typographers, the majority of creative people have difficulty in recognising and identifying individual typefaces. Therefore, the primary purpose of the book is to satisfy this need and simplify this essential task as fully as possible.

A secondary purpose is to help in the process of typeface selection. The graphic designer often has difficulty in obtaining good, comprehensive reference material despite an abundance of typefounders' and typesetters' catalogues. It is the aim of this book to make this job easier and to contribute to the educational experience in the process.

This book is divided into two parts, *Text* and *Decorative* (non-continuous text) typefaces. The classification system used in each part is entirely new and does not follow previous established type classifications. The typefaces selected were all available at the time of compilation of the book and all the major international typefounders' current lists were consulted so as to make the choice as comprehensive as possible. Readers should note that 'bastard' versions of well-known typefaces have not been included but are cross-referenced in the index. The possible number of *Decorative* typefaces is endless so, with limited space, selection has been confined to a cross-section of the more commonly-used designs. (NB. It is not the purpose of this book to act as a complete typeface dictionary or specimen book.)

The listing of *Text* typefaces are all, as far as possible, in the normal weight of type for text setting (i.e. regular roman). It was not the editor's intention to include the many other variations of one typeface family (e.g. light, bold, italic, condensed etc.) as it is the regular weight which is most commonly used and which establishes the 'style' characteristics of a particular typeface. In order to obtain information on the range of different weights and variations of a typeface it is suggested that readers should consult their own typesetters.

Whilst the selection and compilation of the typefaces in this book were carried out with great care some may have been omitted which readers feel should be included. Your suggestions, submitted through the publisher, will be welcome.

Christopher Perfect
Gordon Rookledge

PREFACE
By Adrian Frutiger

The capital letters of our alphabet are already 2000 years old. Their basic forms were carved into triumphal monuments by the stone-masons of Ancient Rome. Our lower-case letters have not fundamentally changed for 1000 years, since monastic scribes first began to form words in the Carolingian miniscule script, rounding off the letters with flowing penmanship.

Letter-forms, whether carved, handwritten or printed, have always reflected the spirit of their times, being constantly renewed by individual scribes and typefounders, and not least by the techniques of typesetting and printing.

During recent decades, the advent of phototypesetting and rub-off lettering has brought a vast increase in the number of new typefaces. These resources contain both the best and the worst of type and their multitude can be bewildering to the user. To clarify the matter, this mass of typefaces has repeatedly been classified according to historical periods, styles or typesetting techniques. Nowadays, such simple classifications are no longer sufficient, owing to the large number of variations, often unhelpful, of individual letter-forms.

Publication of the typefinder has brought a completely new aid to the world of typography. For the first time, it provides a logical grouping of all existing alphabets, together with clear descriptions of individual letters. The tangle of typefaces has been combed out so as to produce new divisions and classifications of alphabets that were previously jumbled together in piles of heavy specimen books.

For the creative typographer, whose job is to present words to the reader in a correct and completely legible form, the present work is a completely new aid, enabling him to appreciate typefaces in a new dimension and dress the printed message in the right clothing.

Modern reproduction techniques have not made it any easier to deal with type. Specification of the page image is increasingly falling into the hands of untrained people. We hope that the present reference book will be distributed beyond the strictly professional community to reach the uninitiated user of type and serve as an aid to decision-making. In this sense I see the new, enlarged edition of the typefinder as the clearest guide, with the very worthy task of preserving the authenticity of the printed word.

The authors and publisher of this authoritative work have earned the gratitude of the entire graphic world, and indirectly of the reading public as a whole. I hope that it will be accepted as a world standard.

Adrian Frutiger

INTRODUCTION

It is seven years since Rookledge's International typefinder was first published as a single reference work for the correct identification of typefaces. During this time it has proved an invaluable tool for everyone who works with type. For this new edition the opportunity has been taken to expand the scope of the book as well as correct a few minor errors in the original.

The three main parts of the original typefinder have been retained. They are as follows:

1. An at-a-glance guide to typeface classification, with a substantial typeface catalogue grouped according to eight classifications for comparative study.
2. Letter-by-letter recognition (earmark) tables with cross-references to the typeface catalogue.
3. A fully cross-referenced index, bibliography and notes for further reading.

The original typefinder leads the user to the correct identification of a typeface specimen by a process of visual inspection and elimination. The first step in the process is the fitting of the face into one of eight basic categories, using the classification guide. This edition keeps this successful method but prefaces each category with an introduction examining the historical background to each category of typeface design.

The first edition contained 700 typefaces, this new edition updates these with the addition of selected faces released since that date.

The final new feature for this edition is an eight page section devoted to some of the leading people behind the typefaces. Alphabetically arranged, it provides biographical notes on over fifty type designers from Gutenberg to the present day. Entries are cross-referenced to the typefaces included in the typefinder. This section of the typefinder is an abridged list from Rookledge's International Handbook of Type Designers, to be published by Sarema Press later this year (1990).

Whilst the selection and compilation of the typefaces in this book were carried out with great care some may have been omitted which readers feel should be included. Your suggestions, submitted through the publisher, will be welcome.

Phil Baines
Gordon Rookledge

pt. I:

text

typefaces

TEXT TYPEFACE CATEGORIES

THIS PART OF the book contains typefaces which are commonly used for continuous text setting. The characteristic features of each of the eight typeface categories are described below and are illustrated on the opposite page.

The classification system used in this book is entirely new and is based on the grouping of typefaces according to specific design features. This will sometimes mean that typefaces of a similar historical origin fall into different categories. This book, therefore, does not follow established classifications such as the British Standards Typeface Nomenclature and Classification System (BS 2961). (NB. a comparison to this can be found in the Appendix at the back of the book.)

Each category is further divided into smaller groups according to more specific design features which are explained at the beginning of each section. Typeface specimens are then arranged alphabetically within each group and have an individual specimen number which is cross-referenced to both the index and 'Earmark' Tables starting on p. 97.

NB. There is a small overlap between the *Text* and *Decorative* parts of the book. For instance, some *Decorative* typefaces in special circumstances may be used for continuous text setting and vice-versa.

Categories 1 to 5 are all variations of the roman serif design and begin with:

1. Sloping e-Bar (Venetian Serif). *Nos. 1-34*

Typefaces in this category all have a sloping bar on the lower case e. All roman serif typefaces with this feature, *plus those which have slab or wedge serif characteristics*, will be found here. Generally, these typefaces are of a heavy appearance and have poor contrast between thick and thin strokes. They usually have oblique ascender serifs.

2. Angled Stress/Oblique Serifs (Old Style Serif) *Nos. 35-53*

Typefaces in this group are characterised by an angled stress on the bowls of letters (e.g. the lower case o) and have oblique serifs on the ascenders of lower case letters. The foot serif on the lower case d is also oblique. There is a stronger contrast between the thick and thin strokes of letters than in Category 1.

3. Vertical Stress/Oblique Serifs (Transitional Serif) *Nos. 54-110*

Typefaces in this category have vertical stress (or nearly so) on the bowls of letters (such as the lower case o) but still have distinct oblique serifs on the ascenders. The serif foot of the lower case d is usually horizontal but sometimes slightly oblique. The contrast between the thick and thin strokes of letters is generally more pronounced than in Category 2. All typefaces have bracketed serifs.

4. Vertical Stress/Straight Serifs (New Transitional Serif) *Nos. 111-150*

All typefaces in this group have a definite vertical stress and serifs are normally all horizontal (straight). However, a small number have slightly oblique serifs. These typefaces generally have little contrast between the thick and thin strokes and the serifs are usually bracketed.

5. Abrupt Contrast/Straight Serifs (Modern Serif) *Nos. 151-187*

These typefaces feature a strong and abrupt contrast between the thick and thin strokes of letters and all serifs are horizontal (straight). The overall stress is clearly vertical. Serifs can be line (unbracketed) or slightly bracketed and typefaces can vary in colour from light to black face.

6. Slab Serif. *Nos. 188-217*

These typefaces are characterised by a generally heavy appearance with thick 'slab' serifs often the same thickness as the main stem of the letters. Serifs can be square (unbracketed) or bracketed. *(NB. Slab serif style typefaces with a sloping bar on the lower case e will be found in Category 1.)*

7. Wedge Serif (Hybrid Serif). *Nos. 218-240*

This category contains typefaces which are not always clearly serif or sans serif (i.e. hybrids). It includes typefaces both of a general serif-style but with only a thickening at the terminals of letters and sans serif-style typefaces with very small line serifs on the terminals. It includes other groups with wedge-shaped serifs and half serifs. *(NB. Wedge serif-style typefaces with a sloping bar on the lower case e are to be found in Category 1.)*

8. Sans Serif. *Nos. 245-304*

Typefaces with no serifs. Generally, with little or no difference between strokes (i.e. monoline.) These typefaces are primarily divided according to whether the capital G has a spur or not and if it has, whether it is of a wide, medium or narrow design. The category also includes groups of typefaces of a special shape (such as rounded).

The Typefinding Process

1. To identify a typeface, first decide into which of the main categories shown opposite the typeface specimen you wish to identify belongs.

2. By using the thumb index on the edge of the page turn to the appropriate category introduction page.

3. From the 'contents' list given there select the specific group within the category to which your specimen relates.

4. Read off the specimen numbers given for this group and find them in the following listings of typeface specimens.

5. Decide which of the typefaces in the group it equates to with the help of asterisks which show letters with special or 'style' characteristics.

Text Typeface 'Earmark' Tables

These will be found at the end of this part of the book, beginning on p. 97, and offer an alternative but companion method of identifying *Text* typefaces by comparing to 'earmarks' or features on individual letters. The tables are divided into two parts, 'Common' and 'Special Earmarks', and letters are arranged in a continuous sequence from a to z in both capital and lower case forms (plus ampersand and figures.)

Type categories	*General characteristics*					
1. Sloping e-Bar (Venetian Serif) *Nos 1-34* e.g. **6** Kennerley, **19** Centaur, **30** ITC Souvenir, and **32** Italian Old Style (Monotype).	*little contrast*	*e-bar sloped*	*angled or vertical stress*	*oblique ascender serif (not always)*	*foot serif often oblique (not always)*	*oblique lower case serif (not always)*
2. Angled Stress/Oblique Serifs (Old Style Serif) *Nos 35-53* e.g. **35** Bembo, **39** Plantin, **44** Trump Mediaeval and **53** Times New Roman (Monotype).	*medium contrast*	*e-bar horizontal*	*angled stress*	*oblique ascender serif*	*oblique foot serif*	*oblique lower case serif*
3. Vertical Stress/Oblique Serifs (Transitional Serif) *Nos 54-110* e.g. **61** Caslon 540, **78** Baskerville 169 (Monotype), **92** Garamond (Stempel) and **105** Romulus.	*good contrast*	*e-bar horizontal*	*stress vertical (or nearly so)*	*oblique serifs*	*foot serif usually level (not always)*	*oblique lower case serif*
4. Vertical Stress/Straight Serifs (New Transitional Serif) *Nos. 151-187* e.g. **111** Joanna, **119** Century Schoolbook, **123** Cheltenham, and **138** Melior.	*little contrast*	*e-bar horizontal*	*vertical stress*		*straight serifs (some slightly oblique)*	*straight serif in lower case (some oblique)*
5. Abrupt Contrast/Straight Serifs (Modern Serif) *Nos 151-187* e.g. **153** Bauer Bodoni, **161** Walbaum (Linotype), **174** Caledonia and **185** Scotch Roman.	*abrupt contrast*	*e-bar horizontal*	*vertical stress*	*line or bracketed serifs*	*straight serifs*	*straight serifs*
6. Slab Serif *Nos 188-217* e.g. **197** Rockwell, **203** Schadow Antiqua, **209** Clarendon (Linotype), and **214** ITC American Typewriter.	*little or no contrast*	*square slab serifs* — *single storey*, *double storey*		*bracketed serifs* — *single storey*, *double storey*		*rounded serif*
7. Wedge Serif (Hybrid Serif) *Nos 218-240* e.g. **218** Albertus, **233** Meridien, **236** Copperplate Gothic and **240** Romic.	*poor contrast*	*wedge-ended serifs*	*wedge-shaped serifs*		*fine line terminals*	*half serif only*
8. Sans Serif *Nos 245-304* e.g. **254** Futura, **259** Gill Sans, **267** Univers 55 and **279** Helvetica.	*little or no contrast*	*wide* / *medium* / *narrow* — *no spur*		*wide* / *medium* / *narrow* — *spur*		*special shape (rounded)*

I. SLOPING e-BAR
(Venetian Serif) Nos I-34

Typefaces in this category all have a sloping bar on the lower case e. All roman serif typefaces with this feature, *plus those which have slab or wedge characteristics*, will be found here. Generally, these typefaces are of a heavy appearance and have poor contrast between thick and thin strokes. They usually have oblique ascender serifs.

When printing from moveable metal type was first perfected by Gutenberg and his partners in Mainz, Germany, in 1455, the letterforms they used were of course those of the middle ages, a heavy black script called textura. German printers moved to Italy, the centre of the Renaissance, and within ten years a new style of type appeared which became known as *roman*. Although imperfect, it was the type of a new age.

Venice became the centre of fine printing and it was there that the Frenchman Nicholas
16 Jenson designed and cut his famous type in about 1470. The letters have a calligraphic
(oblique) stress but the change from thick to thin strokes is gradual whilst the serifs are
strong and steeply sloped. The most obvious characteristic is the sloping bar to the lower
case e.

A generation later, the types of Manutius ousted Jenson's which were then largely ignored by all but a few experts for four centuries. When William Morris, the leader of the Arts and Crafts movement, turned his attention to typography it was to Jenson that he looked for inspiration. His Golden type of 1892 was based on Jenson's type of 1470.

In this century there have been several notable revivals such as E. F. Detterer's Eusebius
19 (for Ludlow) and Bruce Rodgers' Centaur of 1915 (Monotype 1929).

I. SLOPING e-BAR
(Venetian Serif) Nos I-34

Specimen nos		*Basic characteristics*		*Secondary characteristics*	
I-5	o	*steeply inclined axis on bowls of letters*			e.g. **5** Windsor
6-12	o	*less steeply inclined axis*	q	*short descenders long serifs*	e.g. **7** Lavenham
13	"		q	*short descenders short serifs*	e.g. **13** Della Robbia
14-18	"		q	*longer descenders weak contrast*	e.g. **17** Schneidler Old Style
19-21	"		q	*longer descenders strong contrast*	e.g. **19** Centaur
22-27	o	*vertical axis*	r	*roman serifs*	e.g. **25** Lutetia
28-31	"		r	*wedge serifs*	e.g. **30** ITC Souvenir
32	o	*inclined axis*	d	*roman and slab serifs (mixed)*	e.g. **32** Italian Old Style (Monotype)
33-34	o	*vertical or slightly inclined axis*	d	*slab serifs on ascenders*	e.g. **34** Jenson Old Style

***NB.** Typefaces in each group are arranged in alphabetical order.*

SLOPING E-BAR
(VENETIAN SERIF)

e

Bellini
Erasmus
Hollandse Mediaeval
Pastonchi
Windsor
Kennerley
Lavenham
Raleigh
Surrey Old Style
Trajanus

steeply inclined axis

1 Bellini

ABCDEFGHIJKLMNOPQRSTUVWXYZ&

2 Erasmus

ABCDEFGHIJKLMNOPQRSTUVWXYZ&

3 Hollandse Mediaeval

ABCDEFGHIJKLMNOPQRSTUVWXYZ&

4 Pastonchi

ABCDEFGHIJKLMNOPQRSTUVWXYZ&

5 Windsor

ABCDEFGHIJKLMNOPQRSTUVWXYZ&

less steeply inclined axis

short descenders long serifs

6 Kennerley

ABCDEFGHIJKLMNOPQRSTUVWXYZ&

7 Lavenham

ABCDEFGHIJKLMNOPQRSTUVWXYZ&

8 Raleigh

ABCDEFGHIJKLMNOPQRSTUVWXYZ&

9 Surrey Old Style

ABCDEFGHIJKLMNOPQRSTUVWXYZ&

10 Trajanus

ABCDEFGHIJKLMNOPQRSTUVWXYZ&

** These letters show special or 'style' characteristics. (NB. J, Q, & and g will usually vary from one typeface to another).*

SLOPING E-BAR
(VENETIAN SERIF)
e

Bellini
Erasmus
Hollandse Mediaeval
Pastonchi
Windsor
Kennerley
Lavenham
Raleigh
Surrey Old Style
Trajanus

Bellini **1**

abcdefghijklmnopqrstuvwxyz1234567890

Erasmus **2**

abcdefghijklmnopqrstuvwxyz1234567890

Hollandse Mediaeval **3**

abcdefghijklmnopqrstuvwxyz1234567890

Pastonchi **4**

abcdefghijklmnopqrstuvwxyz1234567890

Windsor **5**

abcdefghijklmnopqrstuvwxyz 1234567890

Kennerley **6**

abcdefghijklmnopqrstuvwxyz1234567890

Lavenham **7**

abcdefghijklmnopqrstuvwxyz1234567890

Raleigh **8**

abcdefghijklmnopqrstuvwxyz1234567890

Surrey Old Style **9**

abcdefghijklmnopqrstuvwxyz1234567890

Trajanus **10**

abcdefghijklmnopqrstuvwxyz1234567890

NB. On lower case letters generally look at the x height and length of ascenders and descenders.

SLOPING E-BAR (VENETIAN SERIF)

- Verona
- Worcester Round
- Della Robbia
- Bauer Text
- Cloister
- Jenson
- Schneidler Old Style
- Seneca
- Centaur
- Horley Old Style

11 Verona

ABCDEFGHIJKLMNOPQRSTUVWXYZ&

12 Worcester Round

ABCDEFGHIJKLMNOPQRSTUVWXYZ&

less steeply inclined axis
short descenders
short serifs

13 Della Robbia

ABCDEFGHIJKLMNOPQRSTUVWXYZ&

less steeply inclined axis
longer descenders
weak contrast

14 Bauer Text

ABCDEFGHIJKLMNOPQRSTUVWXYZ&

15 Cloister

ABCDEFGHIJKLMNOPQRSTUVWXYZ&

16 Jenson

ABCDEFGHIJKLMNOPQRSTUVWXYZ

17 Schneidler Old Style

ABCDEFGHIJKLMNOPQRSTUVWXYZ&

18 Seneca

ABCDEFGHIJKLMNOPQRSTUVWXYZ&

less steeply inclined axis
longer descenders
strong contrast

19 Centaur

ABCDEFGHIJKLMNOPQRSTUVWXYZ&

20 Horley Old Style

ABCDEFGHIJKLMNOPQRSTUVWXYZ&

** These letters show special or 'style' characteristics. (NB. J, Q, & and g will usually vary from one typeface to another).*

SLOPING E-BAR
(VENETIAN SERIF)
e

Verona
Worcester Round
Della Robbia
Bauer Text
Cloister
Jenson
Schneidler Old Style
Seneca
Centaur
Horley Old Style

Verona **11**

abcdefghijklmnopqrstuvwxyz 1234567890

Worcester Round **12**

abcdefghijklmnopqrstuvwxyz1234567890

Della Robbia **13**

abcdefghijklmnopqrstuvwxyz 1234567890

Bauer Text **14**

abcdefghijklmnopqrstuvwxyz1234567890

Cloister **15**

abcdefghijklmnopqrstuvwxyz1234567890

Jenson **16**

abcdefghijklmnopqrstuvwxyz 1234567890

Schneidler Old Style **17**

abcdefghijklmnopqrstuvwxyz1234567890

Seneca **18**

abcdefghijklmnopqrstuvwxyz1234567890

Centaur **19**

abcdefghijklmnopqrstuvwxyz1234567890

Horley Old Style **20**

abcdefghijklmnopqrstuvwxyz1234567890

NB. On lower case letters generally look at the x height and length of ascenders and descenders.

SLOPING E-BAR (VENETIAN SERIF)

Deepdene
Brighton
Clearface Bold 157 (Monotype)
ITC Clearface
Lutetia
Stratford
ITC Tiffany
ITC Benguiat
Seagull
ITC Souvenir

21 Deepdene

ABCDEFGHIJKLMNOPQRSTUVWXYZ&

vertical axis roman serifs

22 Brighton

ABCDEFGHIJKLMNOPQRSTUVWXYZ&

23 Clearface Bold 157 (Monotype)

ABCDEFGHIJKLMNOPQRSTUVWXYZ&

24 ITC Clearface

ABCDEFGHIJKLMNOPQRSTUVWXYZ&

25 Lutetia

ABCDEFGHIJKLMNOPQRSTUVWXYZ&

26 Stratford

ABCDEFGHIJKLMNOPQRSTUVWXYZ&

27 ITC Tiffany

ABCDEFGHIJKLMNOPQRSTUVWXYZ&

vertical axis wedge serifs

28 ITC Benguiat

ABCDEFGHIJKLMNOPQRSTUVWXYZ&

29 Seagull

ABCDEFGHIJKLMNOPQRSTUVWXYZ&

30 ITC Souvenir

ABCDEFGHIJKLMNOPQRSTUVWXYZ&

* *These letters show special or 'style' characteristics. (NB. J, Q, & and g will usually vary from one typeface to another).*

Deepdene **21**

abcdefghijklmnopqrstuvwxyz1234567890

Brighton **22**

abcdefghijklmnopqrstuvwxyz1234567890

Clearface Bold 157 (Monotype) **23**

abcdefghijklmnopqrstuvwxyz1234567890

ITC Clearface **24**

abcdefghijklmnopqrstuvwxyz1234567890

Lutetia **25**

abcdefghijklmnopqrstuvwxyz1234567890

Stratford **26**

abcdefghijklmnopqrstuvwxyz1234567890

ITC Tiffany **27**

abcdefghijklmnopqrstuvwxyz1234567890

ITC Benguiat **28**

abcdefghijklmnopqrstuvwxyz1234567890

Seagull **29**

abcdefghijklmnopqrstuvwxyz1234567890

ITC Souvenir **30**

abcdefghijklmnopqrstuvwxyz1234567890

NB. On lower case letters generally look at the x height and length of ascenders and descenders.

SLOPING E-BAR (VENETIAN SERIF)

e

-OPING E-BAR
ENETIAN SERIF)
e

'endôme
:alian Old Style
Monotype)
TC Italia
enson Old Style
Guardi 55 (Linotype)

31 Vendôme

ABC*DEFGHIJKLMN*OPQRS*T*UVWXYZ&

inclined axis
roman and slab serifs

32 Italian Old Style (Monotype)

ABC*DEFG*HIJKLMNOPQRSTUVWXYZ&

vertical or slightly inclined axis
slab serifs on ascenders

33 ITC Italia

A*BC*DEFG*HIJ*KLMNOPQR*STUVWXYZ&

34 Jenson Old Style

ABCDEFGHIJKLMNOPQRS*TUVWXYZ&

new entry

34A Guardi 55 (Linotype)

ABCDEFGHIJKLMNOPQRS*T*UVWXYZ&

* *These letters show special or 'style' characteristics. (NB. J, Q, & and g will usually vary from one typeface to another).*

Vendôme **31**

abcdefghijklmnopqrstuvwxyz1234567890

Italian Old Style (Monotype) **32**

abcdefghijklmnopqrstuvwxyz1234567890

ITC Italia **33**

abcdefghijklmnopqrstuvwxyz1234567890

Jenson Old Style **34**

abcdefghijklmnopqrstuvwxyz1234567890

Guardi 55 (Linotype) **34A**

abcdefghijklmnopqrstuvwxyz 1234567890

NB. On lower case letters generally look at the x height and length of ascenders and descenders.

SLOPING E-BA
(VENETIAN SERIF
e

Vendôme
Italian Old Style (Monotype
ITC Italia
Jenson Old Style
Guardi 55 (Linotype

2. ANGLED STRESS/OBLIQUE SERIFS
(Old Style Serif) Nos 35-53

Typefaces in this group are characterised by an angled stress on the bowls of letters (e.g. the lower case o) and have oblique serifs on the ascenders of the lower case letters. The foot of the lower case d is also oblique. There is a stronger contrast between the thick and thin strokes of letters than in Category 1.

In 1495 the great Renaissance publisher and printer Aldus Manutius published *Erotomata* using a new set of types which were a development from the earlier *venetian* types of Nicholas Jenson and which became the basic model for European type design for the next two hundred and fifty years. Printers of each generation from Manutius to Caslon used this basic letter form with differences in emphasis only.

The design followed the underlying principles of Jenson's type, a calligraphic stress and oblique serifs and the most obvious difference is a straight cross-bar to the lower case e, but Aldus' type had a better balanced set of capitals and lower case and the fit of the letters together was more even. These factors and Aldus' position as a pioneer of cheap and accurate editions ensured their success.

91-95/96 The design was further refined in France from 1540 onwards by Claude Garamond* and
66 later, Jean Jannon and Robert Granjon. French types were bought by Dutch printers such as
39, 107 Christopher Plantin and Christoffel Van Dijck (who darkened the design a little), and their
types in turn were bought by English printers, notably Dr. Fell of Cambridge. William
59-61/99 Caslon was the first English typefounder to satisfy the home market, and his types (started
in 1725), the last of this category, followed Dutch models.

In this century, the *old style* has enjoyed enormous success following the various
35 'revivals' of designs such as Garamond, Bembo, Granjon, &c. In addition, the most
52/53 successful book typeface yet produced, Stanley Morison's Times New Roman, is a version of
this style.

*The types in the typefinder are arranged for easy recognition and identification first and foremost, thus faces such as Garamond, Van Dijck and Granjon, which academically/historically are *old style*, are included for typefinding purposes in category 3.

A note about italics.
The first italic typeface is usually accepted as that of Aldus Manutius, first used in 1501; mean and cramped it was designed to save space in pocket editions. Other early italics took as their models the cursive formal hand of the Italian writing masters such as Arrighi in Rome and Tagliente in Venice. Although only a lower-case matched with roman capitals the italic was originally used as an independent face. Today it is regarded generally as an accompaniment to a roman and is little used alone.

2. ANGLED STRESS/OBLIQUE SERIFS
(Old Style Serif) Nos 35-53

Specimen nos	Basic characteristics	Secondary characteristics	
35-41	od *angled stress definite oblique serifs (including foot serif)*	W *crossed centre strokes*	e.g. **35** Bembo
42-44	"	W *centre strokes joining at cap height (or nearly so)*	e.g. **44** Trump Mediaeval
45-46	"	W *no centre serif*	e.g. **45** Berling
47-53	"	W *stepped centre strokes*	e.g. **53** Times New Roman

NB. *Typefaces in each group are arranged in alphabetical order.*

ANGLED STRESS
OBLIQUE SERIFS
(OLD STYLE SERIF)
od

ANGLED STRESS OBLIQUE SERIFS (OLD STYLE SERIF)

od

Bembo
Bernhard Modern
Goudy Old Style
News Plantin
Plantin
Poliphilus
Trajon
Leamington
Missal
Trump Mediaeval

capital W with crossed centre strokes

35 Bembo

ABCDEFGHIJKLMNOPQRSTUVWXYZ&

36 Bernhard Modern

ABCDEFGHIJKLMNOPQRSTUVWXYZ&

37 Goudy Old Style

ABCDEFGHIJKLMNOPQRSTUVWXYZ&

38 News Plantin

ABCDEFGHIJKLMNOPQRSTUVWXYZ&

39 Plantin

ABCDEFGHIJKLMNOPQRSTUVWXYZ&

40 Poliphilus

ABCDEFGHIJKLMNOPQRSTUVWXYZ&

41 Trajon

ABCDEFGHIJKLMNOPQRSTUVWXYZ&

capital W with centre strokes joining at cap height (or nearly so)

42 Leamington

ABCDEFGHIJKLMNOPQRSTUVWXYZ&

43 Missal

ABCDEFGHIJKLMNOPQRSTUVWXYZ&

44 Trump Mediaeval

ABCDEFGHIJKLMNOPQRSTUVWXYZ&

** These letters show special or 'style' characteristics. (NB. J, Q, & and g will usually vary from one typeface to another).*

Bembo 35

* * * *
abcdefghijklmnopqrstuvwxyz1234567890

Bernhard Modern 36

* * * *
abcdefghijklmnopqrstuvwxyz1234567890

Goudy Old Style 37

* * *
abcdefghijklmnopqrstuvwxyz1234567890

News Plantin 38

* * * * * * *
abcdefghijklmnopqrstuvwxyz1234567890

Plantin 39

* * * * * * *
abcdefghijklmnopqrstuvwxyz1234567890

Poliphilus 40

* * * * * *
abcdefghijklmnopqrstuvwxyz1234567890

Trajon 41

* * * * * *
abcdefghijklmnopqrstuvwxyz1234567890

Leamington 42

* * * *
abcdefghijklmnopqrstuvwxyz1234567890

Missal 43

* *
abcdefghijklmnopqrstuvwxyz1234567890

Trump Mediaeval 44

* * * * * *
abcdefghijklmnopqrstuvwxyz1234567890

NB. On lower case letters generally look at the x height and length of ascenders and descenders.

od

ANGLED STRESS OBLIQUE SERIFS (OLD STYLE SERIF)

Berling
Nicholas Cochin
Albertina
Emerson
Goudy Catalogue
Life
Minister
Times Roman (Linotype)
Times New Roman (Monotype)
Calisto (Monotype)

capital W with no centre serif

45 Berling

ABCDEFGHIJKLMNOPQRSTUVWXYZ&

46 Nicholas Cochin

ABCDEFGHIJKLMNOPQRSTUVWXYZ&

capital W with stepped centre strokes

47 Albertina

ABCDEFGHIJKLMNOPQRSTUVWXYZ&

48 Emerson

ABCDEFGHIJKLMNOPQRSTUVWXYZ&

49 Goudy Catalogue

ABCDEFGHIJKLMNOPQRSTUVWXYZ&

50 Life

ABCDEFGHIJKLMNOPQRSTUVWXYZ&

51 Minister

ABCDEFGHIJKLMNOPQRSTUVWXYZ&

52 Times Roman (Linotype)

ABCDEFGHIJKLMNOPQRSTUVWXYZ&

53 Times New Roman (Monotype)

ABCDEFGHIJKLMNOPQRSTUVWXYZ&

new entry

53A Calisto (Monotype)

ABCDEFGHIJKLMNOPQRSTUVWXYZ&

** These letters show special or 'style' characteristics. (NB. J, Q, & and g will usually vary from one typeface to another).*

Berling **45**

abcdefghijklmnopqrstuvwxyz1234567890

Nicholas Cochin **46**

abcdefghijklmnopqrstuvwxyz1234567890

Albertina **47**

abcdefghijklmnopqrstuvwxyz1234567890

Emerson **48**

abcdefghijklmnopqrstuvwxyz 1234567890

Goudy Catalogue **49**

abcdefghijklmnopqrstuvwxyz1234567890

Life **50**

abcdefghijklmnopqrstuvwxyz1234567890

Minister **51**

abcdefghijklmnopqrstuvwxyz1234567890

Times Roman (Linotype) **52**

abcdefghijklmnopqrstuvwxyz1234567890

Times New Roman (Monotype) **53**

abcdefghijklmnopqrstuvwxyz1234567890

Calisto (Monotype) **53A**

abcdefghijklmnopqrstuvwxyz1234567890

NB. On lower case letters generally look at the x height and length of ascenders and descenders.

ANGLED STRESS
OBLIQUE SERIFS
(OLD STYLE SERIF)
od

Berling
Nicholas Cochin
Albertina
Emerson
Goudy Catalogue
Life
Minister
Times Roman (Linotype)
Times New Roman (Monotype)
Calisto (Monotype)

3. VERTICAL STRESS/OBLIQUE SERIFS
(Transitional Serif) Nos 54-110

Typefaces in this category have vertical stress (or nearly so) on the bowls of letters (such as the lower case o) but still have distinct oblique serifs on the ascenders. The serif foot of the lower case d is usually horizontal but sometimes slightly oblique. The contrast between the thick and the thin strokes of the letters is generally more pronounced than in category 2. All typefaces have bracketed serifs.

Transitional faces first appeared in England and France in the eighteenth century. The transition implied by the name was from the *old style** with its oblique stress (Jenson, Bembo &c.) to the *modern* faces of Didot and Bodoni with their vertical shading and abrupt contrast between thick and thin strokes.

89/90 The first transitional faces are generally accepted as being Pierre Simon **Fournier**'s roman
77-80 of 1750 and John **Baskerville**'s of 1757, although both were preceded by Phillippe Grandjean's
Romain du Roi of 1702.† With their vertical stress and greater contrast between thick and
thin strokes, all three typefaces marked a definite break from the past.

Baskerville's type and typography (his generous use of space and lack of ornament) was frowned upon in Britain during his lifetime but was very popular and highly influential on the Continent. His roman type is now regarded as the archetypal transitional type and has been an important source of modern designs such as G.W. Jones' **Georgian** of 1925 and
65 Giovanni Mardersteig's **Fontana** of 1936 (Monotype 1961).

*The types in the typefinder are arranged for easy recognition and identification first and foremost, thus faces such as Garamond, Van Dijck and Granjon, which academically/historically are *old style*, are included for typefinding purposes in this category.
†The **Romain du Roi** was cut for the exclusive use of Louis XIV's *Imprimerie Royale* and was supposedly based on a mathematically drawn alphabet.

3. VERTICAL STRESS/OBLIQUE SERIFS
(Transitional Serif) Nos 54-110

Specimen nos	*Basic characteristics*	*Secondary characteristics*		
54-72	W *centre strokes joining at cap height*	M *parallel (or nearly so)*		e.g. **59** Caslon Old Face No 2
73-74	„	M *definitely splayed*		e.g. **73** Ehrhardt
75-86	W *with no centre serif*			e.g. **78** Baskerville 169 (Monotype)
87-88	W *crossed centre strokes*	M *with serifs at cap height*	W *centre strokes joining at cap height*	e.g. **88** Sabon
89	„	„	W *crossed centre strokes*	e.g. **89** Barbou
90-97	„	„	W *centre strokes stepped*	e.g. **91** Garamond 156 (Monotype)
98	„	M *no serifs at cap height*		e.g. **98** Weiss
99-107	W *stepped centre strokes*	M *parallel (or nearly so)*		e.g. **100** Concorde
108-110	„	M *definitely splayed*		e.g. **108** De Roos

***NB.** Typefaces in each group are arranged in alphabetical order.*

VERTICAL STRESS
OBLIQUE SERIFS
(TRANSITIONAL SERIF)
od

capital W with centre strokes joining at cap height (or nearly so)
M parallel (or nearly so)

54 Fry's Baskerville

ABCDEFGHIJKLMNOPQRSTUVWXYZ&

55 Binny Old Style

ABCDEFGHIJKLMNOPQRSTUVWXYZ&

56 Bookman

ABCDEFGHIJKLMNOPQRSTUVWXYZ&

57 ITC Bookman

ABCDEFGHIJKLMNOPQRSTUVWXYZ&

58 Bulmer

ABCDEFGHIJKLMNOPQRSTUVWXYZ&

59 Caslon Old Face No 2

ABCDEFGHIJKLMNOPQRSTUVWXYZ&

60 Caslon 128 (Monotype)

ABCDEFGHIJKLMNOPQRSTUVWXYZ&

61 Caslon 540

ABCDEFGHIJKLMNOPQRSTUVWXYZ&

62 Century Old Style

ABCDEFGHIJKLMNOPQRSTUVWXYZ&

63 Chiswell Old Face

ABCDEFGHIJKLMNOPQRSTUVWXYZ&

** These letters show special or 'style' characteristics. (NB. J, Q, & and g will usually vary from one typeface to another).*

VERTICAL STRESS OBLIQUE SERIFS (TRANSITIONAL SERIF)

od

Fry's Baskerville
Binny Old Style
Bookman
ITC Bookman
Bulmer
Caslon Old Face No 2
Caslon 128 (Monotype)
Caslon 540
Century Old Style
Chiswell Old Face

Fry's Baskerville **54**

*　*　*　*
abcdefghijklmnopqrstuvwxyz1234567890

Binny Old Style **55**

*　*
abcdefghijklmnopqrstuvwxyz1234567890

Bookman **56**

*　*
abcdefghijklmnopqrstuvwxyz1234567890

ITC Bookman **57**

*
abcdefghijklmnopqrstuvwxyz1234567890

Bulmer **58**

*　*　*
abcdefghijklmnopqrstuvwxyz1234567890

Caslon Old Face No 2 **59**

*　*　*　*
abcdefghijklmnopqrstuvwxyz1234567890

Caslon 128 (Monotype) **60**

*　*　*　*
abcdefghijklmnopqrstuvwxyz1234567890

Caslon 540 **61**

*　*　*　*
abcdefghijklmnopqrstuvwxyz1234567890

Century Old Style **62**

*　*　*　*　*
abcdefghijklmnopqrstuvwxyz1234567890

Chiswell Old Face **63**

*　*
abcdefghijklmnopqrstuvwxyz 1234567890

NB. On lower case letters generally look at the x height and length of ascenders and descenders.

VERTICAL STRESS OBLIQUE SERIFS (TRANSITIONAL SERIF)

od

Fry's Baskerville
Binny Old Style
Bookman
ITC Bookman
Bulmer
Caslon Old Face No 2
Caslon 128 (Monotype)
Caslon 540
Century Old Style
Chiswell Old Face

VERTICAL STRESS OBLIQUE SERIFS (TRANSITIONAL SERIF)

od

Concorde Nova
Fontana
Granjon
Imprint
Monticello
Old Style No 2
Old Style No 7
Olympian
Ronaldson
Ehrhardt

64 Concorde Nova

ABCDEFGHIJKLMNOPQRSTUVWXYZ&

65 Fontana

ABCDEFGHIJKLMNOPQRSTUVWXYZ&

66 Granjon

ABCDEFGHIJKLMNOPQRSTUVWXYZ&

67 Imprint

ABCDEFGHIJKLMNOPQRSTUVWXYZ&

68 Monticello

ABCDEFGHIJKLMNOPQRSTUVWXYZ&

69 Old Style No 2

ABCDEFGHIJKLMNOPQRSTUVWXYZ&

70 Old Style No 7

ABCDEFGHIJKLMNOPQRSTUVWXYZ&

71 Olympian

ABCDEFGHIJKLMNOPQRSTUVWXYZ&

72 Ronaldson

ABCDEFGHIJKLMNOPQRSTUVWXYZ&

capital W with centre strokes joining at cap height (or nearly so)
M definitely splayed

73 Ehrhardt

ABCDEFGHIJKLMNOPQRSTUVWXYZ&

* *These letters show special or 'style' characteristics. (NB. J, Q, & and g will usually vary from one typeface to another).*

Concorde Nova **64**

abcdefghijklmnopqrstuvwxyz1234567890

Fontana **65**

abcdefghijklmnopqrstuvwxyz1234567890

Granjon **66**

abcdefghijklmnopqrstuvwxyz1234567890

Imprint **67**

abcdefghijklmnopqrstuvwxyz1234567890

Monticello **68**

abcdefghijklmnopqrstuvwxyz1234567890

Old Style No 2 **69**

abcdefghijklmnopqrstuvwxyz1234567890

Old Style No 7 **70**

abcdefghijklmnopqrstuvwxyz1234567890

Olympian **71**

abcdefghijklmnopqrstuvwxyz1234567890

Ronaldson **72**

abcdefghijklmnopqrstuvwxyz 1234567890

Ehrhardt **73**

abcdefghijklmnopqrstuvwxyz1234567890

NB. On lower case letters generally look at the x height and length of ascenders and descenders.

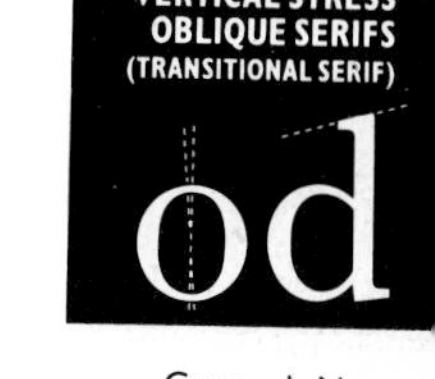
VERTICAL STRESS
OBLIQUE SERIFS
(TRANSITIONAL SERIF)
od

Concorde Nova
Fontana
Granjon
Imprint
Monticello
Old Style No 2
Old Style No 7
Olympian
Ronaldson
Ehrhardt

74 Galliard

ABCDEFGHIJKLMNOPQRSTUVWXYZ&

capital W with no centre serif

75 Aldus

ABCDEFGHIJKLMNOPQRSTUVWXYZ&

76 Aster

ABCDEFGHIJKLMNOPQRSTUVWXYZ&

77 Baskerville (Berthold)

ABCDEFGHIJKLMNOPQRSTUVWXYZ&

78 Baskerville 169 (Monotype)

ABCDEFGHIJKLMNOPQRSTUVWXYZ&

79 Baskerville (Linotype)

ABCDEFGHIJKLMNOPQRSTUVWXYZ&

80 Baskerville No 2

ABCDEFGHIJKLMNOPQRSTUVWXYZ&

81 Cartier

ABCDEFGHIJKLMNOPQRSTUVWXYZ&

82 Congress

ABCDEFGHIJKLMNOPQRSTUVWXYZ&

83 Lectura

ABCDEFGHIJKLMNOPQRSTUVWXYZ&

** These letters show special or 'style' characteristics. (NB. J, Q, & and g will usually vary from one typeface to another).*

VERTICAL STRESS OBLIQUE SERIFS (TRANSITIONAL SERIF)

od

Galliard
Aldus
Aster
Baskerville (Berthold)
Baskerville 169 (Monotype)
Baskerville (Linotype)
Baskerville No. 2
Cartier
Congress
Lectura

Galliard **74**

* * * * * *
abcdefghijklmnopqrstuvwxyz1234567890

Aldus **75**

* * * * * *
abcdefghijklmnopqrstuvwxyz1234567890

Aster **76**

* * * * *
abcdefghijklmnopqrstuvwxyz1234567890

Baskerville (Berthold) **77**

* * * * *
abcdefghijklmnopqrstuvwxyz 1234567890

Baskerville 169 (Monotype) **78**

* * * * *
abcdefghijklmnopqrstuvwxyz1234567890

Baskerville (Linotype) **79**

* * * * *
abcdefghijklmnopqrstuvwxyz1234567890

Baskerville No 2 **80**

* * * *
abcdefghijklmnopqrstuvwxyz1234567890

Cartier **81**

* * *
abcdefghijklmnopqrstuvwxyz1234567890

Congress **82**

* * * *
abcdefghijklmnopqrstuvwxyz1234567890

Lectura **83**

* * * * *
abcdefghijklmnopqrstuvwxyz1234567890

NB. On lower case letters generally look at the x height and length of ascenders and descenders.

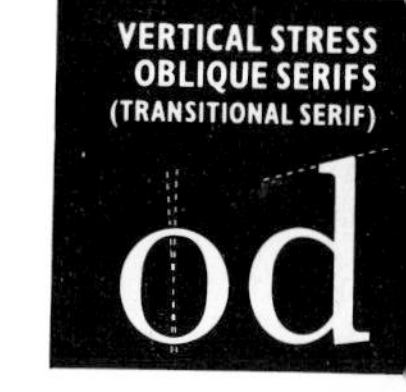
VERTICAL STRESS
OBLIQUE SERIFS
(TRANSITIONAL SERIF)
od

Galliard
Aldus
Aster
Baskerville (Berthold)
Baskerville 169 (Monotype)
Baskerville (Linotype)
Baskerville No. 2
Cartier
Congress
Lectura

VERTICAL STRESS OBLIQUE SERIFS (TRANSITIONAL SERIF)

od

Palatino
Poppl Pontifex
Times Europa
Quadriga Antiqua
Sabon
Barbou
Fournier
Garamond 156 (Monotype)
Garamond (Stempel)
Garamond 3 (Linotype)

84 Palatino

ABCDEFGHIJKLMNOPQRSTUVWXYZ&

85 Poppl Pontifex

ABCDEFGHIJKLMNOPQRSTUVWXYZ&

86 Times Europa

ABCDEFGHIJKLMNOPQRSTUVWXYZ&

capital W with crossed centre strokes
M with serifs at cap height
lower case w with centre strokes joining at cap height

87 Quadriga Antiqua

ABCDEFGHIJKLMNOPQRSTUVWXYZ&

88 Sabon

ABCDEFGHIJKLMNOPQRSTUVWXYZ&

capital W with crossed strokes
M with serifs on tops
lower case w with crossed centre strokes

89 Barbou

ABCDEFGHIJKLMNOPQRSTUVWXYZ&

capital W with crossed centre strokes
M with serifs on tops
lower case w with stepped centre strokes

90 Fournier

ABCDEFGHIJKLMNOPQRSTUVWXYZ&

91 Garamond 156 (Monotype)

ABCDEFGHIJKLMNOPQRSTUVWXYZ&

92 Garamond (Stempel)

ABCDEFGHIJKLMNOPQRSTUVWXYZ&

93 Garamond 3 (Linotype)

ABCDEFGHIJKLMNOPQRSTUVWXYZ&

** These letters show special or 'style' characteristics. (NB. J, Q, & and g will usually vary from one typeface to another).*

Palatino **84**

abcdefghijklmnopqrstuvwxyz1234567890

Poppl Pontifex **85**

abcdefghijklmnopqrstuvwxyz1234567890

Times Europa **86**

abcdefghijklmnopqrstuvwxyz1234567890

Quadriga Antiqua **87**

abcdefghijklmnopqrstuvwxyz1234567890

Sabon **88**

abcdefghijklmnopqrstuvwxyz1234567890

Barbou **89**

abcdefghijklmnopqrstuvwxyz 1234567890

Fournier **90**

abcdefghijklmnopqrstuvwxyz1234567890

Garamond 156 (Monotype) **91**

abcdefghijklmnopqrstuvwxyz1234567890

Garamond (Stempel) **92**

abcdefghijklmnopqrstuvwxyz1234567890

Garamond 3 (Linotype) **93**

abcdefghijklmnopqrstuvwxyz1234567890

NB. On lower case letters generally look at the x height and length of ascenders and descenders.

VERTICAL STRESS OBLIQUE SERIFS (TRANSITIONAL SERIF)

od

Palatino
Poppl Pontifex
Times Europa
Quadriga Antiqua
Sabon
Barbou
Fournier
Garamond 156 (Monotype)
Garamond (Stempel)
Garamond 3 (Linotype)

VERTICAL STRESS OBLIQUE SERIFS (TRANSITIONAL SERIF)

Garamond (Berthold)
ITC Garamond
Garamont (Amsterdam)
Spectrum
Weiss
Caslon 3
Concorde
ITC Cushing
Dante
Gazette

94 Garamond (Berthold)

ABCDEFGHIJKLMNOPQRSTUVWXYZ&

95 ITC Garamond

ABCDEFGHIJKLMNOPQRSTUVWXYZ&

96 Garamont (Amsterdam)

ABCDEFGHIJKLMNOPQRSTUVWXYZ&

97 Spectrum

ABCDEFGHIJKLMNOPQRSTUVWXYZ&

capital W with crossed centre strokes
M with no serifs at cap height

98 Weiss

ABCDEFGHIJKLMNOPQRSTUVWXYZ&

capital W with stepped centre strokes
M parallel (or nearly so)

99 Caslon 3

ABCDEFGHIJKLMNOPQRSTUVWXYZ&

100 Concorde

ABCDEFGHIJKLMNOPQRSTUVWXYZ&

101 ITC Cushing

ABCDEFGHIJKLMNOPQRSTUVWXYZ&

102 Dante

ABCDEFGHIJKLMNOPQRSTUVWXYZ&

103 Gazette

ABCDEFGHIJKLMNOPQRSTUVWXYZ&

** These letters show special or 'style' characteristics. (NB. J, Q, & and g will usually vary from one typeface to another).*

Garamond (Berthold) **94**

* * *
abcdefghijklmnopqrstuvwxyz1234567890

ITC Garamond **95**

* * *
abcdefghijklmnopqrstuvwxyz1234567890

Garamont (Amsterdam) **96**

* * * *
abcdefghijklmnopqrstuvwxyz1234567890

Spectrum **97**

* * *
abcdefghijklmnopqrstuvwxyz1234567890

Weiss **98**

* * * * *
abcdefghijklmnopqrstuvwxyz1234567890

Caslon 3 **99**

* * * *
abcdefghijklmnopqrstuvwxyz1234567890

Concorde **100**

* *
abcdefghijklmnopqrstuvwxyz1234567890

ITC Cushing **101**

* * * * *
abcdefghijklmnopqrstuvwxyz1234567890

Dante **102**

* * * *
abcdefghijklmnopqrstuvwxyz1234567890

Gazette **103**

* * * * * * * * *
abcdefghijklmnopqrstuvwxyz1234567890

NB. On lower case letters generally look at the x height and length of ascenders and descenders.

VERTICAL STRESS OBLIQUE SERIFS (TRANSITIONAL SERIF)

od

Garamond (Berthold)
ITC Garamond
Garamont (Amsterdam)
Spectrum
Weiss
Caslon 3
Concorde
ITC Cushing
Dante
Gazette

104 ITC Isbell

ABCDEFGHIJKLMNOPQRSTUVWXYZ&

105 Romulus

ABCDEFGHIJKLMNOPQRSTUVWXYZ&

106 Rotation

ABCDEFGHIJKLMNOPQRSTUVWXYZ&

107 Van Dijck

ABCDEFGHIJKLMNOPQRSTUVWXYZ&

capital W with stepped centre strokes

M definitely splayed

108 De Roos

ABCDEFGHIJKLMNOPQRSTUVWXYZ&

109 Janson

ABCDEFGHIJKLMNOPQRSTUVWXYZ&

110 Rundfunk

ABCDEFGHIJKLMNOPQRSTUVWXYZ&

** These letters show special or 'style' characteristics. (NB. J, Q, & and g will usually vary from one typeface to another).*

VERTICAL STRESS OBLIQUE SERIFS (TRANSITIONAL SERIF)

ITC Isbell
Romulus
Rotation
Van Dijck
De Roos
Janson
Rundfunk

ITC Isbell **104**

* * * * * *
abcdefghijklmnopqrstuvwxyz1234567890

Romulus **105**

* * * *
abcdefghijklmnopqrstuvwxyz1234567890

Rotation **106**

* * * *
abcdefghijklmnopqrstuvwxyz1234567890

Van Dijck **107**

* * *
abcdefghijklmnopqrstuvwxyz1234567890

De Roos **108**

* * * * * *
abcdefghijklmnopqrstuvwxyz 1234567890

Janson **109**

* *
abcdefghijklmnopqrstuvwxyz1234567890

Rundfunk **110**

* * *
abcdefghijklmnopqrstuvwxyz1234567890

NB. On lower case letters generally look at the x height and length of ascenders and descenders.

VERTICAL STRESS
OBLIQUE SERIFS
(TRANSITIONAL SERIF)

od

ITC Isbell
Romulus
Rotation
Van Dijck
De Roos
Janson
Rundfunk

4. VERTICAL STRESS/STRAIGHT SERIFS
(New Transitional Serif) Nos 111-150

All typefaces in this group* have a definite vertical stress and serifs are normally all horizontal (straight). However, a small number have slightly oblique serifs. These typefaces generally have little contrast between the thick and thin strokes and serifs are usually bracketed.

*These typefaces appear together because of stylistic similarities which will aid identification and recognition. They are nearly all late nineteenth or twentieth century designs which draw on several historical precedents for their inspiration and (with the exception of nos. 118-122: see footnote, p.64) cannot be easily grouped elsewhere.

4. VERTICAL STRESS/STRAIGHT SERIFS
(New Transitional Serif) Nos 111-150

Specimen nos	Basic characteristics	Secondary characteristics		
111-112	rd *horizontal line serifs (or nearly so)*	n *line serifs*		e.g. **111** Joanna
113-117	rd *horizontal bracketed serifs (or nearly so)*	W *centre strokes joining at cap height*	n *light face*	e.g. **117** Primer
118-122	"	"	n *black face*	e.g. **121** Ionic 5
123-127	"	W *crossed centre strokes*		e.g. **123** Cheltenham
128-132	"	W *stepped centre strokes*		e.g. **130** Columbia
133-140	"	W *no centre serif*		e.g. **138** Melior
141-146	rd *some definite oblique bracketed serifs*	n *weak contrast*		e.g. **146** Textype
147-150	"	n *good contrast*		e.g. **147** Cochin

NB. *Typefaces in each group are arranged in alphabetical order.*

VERTICAL STRESS
STRAIGHT SERIFS
(NEW TRANSITIONAL)
od

horizontal line serifs (or nearly so)

111 Joanna

ABCDEFGHIJKLMNOPQRSTUVWXYZ&

112 Maximus

ABCDEFGHIJKLMNOPQRSTUVWXYZ&

horizontal bracketed serifs (or nearly so)
capital W with centre strokes joining at cap height (or nearly so)
light face

113 Breughel 55

ABCDEFGHIJKLMNOPQRSTUVWXYZ&

114 Century Expanded

ABCDEFGHIJKLMNOPQRSTUVWXYZ&

VERTICAL STRESS STRAIGHT SERIFS (NEW TRANSITIONAL)

od

Joanna
Maximus
Breughel 55
Century Expanded
Excelsior
Perpetua
Primer
Aurora
Century Schoolbook
Corona

115 Excelsior

ABCDEFGHIJKLMNOPQRSTUVWXYZ&

116 Perpetua

ABCDEFGHIJKLMNOPQRSTUVWXYZ&

117 Primer

ABCDEFGHIJKLMNOPQRSTUVWXYZ&

horizontal bracketed serifs (or nearly so)
capital W with centre strokes joining at cap height (or nearly so)
black face

118 Aurora

ABCDEFGHIJKLMNOPQRSTUVWXYZ

119 Century Schoolbook

ABCDEFGHIJKLMNOPQRSTUVWXYZ&

120 Corona

ABCDEFGHIJKLMNOPQRSTUVWXYZ&

** These letters show special or 'style' characteristics. (NB. J, Q, & and g will usually vary from one typeface to another).*

Joanna **111**

abcdefghijklmnopqrstuvwxyz1234567890

Maximus **112**

abcdefghijklmnopqrstuvwxyz1234567890

Breughel 55 **113**

abcdefghijklmnopqrstuvwxyz1234567890

Century Expanded **114**

abcdefghijklmnopqrstuvwxyz1234567890

Excelsior **115**

abcdefghijklmnopqrstuvwxyz1234567890

Perpetua **116**

abcdefghijklmnopqrstuvwxyz1234567890

Primer **117**

abcdefghijklmnopqrstuvwxyz1234567890

Aurora **118**

abcdefghijklmnopqrstuvwxyz1234567890

Century Schoolbook **119**

abcdefghijklmnopqrstuvwxyz1234567890

Corona **120**

abcdefghijklmnopqrstuvwxyz1234567890

NB. On lower case letters generally look at the x height and length of ascenders and descenders.

VERTICAL STRESS STRAIGHT SERIFS (NEW TRANSITIONAL)

od

Joanna
Maximus
Breughel 55
Century Expanded
Excelsior
Perpetua
Primer
Aurora
Century Schoolbook
Corona

121 Ionic 5

ABCDEFGHIJKLMNOPQRSTUVWXYZ&

122 Nimrod

ABCDEFGHIJKLMNOPQRSTUVWXYZ&

horizontal bracketed serifs (or nearly so) capital W with crossed centre strokes

123 Cheltenham

ABCDEFGHIJKLMNOPQRSTUVWXYZ&

124 Cheltenham Nova

ABCDEFGHIJKLMNOPQRSTUVWXYZ&

VERTICAL STRESS STRAIGHT SERIFS (NEW TRANSITIONAL)

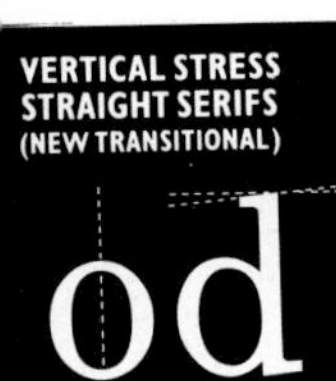
od

Ionic 5
Nimrod
Cheltenham
Cheltenham Nova
Comenius
Gloucester Old Style
Sorbonne
Bramley
ITC Cheltenham
Columbia

125 Comenius

ABCDEFGHIJKLMNOPQRSTUVWXYZ&

126 Gloucester Old Style

ABCDEFGHIJKLMNOPQRSTUVWXYZ&

127 Sorbonne

ABCDEFGHIJKLMNOPQRSTUVWXYZ&

horizontal bracketed serifs (or nearly so) capital W with stepped centre strokes

128 Bramley

ABCDEFGHIJKLMNOPQRSTUVWXYZ&

129 ITC Cheltenham

ABCDEFGHIJKLMNOPQRSTUVWXYZ&

130 Columbia

ABCDEFGHIJKLMNOPQRSTUVWXYZ&

* *These letters show special or 'style' characteristics. (NB. J, Q, & and g will usually vary from one typeface to another).*

Ionic 5 **121**

*   *   *   *   *

abcdefghijklmnopqrstuvwxyz1234567890

Nimrod **122**

*   *   *   *

abcdefghijklmnopqrstuvwxyz1234567890

Cheltenham **123**

*   *   *   *   *   *   *   *   *   *

abcdefghijklmnopqrstuvwxyz1234567890

Cheltenham Nova **124**

*   *   *   *   *   *   *   *   *

abcdefghijklmnopqrstuvwxyz1234567890

Comenius **125**

*   *   *   *   *   *   *   *

abcdefghijklmnopqrstuvwxyz1234567890

Gloucester Old Style **126**

*   *   *   *   *   *   *   *   *

abcdefghijklmnopqrstuvwxyz1234567890

Sorbonne **127**

*   *   *   *

abcdefghijklmnopqrstuvwxyz1234567890

Bramley **128**

*   *   *   *   *

abcdefghijklmnopqrstuvwxyz1234567890

ITC Cheltenham **129**

*   *   *   *   *   *   *   *

abcdefghijklmnopqrstuvwxyz1234567890

Columbia **130**

**   *   *

abcdefghijklmnopqrstuvwxyz1234567890

NB. On lower case letters generally look at the x height and length of ascenders and descenders.

VERTICAL STRESS STRAIGHT SERIFS (NEW TRANSITIONAL)

od

131 French Round Face

ABCDEFGHIJKLMNOPQRSTUVWXYZ&

132 Goudy Modern

ABCDEFGHIJKLMNOPQRSTUVWXYZ&

horizontal serifs (or nearly so)

no centre serif on capital W

133 Apollo

ABCDEFGHIJKLMNOPQRSTUVWXYZ&

134 Athenaeum

ABCDEFGHIJKLMNOPQRSTUVWXYZ&

VERTICAL STRESS
STRAIGHT SERIFS
(NEW TRANSITIONAL)
od

French Round Face
Goudy Modern
Apollo
Athenaeum
Diotima
Franklin Antiqua
Impressum
Melior
Orion
Renault

135 Diotima

ABCDEFGHIJKLMNOPQRSTUVWXYZ&

136 Franklin Antiqua

ABCDEFGHIJKLMNOPQRSTUVWXYZ&

137 Impressum

ABCDEFGHIJKLMNOPQRSTUVWXYZ&

138 Melior

ABCDEFGHIJKLMNOPQRSTUVWXYZ&

139 Orion

ABCDEFGHIJKLMNOPQRSTUVWXYZ&

140 Renault

ABCDEFGHIJKLMNOPQRSTUVWXYZ&

** These letters show special or 'style' characteristics. (NB. J, Q, & and g will usually vary from one typeface to another).*

French Round Face **131**

* * * * * * *
abcdefghijklmnopqrstuvwxyz1234567890

Goudy Modern **132**

* * * *
abcdefghijklmnopqrstuvwxyz1234567890

Apollo **133**

* * * * * * * *
abcdefghijklmnopqrstuvwxyz1234567890

Athenaeum **134**

* *
abcdefghijklmnopqrstuvwxyz1234567890

Diotima **135**

* * * * *
abcdefghijklmnopqrstuvwxyz1234567890

Franklin Antiqua **136**

* * *
abcdefghijklmnopqrstuvwxyz1234567890

Impressum **137**

* * * *
abcdefghijklmnopqrstuvwxyz1234567890

Melior **138**

* * * * *
abcdefghijklmnopqrstuvwxyz1234567890

Orion **139**

* *
abcdefghijklmnopqrstuvwxyz1234567890

Renault **140**

* * *
abcdefghijklmnopqrstuvwxyz1234567890

NB. On lower case letters generally look at the x height and length of ascenders and descenders.

VERTICAL STRESS
STRAIGHT SERIFS
(NEW TRANSITIONAL
od

some definite oblique bracketed serifs
weak contrast

141 Dominante

ABCDEFGHIJKLMNOPQRSTUVWXYZ&

142 Lo-type

ABCDEFGHIJKLMNOPQRSTUVWXYZ&

143 Menhart

ABCDEFGHIJKLMNOPQRSTUVWXYZ&

144 Paragon

ABCDEFGHIJKLMNOPQRSTUVWXYZ

145 Primus Antiqua

ABCDEFGHIJKLMNOPQRSTUVWXYZ&

146 Textype

ABCDEFGHIJKLMNOPQRSTUVWXYZ&

some definite oblique bracketed serifs
good contrast

147 Cochin

ABCDEFGHIJKLMNOPQRSTUVWXYZ&

148 Electra

ABCDEFGHIJKLMNOPQRSTUVWXYZ&

149 Iridium

ABCDEFGHIJKLMNOPQRSTUVWXYZ&

150 ITC Zapf International

ABCDEFGHIJKLMNOPQRSTUVWXYZ&

** These letters show special or 'style' characteristics. (NB. J, Q, & and g will usually vary from one typeface to another).*

VERTICAL STRESS STRAIGHT SERIFS (NEW TRANSITIONAL)

od

Dominante
Lo-Type
Menhart
Paragon
Primus Antiqua
Textype
Cochin
Electra
Iridium
ITC Zapf International

Dominante **141**

* * * * *
abcdefghijklmnopqrstuvwxyz1234567890

Lo-type **142**

* * * *
abcdefghijklmnopqrstuvwxyz1234567890

Menhart **143**

* * * * *
abcdefghijklmnopqrstuvwxyz1234567890

Paragon **144**

* * * *
abcdefghijklmnopqrstuvwxyz1234567890

Primus Antiqua **145**

* * * * *
abcdefghijklmnopqrstuvwxyz1234567890

Textype **146**

* * * * *
abcdefghijklmnopqrstuvwxyz1234567890

Cochin **147**

* * * * *
abcdefghijklmnopqrstuvwxyz1234567890

Electra **148**

* * * * * *
abcdefghijklmnopqrstuvwxyz1234567890

Iridium **149**

* * * *
abcdefghijklmnopqrstuvwxyz1234567890

ITC Zapf International **150**

* * * *
abcdefghijklmnopqrstuvwxyz1234567890

NB. On lower case letters generally look at the x height and length of ascenders and descenders.

VERTICAL STRESS STRAIGHT SERIFS (NEW TRANSITIONAL)

od

5. ABRUPT CONTRAST/STRAIGHT SERIFS
(Modern Serif) Nos 151-187

These typefaces feature a strong and abrupt contrast between the thick and thin strokes of letters and all serifs are horizontals (straight). The overall stress is nearly vertical. Serifs can be line (unbracketed) or slightly bracketed and typefaces can vary in colour from light to black face.

After Baskerville, designers took the trends of greater contrast and vertical stress a stage further. In Britain, influenced as much by contemporary copper-plates as by Baskerville's
58,172,185/186 types, William Martin (Bulmer; c. 1790) and Richard Austin (Bell; 1788, Scotch Roman; c. 1812) condensed the basic letterform and sharpened the serifs.

156 On the Continent the trend was taken further and the types of Firmin Didot (c. 1784),
153/154/162/163 Giovanni Batista Bodoni (1798) and Justus Erich Walbaum (c. 1800) took the design to its
161/167/168/187 limits as a text face. The thin strokes and serifs were now simply hairlines and demanded the most exacting presswork and high quality paper to achieve the desired, almost dazzling effect. The resultant characters were 'designed' rather than 'drawn' and the abrupt vertical stress makes them difficult to read in any quantity without generous leading. Unfortunately the *modern* design became the standard typeface for much of the nineteenth century and these defects were ignored. Insensitive *modern* typefaces and poor typography (loose letter and word spacing in particular) led to William Morris's typographic revolution of the 1890's.*

Although not used much as book types today the *moderns* (particularly Bodoni and Walbaum) continue to be popular for display and magazine work where their brilliance can be better appreciated.

*See also the introduction to category 1, p. 14.

5. ABRUPT CONTRAST/STRAIGHT SERIFS
(Modern Serif) Nos 151-187

Specimen nos	Basic characteristics	Secondary characteristics	
151-161	N *line serifs*	n *light face*	e.g. **161** Walbaum (Linotype)
162-169	"	n *black face*	e.g. **162** Bodoni 135 (Monotype)
170-187	N *bracketed serifs*		e.g. **185** Scotch Roman (Monotype)

***NB.** Typefaces in each group are arranged in alphabetical order.*

ABRUPT CONTRAST
STRAIGHT SERIFS
(MODERN SERIF)
od

line serifs light face

151 Auriga

ABCDEFGHIJKLMNOPQRSTUVWXYZ&

152 Basilia

ABCDEFGHIJKLMNOPQRSTUVWXYZ&

153 Bauer Bodoni

ABCDEFGHIJKLMNOPQRSTUVWXYZ&

154 Bodoni Book (Linotype)

ABCDEFGHIJKLMNOPQRSTUVWXYZ&

155 Corvinus

ABCDEFGHIJKLMNOPQRSTUVWXYZ &

ABRUPT CONTRAST STRAIGHT SERIFS (MODERN SERIF)

Auriga
Basilia
Bauer Bodoni
Bodoni Book (Linotype)
Corvinus
Didot
Egmont
Fairfield
Tiemann
Torino

156 Didot

ABCDEFGHIJKLMNOPQRSTUVWXYZ&

157 Egmont

ABCDEFGHIJKLMNOPQRSTUVWXYZ&

158 Fairfield

ABCDEFGHIJKLMNOPQRSTUVWXYZ&

159 Tiemann

ABCDEFGHIJKLMNOPQRSTUVWXYZ&

160 Torino

ABCDEFGHIJKLMNOPQRSTUVWXYZ&

** These letters show special or 'style' characteristics. (NB. J, Q, & and g will usually vary from one typeface to another).*

* * * * *
abcdefghijklmnopqrstuvwxyz1234567890 Auriga **151**

* * *
abcdefghijklmnopqrstuvwxyz1234567890 Basilia **152**

* * * * *
abcdefghijklmnopqrstuvwxyz1234567890 Bauer Bodoni **153**

* * *
abcdefghijklmnopqrstuvwxyz1234567890 Bodoni Book (Linotype) **154**

* * * * *
abcdefghijklmnopqrstuvwxyz 1234567890 Corvinus **155**

* * * * * *
abcdefghijklmnopqrstuvwxyz1234567890 Didot **156**

* * * * *
abcdefghijklmnopqrstuvwxyz1234567890 Egmont **157**

* * * *
abcdefghijklmnopqrstuvwxyz1234567890 Fairfield **158**

* * *
abcdefghijklmnopqrstuvwxyz1234567890 Tiemann **159**

* * * *
abcdefghijklmnopqrstuvwxyz1234567890 Torino **160**

NB. On lower case letters generally look at the x height and length of ascenders and descenders.

ABRUPT CONTRAST STRAIGHT SERIFS (MODERN SERIF)

Auriga
Basilia
Bauer Bodoni
Bodoni Book (Linotype)
Corvinus
Didot
Egmont
Fairfield
Tiemann
Torino

161 Walbaum (Linotype)

ABCDEFGHIJKLMNOPQRSTUVWXYZ&

line serifs
black face

162 Bodoni 135 (Monotype)

ABCDEFGHIJKLMNOPQRSTUVWXYZ&

163 Bodoni (Haas)

ABCDEFGHIJKLMNOPQRSTUVWXYZ&

164 Craw Modern

ABCDEFGHIJKLMNOPQRSTUVWXYZ&

165 ITC Fenice

ABCDEFGHIJKLMNOPQRSTUVWXYZ&

ABRUPT CONTRAST STRAIGHT SERIFS (MODERN SERIF)

od

Walbaum (Linotype)
Bodoni 135 (Monotype)
Bodoni (Haas)
Craw Modern
ITC Fenice
Modern (Linotype)
Walbaum Book (Berthold)
Walbaum (Monotype)
ITC Zapf Book
Albion 42

166 Modern (Linotype)

ABCDEFGHIJKLMNOPQRSTUVWXYZ&

167 Walbaum Book (Berthold)

ABCDEFGHIJKLMNOPQRSTUVWXYZ&

168 Walbaum (Monotype)

ABCDEFGHIJKLMNOPQRSTUVWXYZ&

169 ITC Zapf Book

ABCDEFGHIJKLMNOPQRSTUVWXYZ&

bracketed serifs

170 Albion 42

ABCDEFGHIJKLMNOPQRSTUVWXYZ&

* *These letters show special or 'style' characteristics. (NB. J, Q, & and g will usually vary from one typeface to another).*

Walbaum (Linotype) **161**

* * * * * *
abcdefghijklmnopqrstuvwxyz1234567890

Bodoni 135 (Monotype) **162**

* * * * *
abcdefghijklmnopqrstuvwxyz1234567890

Bodoni (Haas) **163**

* * * * *
abcdefghijklmnopqrstuvwxyz1234567890

Craw Modern **164**

* * * * * *
abcdefghijklmnopqrstuvwxyz1234567890

ITC Fenice **165**

* * * * *
abcdefghijklmnopqrstuvwxyz1234567890

Modern (Linotype) **166**

* * * * * *
abcdefghijklmnopqrstuvwxyz1234567890

Walbaum Book (Berthold) **167**

* * * *
abcdefghijklmnopqrstuvwxyz1234567890

Walbaum (Monotype) **168**

* * * *
abcdefghijklmnopqrstuvwxyz1234567890

ITC Zapf Book **169**

* * * *
abcdefghijklmnopqrstuvwxyz1234567890

Albion 42 **170**

* * * * * *
abcdefghijklmnopqrstuvwxyz1234567890

NB. On lower case letters generally look at the x height and length of ascenders and descenders.

ABRUPT CONTRAST STRAIGHT SERIFS (MODERN SERIF)

od

Walbaum (Linotype)
Bodoni 135 (Monotype)
Bodoni (Haas)
Craw Modern
ITC Fenice
Modern (Linotype)
Walbaum Book (Berthold)
Walbaum (Monotype)
ITC Zapf Book
Albion 42

171 Augustea

ABCDEFGHIJKLMNOPQRSTUVWXYZ&

172 Bell

ABCDEFGHIJKLMNOPQRSTUVWXYZ&

173 Bruce Old Style

ABCDEFGHIJKLMNOPQRSTUVWXYZ&

174 Caledonia

ABCDEFGHIJKLMNOPQRSTUVWXYZ&

175 ITC Century

ABCDEFGHIJKLMNOPQRSTUVWXYZ&

176 Century Nova

ABCDEFGHIJKLMNOPQRSTUVWXYZ&

177 De Vinne

ABCDEFGHIJKLMNOPQRSTUVWXYZ&

178 Madison

ABCDEFGHIJKLMNOPQRSTUVWXYZ&

179 Modern No 20

ABCDEFGHIJKLMNOPQRSTUVWXYZ&

180 Neo Didot

ABCDEFGHIJKLMNOPQRSTUVWXYZ&

ABRUPT CONTRAST STRAIGHT SERIFS (MODERN SERIF)

od

Augustea
Bell
Bruce Old Style
Caledonia
ITC Century
Century Nova
De Vinne
Madison
Modern No 20
Neo Didot

** These letters show special or 'style' characteristics. (NB. J, Q, & and g will usually vary from one typeface to another).*

Augustea **171**

* * * * * *
abcdefghijklmnopqrstuvwxyz1234567890

Bell **172**

* * * * * *
abcdefghijklmnopqrstuvwxyz1234567890

Bruce Old Style **173**

* * * * *
abcdefghijklmnopqrstuvwxyz1234567890

Caledonia **174**

* * * * *
abcdefghijklmnopqrstuvwxyz1234567890

ITC Century **175**

* * * * * * *
abcdefghijklmnopqrstuvwxyz1234567890

Century Nova **176**

* * * * * * * *
abcdefghijklmnopqrstuvwxyz1234567890

De Vinne **177**

* * * *
abcdefghijklmnopqrstuvwxyz1234567890

Madison **178**

* * * *
abcdefghijklmnopqrstuvwxyz1234567890

Modern No 20 **179**

* * * *
abcdefghijklmnopqrstuvwxyz1234567890

Neo Didot **180**

* * *
abcdefghijklmnopqrstuvwxyz1234567890

NB. On lower case letters generally look at the x height and length of ascenders and descenders.

ABRUPT CONTRAST STRAIGHT SERIFS (MODERN SERIF)

od

Augustea
Bell
Bruce Old Style
Caledonia
ITC Century
Century Nova
De Vinne
Madison
Modern No 20
Neo Didot

181 Paganini

ABCDEFGHIJKLMNOPQRSTUVWXYZ&

182 Photina

ABCDEFGHIJKLMNOPQRSTUVWXYZ&

183 Pilgrim

ABCDEFGHIJKLMNOPQRSTUVWXYZ&

184 Promotor

ABCDEFGHIJKLMNOPQRSTUVWXYZ&

185 Scotch Roman (Monotype)

ABCDEFGHIJKLMNOPQRSTUVWXYZ&

186 Scotch 2 (Linotype)

ABCDEFGHIJKLMNOPQRSTUVWXYZ&

187 Walbaum Standard (Berthold)

ABCDEFGHIJKLMNOPQRSTUVWXYZ&

new entries

187A Centennial 55 (Linotype)

ABCDEFGHIJKLMNOPQRSTUVWXYZ&

187B Versailles 55 (Linotype)

ABCDEFGHIJKLMNOPQRSTUVWXYZ&

187C Wilke 55 (Linotype)

ABCDEFGHIJKLMNOPQRSTUVWXYZ&

** These letters show special or 'style' characteristics. (NB. J, Q, & and g will usually vary from one typeface to another).*

ABRUPT CONTRAST
STRAIGHT SERIFS
(MODERN SERIF)
od

Paganini
Photina
Pilgrim
Promotor
Scotch Roman (Monotype)
Scotch 2 (Linotype)
Walbaum Standard (Berthold)
Centennial 55 (Linotype)
Versailles 55 (Linotype)
Wilke 55 (Linotype)

Paganini **181**

* * * *
abcdefghijklmnopqrstuvwxyz1234567890

Photina **182**

* * * * * * * *
abcdefghijklmnopqrstuvwxyz1234567890

Pilgrim **183**

* * * * *
abcdefghijklmnopqrstuvwxyz1234567890

Promotor **184**

* * * * * *
abcdefghijklmnopqrstuvwxyz1234567890

Scotch Roman (Monotype) **185**

* * * * * *
abcdefghijklmnopqrstuvwxyz1234567890

Scotch 2 (Linotype) **186**

* * * * * *
abcdefghijklmnopqrstuvwxyz1234567890

Walbaum Standard (Berthold) **187**

* * * *
abcdefghijklmnopqrstuvwxyz1234567890

Centennial 55 (Linotype) **187A**

*
abcdefghijklmnopqrstuvwxyz1234567890

Versailles 55 (Linotype) **187B**

* * * *
abcdefghijklmnopqrstuvwxyz1234567890

Wilke 55 (Linotype) **187C**

* *
abcdefghijklmnopqrstuvwxyz1234567890

NB. On lower case letters generally look at the x height and length of ascenders and descenders.

ABRUPT CONTRAST STRAIGHT SERIFS (MODERN SERIF)

od

Paganini
Photina
Pilgrim
Promotor
Scotch Roman (Monotype)
Scotch 2 (Linotype)
Walbaum Standard (Berthold)
Centennial 55 (Linotype)
Versailles 55 (Linotype)
Wilke 55 (Linotype)

6. SLAB SERIF
(Egyptians and Clarendons) Nos 188-217

The typefaces in this section are characterised by a generally heavy appearance with thick 'slab' serifs often the same thickness as the main stem of the letters. When the serifs are square (unbracketed) the type is known as an *egyptian*, and when bracketed, as a *clarendon*. (NB Slab serif style typefaces with a sloping cross-bar to the lower case e will be found in Category 1, nos. 1-34).

Egyptian typefaces first appeared in Britain in the early nineteenth century. Figgins Egyptian of 1817, perhaps the first original design of advertising type, was quickly followed by versions from other founders. They were heavy with almost even weight and were designed not for legibility or sensitivity, but impact and aggression, they could not be ignored. Most of the *egyptians* shown in this section are polite twentieth century text
189,196,197 versions of the basic design. Faces such as Beton, Memphis and Rockwell date from the 1920's
253,254 and '30's and are contemporary with *sans serifs* such as Erbar and Futura, sharing with them
190 geometric construction and a single storey lower case 'g'. Calvert (Margaret Calvert 1980), on the other hand, shows more irregularity in character, width and construction, and has an idiosyncratic serif treatment. Versions of the heavy Victorian originals can be found in Part 2 of this book, nos. 453-458.

Clarendons take their name from the first version of this typestyle, cut by Benjamin Fox of the Fann Street Foundry in 1845. They are not as heavy and exaggerated as the *egyptians* and the serifs are strongly bracketed. The first *clarendons* were condensed and designed as a bold face to accompany the *modern* typefaces then in use. Subsequently, expanded versions appeared and later still different weights, but all are characterised by a large x-height (for legibility), a strong horizontal emphasis, and an almost architectural sturdiness. These qualities make them ideal for printing on poor quality paper and the basic design has proved the most successful for newspaper types and also typewriters.*

*Because of other design features, some *clarendons* are to be found in category 4 of this book (nos. 118-122) including one of the most popular newspaper typefaces currently available, Robin Nicholas' **Nimrod, (122)**.

6. SLAB SERIF
(Egyptians and Clarendons) Nos 188-217

Specimen nos	*Basic characteristics*		*Secondary characteristics*		
188-200	I	*square slab*	g	*single storey*	e.g. **197** Rockwell
201-203	"		g	*double storey*	e.g. **203** Schadow Antiqua
204-205	I	*bracketed slab*	g	*single storey*	e.g. **205** Egyptian 505
206-213	"		g	*double storey*	e.g. **209** Clarendon (Linotype)
214-217	I	*rounded slab*			e.g. **214** ITC American Typewriter

NB. *Typefaces in each group are arranged in alphabetical order.*

square slab
single storey g

188 A & S Gallatin

ABCDEFGHIJKLMNOPQRSTUVWXYZ&

189 Beton

ABCDEFGHIJKLMNOPQRSTUVWXYZ&

190 Calvert

ABCDEFGHIJKLMNOPQRSTUVWXYZ&

191 Candida

ABCDEFGHIJKLMNOPQRSTUVWXYZ&

192 City

ABCDEFGHIJKLMNOPQRSTUVWXYZ&

193 Glypha 55

ABCDEFGHIJKLMNOPQRSTUVWXYZ&

194 ITC Lubalin Graph

ABCDEFGHIJKLMNOPQRSTUVWXYZ&

195 ITC Lubalin Graph Extra Light

ABCDEFGHIJKLMNOPQRSTUVWXYZ&

196 Memphis

ABCDEFGHIJKLMNOPQRSTUVWXYZ&

197 Rockwell

ABCDEFGHIJKLMNOPQRSTUVWXYZ&

** These letters show special or 'style' characteristics. (NB. J, Q, & and g will usually vary from one typeface to another).*

SLAB SERIF

II

A & S Gallatin
Beton
Calvert
Candida
City
Glypha 55
ITC Lubalin Graph
ITC Lubalin Graph Extra Light
Memphis
Rockwell

A & S Gallatin **188**

abcdefghijklmnopqrstuvwxyz1234567890

Beton **189**

abcdefghijklmnopqrstuvwxyz1234567890

Calvert **190**

abcdefghijklmnopqrstuvwxyz1234567890

Candida **191**

abcdefghijklmnopqrstuvwxyz1234567890

City **192**

abcdefghijklmnopqrstuvwxyz1234567890

Glypha 55 **193**

abcdefghijklmnopqrstuvwxyz1234567890

ITC Lubalin Graph **194**

abcdefghijklmnopqrstuvwxyz1234567890

ITC Lubalin Graph Extra Light **195**

abcdefghijklmnopqrstuvwxyz1234567890

Memphis **196**

abcdefghijklmnopqrstuvwxyz1234567890

Rockwell **197**

abcdefghijklmnopqrstuvwxyz1234567890

NB. On lower case letters generally look at the x height and length of ascenders and descenders.

SLAB SERIF
II

198 Serifa 55

ABCDEFGHIJKLMNOPQRSTUVWXYZ&

199 Stymie (ATF)

ABCDEFGHIJKLMNOPQRSTUVWXYZ&

200 ITC Stymie Hairline

ABCDEFGHIJKLMNOPQRSTUVWXYZ&

square slab double storey g

201 Antique No 5

ABCDEFGHIJKLMNOPQRSTUVWXYZ&

202 Egyptian 173

ABCDEFGHIJKLMNOPQRSTUVWXYZ&

203 Schadow Antiqua

ABCDEFGHIJKLMNOPQRSTUVWXYZ&

bracketed slab single storey g

204 Aachen

ABCDEFGHIJKLMNOPQRSTUVWXYZ&

205 Egyptian 505

ABCDEFGHIJKLMNOPQRSTUVWXYZ&

bracketed slab double storey g

206 Antique No 3

ABCDEFGHIJKLMNOPQRSTUVWXYZ&

207 Consort

ABCDEFGHIJKLMNOPQRSTUVWXYZ&

** These letters show special or 'style' characteristics. (NB. J, Q, & and g will usually vary from one typeface to another).*

* * * * *

abcdefghijklmnopqrstuvwxyz1234567890 Serifa 55 **198**

* * * *

abcdefghijklmnopqrstuvwxyz1234567890 Stymie (ATF) **199**

* * * *

abcdefghijklmnopqrstuvwxyz1234567890 ITC Stymie Hairline **200**

* * * *

abcdefghijklmnopqrstuvwxyz1234567890 Antique No 5 **201**

* * * * *

abcdefghijklmnopqrstuvwxyz1234567890 Egyptian 173 **202**

* * * * * *

abcdefghijklmnopqrstuvwxyz1234567890 Schadow Antiqua **203**

* * * *

abcdefghijklmnopqrstuvwxyz1234567890 Aachen **204**

* * * * * *

bcdefghijklmnopqrstuvwxyz1234567890 Egyptian 505 **205**

* * * * * *

bcdefghijklmnopqrstuvwxyz1234567890 Antique No 3 **206**

* * * * *

bcdefghijklmnopqrstuvwxyz1234567890 Consort **207**

NB. On lower case letters generally look at the x height and length of ascenders and descenders.

SLAB SERIF

II

Serifa 55
Stymie (ATF)
ITC Stymie Hairline
Antique No 5
Egyptian 173
Schadow Antiqua
Aachen
Egyptian 505
Antique No 3
Consort

208 Clarendon 12 (Monotype)

ABCDEFGHIJKLMNOPQRSTUVWXYZ&

209 Clarendon (Linotype)

ABCDEFGHIJKLMNOPQRSTUVWXYZ&

210 Egyptienne F 55

ABCDEFGHIJKLMNOPQRSTUVWXYZ&

211 New Clarendon

ABCDEFGHIJKLMNOPQRSTUVWXYZ&

212 Egizio

ABCDEFGHIJKLMNOPQRSTUVWXYZ&

213 Fortune

ABCDEFGHIJKLMNOPQRSTUVWXYZ&

rounded slab

214 ITC American Typewriter

ABCDEFGHIJKLMNOPQRSTUVWXYZ&

215 Clarinda Typewriter

ABCDEFGHIJKLMNOPQRSTUVWXYZ&

216 Linotype Typewriter

ABCDEFGHIJKLMNOPQRSTUVWXYZ&

217 Monotype Typewriter 105

ABCDEFGHIJKLMNOPQRSTUVWXYZ

* *These letters show special or 'style' characteristics. (NB. J, Q, & and g will usually vary from one typeface to another).*

SLAB SERIF

II

Clarendon 12 (Monotype)
Clarendon (Linotype)
Egyptienne F 55
New Clarendon
Egizio
Fortune
ITC American Typewriter
Clarinda Typewriter
Linotype Typewriter
Monotype Typewriter 105

Clarendon 12 (Monotype) **208**

abcdefghijklmnopqrstuvwxyz1234567890

Clarendon (Linotype) **209**

abcdefghijklmnopqrstuvwxyz1234567890

Egyptienne F 55 **210**

abcdefghijklmnopqrstuvwxyz1234567890

New Clarendon **211**

abcdefghijklmnopqrstuvwxyz1234567890

Egizio **212**

abcdefghijklmnopqrstuvwxyz1234567890

Fortune **213**

abcdefghijklmnopqrstuvwxyz1234567890

ITC American Typewriter **214**

abcdefghijklmnopqrstuvwxyz1234567890

Clarinda Typewriter **215**

abcdefghijklmnopqrstuvwxyz1234567890

Linotype Typewriter **216**

abcdefghijklmnopqrstuvwxyz1234567890

Monotype Typewriter 105 **217**

abcdefghijklmnopqrstuvwxyz1234567890

NB. On lower case letters generally look at the x height and length of ascenders and descenders.

7. WEDGE SERIF
(Hybrid Serif), Nos 218-240

This category contains typefaces* which are not always clearly serif or sans serif (i.e. hybrids). It includes typefaces both of general serif-style but with only a thickening at the terminals of letters and sans serif style typefaces with very small line serifs on the terminals. It includes other groups with wedge-shaped serifs and half serifs. (N.B. Wedge serif style typefaces with a sloping bar on the lower case e are to be found in category 1.)

*Nos. 230-235 belong (stylistically) to a sub-group of *egyptians* (see introduction to category 5, p.64) called *latins*, they are not of the correct age. All the other typefaces are grouped here for identification and recognition purposes as they cannot be grouped elsewhere. Some bolder versions of these hybrids are also included in part 2, category 6, Modified Serif.

7. WEDGE SERIF
(Hybrid Serif), Nos 218-240

Specimen nos		*Basic characteristics*	
218-229	I or I	*wedge-ended or small wedge serifs*	e.g. **218** Albertus, **229** Romana
230-235	I	*wedge-shaped serifs*	e.g. **233** Meridien
236-238	I	*line-ended serifs*	e.g. **236** Copperplate Gothic
239-240	I	*half serifs*	e.g. **240** Romic

NB. *Typefaces in each group are arranged in alphabetical order.*

WEDGE SERIF
(HYBRID SERIF)

wedge-ended or small wedge serifs

218 Albertus

ABCDEFGHIJKLMNOPQRSTUVWXYZ&

219 Americana

ABCDEFGHIJKLMNOPQRSTUVWXYZ&

220 Flange

ABCDEFGHIJKLMNOPQRSTUVWXYZ&

221 French Old Style

ABCDEFGHI JKLMNOPQRSTUVWXYZ&

222 ITC Friz Quadrata

ABCDEFGHIJKLMNOPQRSTUVWXYZ&

223 Icone

ABCDEFGHIJKLMNOPQRSTUVWXYZ&

224 ITC Korinna

ABCDEFGHIJKLMNOPQRSTUVWXYZ&

225 ITC Newtext

ABCDEFGHIJKLMNOPQRSTUVWXYZ&

226 ITC Novarese

ABCDEFGHIJKLMNOPQRSTUVWXYZ&

227 Poppl-Laudatio

ABCDEFGHIJKLMNOPQRSTUVWXYZ&

* *These letters show special or 'style' characteristics. (NB. J, Q, & and g will usually vary from one typeface to another).*

WEDGE SERIF
(HYBRID SERIF)
II

Albertus **218**

* * * * *

abcdefghijklmnopqrstuvwxyz1234567890

Americana **219**

* * * *

abcdefghijklmnopqrstuvwxyz1234567890

Flange **220**

* * * *

abcdefghijklmnopqrstuvwxyz1234567890

French Old Style **221**

* * * *

abcdefghijklmnopqrstuvwxyz1234567890

ITC Friz Quadrata **222**

* * * * *

abcdefghijklmnopqrstuvwxyz1234567890

Icone **223**

* * * *

abcdefghijklmnopqrstuvwxyz1234567890

ITC Korinna **224**

* *

abcdefghijklmnopqrstuvwxyz1234567890

ITC Newtext **225**

* * * *

abcdefghijklmnopqrstuvwxyz1234567890

ITC Novarese **226**

* * * * *

abcdefghijklmnopqrstuvwxyz1234567890

Poppl-Laudatio **227**

* * * * *

abcdefghijklmnopqrstuvwxyz1234567890

NB. On lower case letters generally look at the x height and length of ascenders and descenders.

WEDGE SERIF
(HYBRID SERIF)
II

228 ITC Quorum

ABCDEFGHIJKLMNOPQRSTUVWXYZ&

229 Romana

ABCDEFGHIJKLMNOPQRSTUVWXYZ&

wedge-shaped serifs

230 ITC Barcelona

ABCDEFGHIJKLMNOPQRSTUVWXYZ&

231 Biltmore

ABCDEFGHIJKLMNOPQRSTUVWXYZ&

232 ITC LSC Book

ABCDEFGHIJKLMNOPQRSTUVWXYZ&

233 Meridien

ABCDEFGHIJKLMNOPQRSTUVWXYZ&

234 Octavian

ABCDEFGHIJKLMNOPQRSTUVWXYZ&

235 Pegasus

ABCDEFGHIJKLMNOPQRSTUVWXYZ&

line-ended serifs

236 Copperplate Gothic

ABCDEFGHIJKLMNOPQRSTUVWXYZ&

237 ITC Serif Gothic

ABCDEFGHIJKLMNOPQRSTUVWXYZ&

** These letters show special or 'style' characteristics. (NB. J, Q, & and g will usually vary from one typeface to another).*

WEDGE SERIF (HYBRID SERIF)

ITC Quorum **228**

abcdefghijklmnopqrstuvwxyz1234567890

Romana **229**

abcdefghijklmnopqrstuvwxyz1234567890

ITC Barcelona **230**

abcdefghijklmnopqrstuvwxyz1234567890

Biltmore **231**

abcdefghijklmnopqrstuvwxyz1234567890

ITC LSC Book **232**

abcdefghijklmnopqrstuvwxyz1234567890

Meridien **233**

abcdefghijklmnopqrstuvwxyz1234567890

Octavian **234**

abcdefghijklmnopqrstuvwxyz1234567890

Pegasus **235**

abcdefghijklmnopqrstuvwxyz1234567890

small capitals

Copperplate Gothic **236**

ABCDEFGHIJKLMNOPQRSTUVWXYZ1234567890

ITC Serif Gothic **237**

abcdefghijklmnopqrstuvwxyz1234567890

NB. On lower case letters generally look at the x height and length of ascenders and descenders.

WEDGE SERIF
(HYBRID SERIF)
II

238 Spartan 140 (Monotype)

ABCDEFGHIJKLMNOPQRSTUVWXYZ&

half serifs

239 Parsons

ABCDEFGHIJKLMNOPQRSTUVWXYZ&

240 Romic

ABCDEFGHIJKLMNOPQRSTUVWXYZ&

new entries

240A Cantoria (Monotype)

ABCDEFGHIJKLMNOPQRSTUVWXYZ&

240B Footlight (Monotype)

ABCDEFGHIJKLMNOPQRSTUVWXYZ&

* *These letters show special or 'style' characteristics. (NB. J, Q, & and g will usually vary from one typeface to another).*

WEDGE SERIF
(HYBRID SERIF)
II

Spartan 140 (Monotype) **238**

1234567890 *no lower case*

Parsons **239**

abcdefghijklmnopqrstuvwxyz1234567890

Romic **240**

abcdefghijklmnopqrstuvwxyz1234567890

Cantoria (Monotype) **240A**

abcdefghijklmnopqrstuvwxyz1234567890

Footlight (Monotype) **240B**

abcdefghijklmnopqrstuvwxyz1234567890

NB. Nos 241-244 have been deleted.

NB. On lower case letters generally look at the x height and length of ascenders and descenders.

Spartan 140 (Monotype)
Parsons
Romic
Cantoria (Monotype)
Footlight (Monotype)

WEDGE SERIF
(HYBRID SERIF)
II

8. SANS SERIF
(sometimes called Grotesque), Nos 245-304

Typefaces with no serifs. Generally, with little or no difference between strokes (i.e. monoline). These typefaces are primarily divided according to whether the capital G has a spur on it or not, and if it has, if it is wide, medium or narrow. The category also includes groups of typefaces of a special shape (such as rounded).

The first *sans serifs* appeared in England in the early nineteenth century – Caslon's so-called Egyptian of 1816: a clumsy, unbalanced set of capitals probably intended for headings and emphasis only – but it was the German founders who developed the lower case in the 1830's.

British *sans serifs* of the nineteenth century tended to be heavy, have capitals of equal
width and *modern*-face features to the G, R, g and t. These can be clearly seen on Grot 9/
Headline Bold. The German faces in contrast, reformed the style, the capitals differ in width
273 and the strokes taper. Berthold's Akzidenz Grotesk/Standard of 1898 is typical and has been
highly influential in the last forty years. American *sans serifs* drew on both sources, often
287 using British forms with German stroke treatment. Morris Fuller Benton's News Gothic of
1908 typifies the approach.

During the first half of this century the development of the sans serif took two routes. In
England in 1916, London Transport began using a *sans serif* especially designed for them by
Edward Johnston, it was a break with previous *sans serifs* because it was based on classical
letterforms. His approach was very closely followed by his pupil and friend Eric Gill with
259/348/424/425/427/ 428/476/482/527 Gill Sans in 1928. In Germany, designs were influenced by the teachings of the Bauhaus and
254 developed along geometric lines. Paul Renner's Futura of 1928 is the most popular of this
kind and has been widely copied.

After World War II, the idea of a *sans serif* typeface with a whole family of related
weights arose on the Continent, especially in Switzerland where Bauhaus principles had
been modified to something akin to pattern making. Adrian Frutiger's Univers series begun
267/481/498 in 1952 is the most ambitious of these typeface families, having twenty-one weights all
carefully worked out and mathematically related from the outset. Max Miedinger's New
279/422/493/494/477/ 529/530/620/624 Haas Grotesque/Helvetica, 1957, was based on Akzidenz Grotesque and has become the most
popular and commercially successful *sans serif*. Although it now has a large family of
weights, these were not all planned from the outset.

More recent developments have concentrated on introducing a little more 'personality' into the typeface and do not fall into any one category outlined above. 'Personality' can be
271/473/483, 291/292 difficult to handle. Both Roger Excoffon's Antique Olive of 1962 and Aldo Novarese's Eurostile of 1964/5 have too much for their own good and now look very dated. On the other hand,
266, 304A Frutiger, 1977 and Ong Chong Wah's Abadi of 1988 are more subtle and more successful.

8. SANS SERIF
(sometimes called Grotesque), Nos 245-304

Specimen nos	Basic characteristics	Secondary characteristics	
245-248	G *wide no spur*	E *wide*	e.g. **245** Adonis
249-257	G *wide no spur*	E *narrow*	e.g. **254** Futura
258-265	G *medium width no spur*	G *round base*	e.g. **259** Gill Sans
266-267	"	G *flatter base*	e.g. **267** Univers 55
268-269	"	G *no bar stressed strokes*	e.g. **268** Optima
270	"	G *no bar unstressed strokes*	e.g. **270** Syntax
271-272	G *narrow no spur (or bar)*		e.g. **271** Antique Olive
273	G *wide with spur*		e.g. **273** Akzidenz Grotesk
274-283	G *medium width with spur*		e.g. **279** Helvetica
284-289	G *narrow with spur*		e.g. **287** News Gothic

NB. *Typefaces in each group are arranged in alphabetical order.*

Specimen nos			
290-294	Gg	*(sans serif) square*	e.g. **291** Eurostile
295	Gg	*sloped*	e.g. **295** ITC Eras
296-301	Gg	*rounded*	e.g. **296** ITC Bauhaus
302-304	G	*electronic or machine-read*	e.g. **303** OCR-A

***N.B.** Typefaces in each group are arranged in alphabetical order.*

SANS SERIF
GG

wide capital G no spur
wide capital E

245 Adonis

ABCDEFGHIJKLMNOPQRSTUVWXYZ&

246 Doric

ABCDEFGHIJKLMNOPQRSTUVWXYZ&

247 2-Line Block Gothic

ABCDEFGHIJKLMNOPQRSTUVWXYZ&

248 4-Line Block Gothic

ABCDEFGHIJKLMNOPQRSTUVWXYZ&

wide capital G no spur
narrow capital E

249 Adsans

ABCDEFGHIJKLMNOPQRSTUVWXYZ&

250 ITC Avant Garde Gothic

ABCDEFGHIJKLMNOPQRSTUVWXYZ&

251 Bernhard Gothic

ABCDEFGHIJKLMNOPQRSTUVWXYZ&

252 20th Century

ABCDEFGHIJKLMNOPQRSTUVWXYZ&

253 Erbar

ABCDEFGHIJKLMNOPQRSTUVWXYZ&

254 Futura

ABCDEFGHIJKLMNOPQRSTUVWXYZ&

** These letters show special or 'style' characteristics. (NB. J, Q, & and g will usually vary from one typeface to another).*

SANS SERIF

GG

Adonis **245**

abcdefghijklmnopqrstuvwxyz1234567890

Doric **246**

abcdefghijklmnopqrstuvwxyz1234567890

small capitals (no lower case)

2-Line Block Gothic **247**

ABCDEFGHIJKLMNOPQRSTUVWXYZ1234567890

small capitals (no lower case)

4-Line Block Gothic **248**

ABCDEFGHIJKLMNOPQRSTUVWXYZ1234567890

Adsans **249**

abcdefghijklmnopqrstuvwxyz1234567890

ITC Avant Garde Gothic **250**

abcdefghijklmnopqrstuvwxyz1234567890

Bernhard Gothic **251**

abcdefghijklmnopqrstuvwxyz1234567890

20th Century **252**

abcdefghijklmnopqrstuvwxyz1234567890

Erbar **253**

abcdefghijklmnopqrstuvwxyz1234567890

Futura **254**

abcdefghijklmnopqrstuvwxyz1234567890

NB. On lower case letters generally look at the x height and length of ascenders and descenders.

255 Neuzeit-Grotesk

ABCDEFGHIJKLMNOPQRSTUVWXYZ&

256 Nobel

ABCDEFGHIJKLMNOPQRSTUVWXYZ&

257 Spartan

ABCDEFGHIJKLMNOPQRSTUVWXYZ&

medium width capital G no spur round base

258 Cable (Klingspor)

ABCDEFGHIJKLMNOPQRSTUVWXYZ&

259 Gill Sans

ABCDEFGHIJKLMNOPQRSTUVWXYZ&

260 Granby

ABCDEFGHIJKLMNOPQRSTUVWXYZ&

261 Grotesque 215

ABCDEFGHIJKLMNOPQRSTUVWXYZ&

262 ITC Kabel

ABCDEFGHIJKLMNOPQRSTUVWXYZ&

263 Metro

ABCDEFGHIJKLMNOPQRSTUVWXYZ&

264 Tempo

ABCDEFGHIJKLMNOPQRSTUVWXYZ&

** These letters show special or 'style' characteristics. (NB. J, Q, & and g will usually vary from one typeface to another).*

Neuzeit Grotesk
Nobel
Spartan
Cable (Klingspor)
Gill Sans
Granby
Grotesque 215
ITC Kabel
Metro
Tempo

SANS SERIF

GG

Neuzeit-Grotesk **255**

abcdefghijklmnopqrstuvwxyz1234567890

Nobel **256**

abcdefghijklmnopqrstuvwxyz1234567890

Spartan **257**

abcdefghijklmnopqrstuvwxyz1234567890

Cable (Klingspor) **258**

abcdefghijklmnopqrstuvwxyz1234567890

Gill Sans **259**

abcdefghijklmnopqrstuvwxyz1234567890

Granby **260**

abcdefghijklmnopqrstuvwxyz1234567890

Grotesque 215 **261**

abcdefghijklmnopqrstuvwxyz1234567890

ITC Kabel **262**

abcdefghijklmnopqrstuvwxyz1234567890

Metro **263**

abcdefghijklmnopqrstuvwxyz1234567890

Tempo **264**

abcdefghijklmnopqrstuvwxyz1234567890

NB. On lower case letters generally look at the x height and length of ascenders and descenders.

Neuzeit Grotesk
Nobel
Spartan
Cable (Klingspor)
Gill Sans
Granby
Grotesque 215
ITC Kabel
Metro
Tempo

SANS SERIF

GG

265 Venus

ABCDEFGHIJKLMNOPQRSTUVWXYZ&

medium with capital G no spur flatter base

266 Frutiger

ABCDEFGHIJKLMNOPQRSTUVWXYZ&

267 Univers 55

ABCDEFGHIJKLMNOPQRSTUVWXYZ&

medium width capital G no spur no bar stressed strokes

268 Optima

ABCDEFGHIJKLMNOPQRSTUVWXYZ&

269 ITC Souvenir Gothic

ABCDEFGHIJKLMNOPQRSTUVWXYZ&

medium width capital G no spur no bar unstressed strokes

270 Syntax

ABCDEFGHIJKLMNOPQRSTUVWXYZ&

narrow capital G no spur no bar

271 Antique Olive

ABCDEFGHIJKLMNOPQRSTUVWXYZ&

272 Clearface Gothic

ABCDEFGHIJKLMNOPQRSTUVWXYZ&

wide capital G with spur

273 Akzidenz Grotesk

ABCDEFGHIJKLMNOPQRSTUVWXYZ&

medium width capital G with spur

274 Berthold Imago

ABCDEFGHIJKLMNOPQRSTUVWXYZ&

** These letters show special or 'style' characteristics. (NB. J, Q, & and g will usually vary from one typeface to another).*

* * * *
abcdefghijklmnopqrstuvwxyz1234567890
Venus **265**

* * * * *
abcdefghijklmnopqrstuvwxyz1234567890
Frutiger **266**

* * * *
abcdefghijklmnopqrstuvwxyz1234567890
Univers 55 **267**

* * * *
abcdefghijklmnopqrstuvwxyz1234567890
Optima **268**

* *
abcdefghijklmnopqrstuvwxyz1234567890
ITC Souvenir Gothic **269**

* * *
abcdefghijklmnopqrstuvwxyz1234567890
Syntax **270**

* * * * *
abcdefghijklmnopqrstuvwxyz1234567890
Antique Olive **271**

* * * *
abcdefghijklmnopqrstuvwxyz1234567890
Clearface Gothic **272**

* * * *
abcdefghijklmnopqrstuvwxyz1234567890
Akzidenz Grotesk **273**

* * * *
abcdefghijklmnopqrstuvwxyz1234567890
Berthold Imago **274**

NB. On lower case letters generally look at the x height and length of ascenders and descenders.

275 Folio

ABCDEFGHIJKLMNOPQRSTUVWXYZ&

276 Franklin Gothic (ATF)

ABCDEFGHIJKLMNOPQRSTUVWXYZ&

277 ITC Franklin Gothic

ABCDEFGHIJKLMNOPQRSTUVWXYZ&

278 Haas Unica

ABCDEFGHIJKLMNOPQRSTUVWXYZ&

279 Helvetica

ABCDEFGHIJKLMNOPQRSTUVWXYZ&

280 Mercator

ABCDEFGHIJKLMNOPQRSTUVWXYZ&

281 Standard

ABCDEFGHIJKLMNOPQRSTUVWXYZ&

282 Transport

ABCDEFGHIJKLMNOPQRSTUVWXYZ&

283 Video

ABCDEFGHIJKLMNOPQRSTUVWXYZ&

narrow capital G with spur

284 Bell Centennial

ABCDEFGHIJKLMNOPQRSTUVWXYZ&

* *These letters show special or 'style' characteristics. (NB. J, Q, & and g will usually vary from one typeface to another).*

Folio
Franklin Gothic (ATF)
ITC Franklin Gothic
Haas Unica
Helvetica
Mercator
Standard
Transport
Video
Bell Centennial

SANS SERIF

GG

* * * * *

abcdefghijklmnopqrstuvwxyz1234567890 Folio **275**

* * * * * *

abcdefghijklmnopqrstuvwxyz1234567890 Franklin Gothic (ATF) **276**

* * * * *

abcdefghijklmnopqrstuvwxyz1234567890 ITC Franklin Gothic **277**

* * * *

abcdefghijklmnopqrstuvwxyz1234567890 Haas Unica **278**

* * * *

abcdefghijklmnopqrstuvwxyz1234567890 Helvetica **279**

* * * * *

abcdefghijklmnopqrstuvwxyz1234567890 Mercator **280**

* * * *

abcdefghijklmnopqrstuvwxyz1234567890 Standard **281**

* * * *

abcdefghijklmnopqrstuvwxyz1234567890 Transport **282**

* * * *

abcdefghijklmnopqrstuvwxyz1234567890 Video **283**

* * ** *

abcdefghijklmnopqrstuvwxyz1234567890 Bell Centennial **284**

NB. On lower case letters generally look at the x height and length of ascenders and descenders.

285 Bell Gothic

ABCDEFGHIJKLMNOPQRSTUVWXYZ&

286 Lightline Gothic

ABCDEFGHIJKLMNOPQRSTUVWXYZ&

287 News Gothic

ABCDEFGHIJKLMNOPQRSTUVWXYZ&

288 Record Gothic

ABCDEFGHIJKLMNOPQRSTUVWXYZ&

289 Trade Gothic

ABCDEFGHIJKLMNOPQRSTUVWXYZ&

square-shaped

290 Bank Gothic

ABCDEFGHIJKLMNOPQRSTUVWXYZ&

291 Eurostile

ABCDEFGHIJKLMNOPQRSTUVWXYZ&

293 Heldustry

ABCDEFGHIJKLMNOPQRSTUVWXYZ&

sloped

295 ITC Eras

ABCDEFGHIJKLMNOPQRSTUVWXYZ&

rounded

297 ITC Benguiat Gothic

ABCDEFGHIJKLMNOPQRSTUVWXYZ&

** These letters show special or 'style' characteristics. (NB. J, Q, & and g will usually vary from one typeface to another).*

Bell Gothic
Lightline Gothic
News Gothic
Record Gothic
Trade Gothic
Bank Gothic
Eurostile
Heldustry
ITC Eras
ITC Benguiat Gothic

GG

Bell Gothic 285

abcdefghijklmnopqrstuvwxyz1234567890

Lightline Gothic 286

abcdefghijklmnopqrstuvwxyz1234567890

News Gothic 287

abcdefghijklmnopqrstuvwxyz1234567890

Record Gothic 288

abcdefghijklmnopqrstuvwxyz1234567890

Trade Gothic 289

abcdefghijklmnopqrstuvwxyz1234567890

mall capitals

Bank Gothic 290

ABCDEFGHIJKLMNOPQRSTUVWXYZ1234567890

Eurostile 291

abcdefghijklmnopqrstuvwxyz1234567890

Heldustry 293

abcdefghijklmnopqrstuvwxyz1234567890

ITC Eras 295

abcdefghijklmnopqrstuvwxyz1234567890

ITC Benguiat Gothic 297

abcdefghijklmnopqrstuvwxyz1234567890

NB. On lower case letters generally look at the x height and length of ascenders and descenders.

298 Berliner Grotesk

ABCDEFGHIJKLMNOPQRSTUVWXYZ&

299 Churchward 70

ABCDEFGHIJKLMNOPQRSTUVWXYZ&

300 ITC Ronda

ABCDEFGHIJKLMNOPQRSTUVWXYZ&

electronic or machine read

302 IC – Alphabet

ABCDEFGHIJKLMNOPQRSTUVWXYZ

303 OCR-A

ABCDEFGHIJKLMNOPQRSTUVWXYZ

304 OCR-B

ABCDEFGHIJKLMNOPQRSTUVWXYZ&

new entries

304A Abadi (Monotype)

ABCDEFGHIJKLMNOPQRSTUVWXYZ&

304B Arial (Monotype)

ABCDEFGHIJKLMNOPQRSTUVWXYZ&

304C Avenir 55 (Linotype)

ABCDEFGHIJKLMNOPQRSTUVWXYZ&

304D Wolters Map Face (Monotype)

ABCDEFGHIJKLMNOPQRSTUVWXYZ&

** These letters show special or 'style' characteristics. (NB. J, Q, & and g will usually vary from one typeface to another).*

Berliner Grotesk **298**

* * * *
abcdefghijklmnopqrstuvwxyz1234567890

Churchward 70 **299**

* * *
abcdefghijklmnopqrstuvwxyz1234567890

ITC Ronda **300**

* * * *
abcdefghijklmnopqrstuvwxyz1234567890

IC – Alphabet **302**

*
1234567890 *no lower case*

OCR-A **303**

* *
1234567890 *no lower case*

OCR-B **304**

* * * * * *
abcdefghijklmnopqrstuvwxyz1234567890

Abadi (Monotype) **304A**

* * * * *
abcdefghijklmnopqrstuvwxyz1234567890

Arial (Monotype) **304B**

*
abcdefghijklmnopqrstuvwxyz1234567890

Avenir 55 (Linotype) **304C**

* * *
abcdefghijklmnopqrstuvwxyz1234567890

Wolters Map Face (Monotype) **304D**

* * * *
abcdefghijklmnopqrstuvwxyz1234567890

NB. On lower case letters generally look at the x height and length of ascenders and descenders.

TEXT TYPEFACE 'EARMARK' TABLES

THESE TABLES OFFER a method of identifying *Text* typefaces (Specimen Nos 1-304) by means of 'earmarks' or special characteristic features on individual letters. They represent an alternative but companion identification process to the *Text* typeface classification system beginning on page 12.

The tables are divided into two parts – 'Common' and 'Special Earmarks', but there is, however, a small overlap between the two parts.

'Common Earmark' Tables

These show typical, commonplace letter features and give examples of typefaces with each feature. 'Common' letters are identifiable either by their general appearance or by 'marked' features or captions. (see illustration below).

poor contrast

119 Century Schoolbook
137 Impressum
145 Primus Antiqua

153 Bauer Bodoni
156 Didot
161 Walbaum (Linotype)

'Special Earmark' Tables

These show more distinctive and unusual identifying features.

'Special earmarks' are indicated on letters by arrows, lines or captions and *Text* typefaces with each feature are listed by number below each. (see illustration below). Each letter has been 'analysed' in parts or by features generally starting from the top and working downwards to the bottom. It should be noted that the general 'style' of typefaces with the same 'earmark' can vary slightly.

27, 60, 63

35, **38**-41, 61-2, 74, 76, 99, 123-4, 132, 147

Figures are divided throughout into two kinds – 'lining' and 'non-lining'. An example of each is given below:

lining

1234567890

non-lining

1234567890

e.g. Baskerville

In both sets of tables, letters are arranged in a continuous sequence from a to z in both capital and lower case forms (plus ampersand and figures). The 'earmarks' of each letter are then divided (by rules) into groups representing *Text* typeface categories used in the book as follows:

Category Nos. 1-4 (Roman Serif)
(Specimen Nos. 1-150)

No. 5 (Modern Serif)
(Specimen Nos. 151-187)

No. 6 (Slab Serif)
(Specimen Nos. 188-217)

No. 7 (Wedge Serif)
(Specimen Nos. 218-240)

No. 8 (Sans Serif)
(Specimen Nos. 245-304)

NB. There are no 'common earmarks' for the Wedge Serif category since it generally comprises of more 'unusual' typefaces.

Looking for 'earmarks'

1. Consult the recommended selection order for 'earmarks' on this page and choose a letter as early in the order as possible.

2. Look in the 'Common Earmark' Tables to see whether or not the specimen letter you have chosen has a 'common earmark'. If it has, then select alternative specimen letters until you find one which has features which do not appear in these tables as 'common features will not generally assist in rapid typeface identification.

3. Find this letter in the following 'Special Earmark' Tables.

4. Look through the listings of illustrated specimen letters which are divided by rules into typeface categories (as listed previously) and match your specimen against the 'earmarks' shown.

5. When you have successfully matched your specimen to one or more of the 'earmarks' then look up in turn the typeface specimens whose numbers are given below each until you identify your particular typeface specimen.

6. If specific typeface identification is not easily obtainable with the specimen letter you have chosen then select alternative letters until a positive 'photofit' picture of the typeface is achieved.

Recommended order for selecting 'earmarks':

Capital letters and ampersand:
Q, &, J, G, W, A, K, C, R, M, E, P, S, T, F, B, N, O, U, X, Y, D, H, Z, L, V, I.

Lower case letters:
g, a, j, y, k, t, f, r, q, w, e, b, s, c, d, p, m, u, x, o, v, h, n, i, l, z.

Figures:
3, 7, 5, 2, 1, 4, 9, 6, 8, 0

'Common Earmarks'

The 'common earmarks' (or typical identifying features) are indicated either by the general appearance of letters or by 'marked' features. The general 'style' of typefaces with the same 'earmark' may vary. Example typefaces with their specimen numbers are listed against each letter.

Throughout these tables 'earmarks' are divided into Text typeface categories by fine horizontal rules as described in the introduction on page 97.

19 Centaur
52 Times Roman (Linotype)
79 Baskerville (Linotype)

flat top

56 Bookman
70 Old Style No. 7
86 Times Europa

A — *wide flat top*

57 ITC Bookman
71 Olympian
138 Melior

35 Bembo
39 Plantin
76 Aster

A

59 Caslon Old Face No. 2
73 Ehrhardt
94 Garamond (Stempel)

A — *poor contrast*

119 Century Schoolbook
137 Impressum
145 Primus Antiqua

A

153 Bauer Bodoni
156 Didot
161 Walbaum (Linotype)

A

196 Memphis
197 Rockwell
199 Stymie (ATF)

A

254 Futura
258 Cable (Klingspor)
264 Tempo

A

259 Gill Sans
267 Univers 55
279 Helvetica

B — *equal size bowls*

24 ITC Clearface
67 Imprint
90 Fournier

B — *bottom heavy*

19 Centaur
79 Baskerville (Linotype)
88 Sabon

B — *poor contrast*

115 Excelsior
119 Century Schoolbook
121 Ionic 5

B

153 Bauer Bodoni
156 Didot
161 Walbaum (Linotype)

B

194 ITC Lubalin Graph
197 Rockwell
198 Serifa 55

B

261 Grotesque 215
265 Univers 55
279 Helvetica

C

5 Windsor
56 Bookman
69 Old Style No. 2

C

49 Goudy Catalogue
52 Times Roman (Linotype)
67 Imprint

C

35 Bembo
39 Plantin
92 Garamond (Stempel)

C

20 Horley Old Style
61 Caslon 540
79 Baskerville (Linotype)

C — *poor contrast*

119 Century Schoolbook
121 Ionic 5
145 Primus Antiqua

C

171 Augustea
179 Modern No. 20
186 Scotch 2 (Linotype)

C

196 Memphis
197 Rockwell
198 Serifa 55

C

254 Futura
257 Spartan
259 Gills Sans

C

256 Nobel
261 Grotesque 215
273 Akzidenz Grotesque

C

267 Univers 55
275 Folio
279 Helvetica

D

39 Plantin
52 Times Roman (Linotype)
69 Old Style No. 2

D — *concave*

49 Goudy Catalogue
91 Garamond (Monotype)
100 Concorde

D — *poor contrast*

114 Century Expanded
119 Century Schoolbook
121 Ionic 5

D

153 Bauer Bodoni
156 Didot
163 Bodoni (Haas)

D

196 Memphis
197 Rockwell
198 Serifa 55

D

267 Univers 55
275 Folio
279 Helvetica

E

5 Windsor
61 Caslon 540
69 Old Style No. 2

E

35 Bembo
39 Plantin
52 Times Roman (Linotype)

E

153 Bauer Bodoni
161 Walbaum (Linotype)
174 Caledonia

E

193 Glypha 55
198 Serifa 55
199 Stymie (ATF)

E — *bracketed slab*

207 Consort
209 Clarendon (Linotype)
212 Egizio

E — *narrow*

253 Erbar
254 Futura
257 Spartan

E — *wider*

267 Univers
279 Helvetica
281 Standard

F

5 Windsor
61 Caslon 540
69 Old Style No. 2

F

35 Bembo
39 Plantin
52 Times Roman (Linotype)

F

153 Bauer Bodoni
161 Walbaum (Linotype)
174 Caledonia

F

193 Glypha 55
198 Serifa 55
199 Stymie (ATF)

F — *bracketed slab*

207 Consort
209 Clarendon (Linotype)
212 Egizio

F — *narrow*

253 Erbar
254 Futura
257 Spartan

F — *wider*

267 Univers 55
279 Helvetica
281 Standard

G

49 Goudy Catalogue
70 Old Style No. 7
80 Baskerville No. 2

G

15 Cloister
97 Spectrum
105 Romulus

G
52 Times Roman (Linotype)
67 Imprint
90 Garamond (Stempel)

G *poor contrast*
119 Century Schoolbook
121 Ionic 5
142 Textype

G
175 ITC Century
177 De Vinne
186 Scotch 2 (Linotype)

G
196 Memphis
198 Serifa 55
199 Stymie (ATF)

G *bracketed slab*
207 Consort
209 Clarendon (Linotype)
212 Egizio

G *circular (or nearly so) no spur*
253 Erbar
254 Futura
257 Spartan

G *with spur*
275 Folio
279 Helvetica
281 Standard

H
39 Plantin
60 Caslon 128
79 Baskerville (Linotype)

H
153 Bauer Bodoni
158 Fairfield
161 Walbaum (Linotype)

H
197 Rockwell
198 Serifa 55
199 Stymie (ATF)

H
207 Consort
209 Clarendon (Linotype)
212 Egizio

H
267 Univers 55
279 Helvetica
281 Standard

I
35 Bembo
39 Plantin
92 Garamond (Stempel)

I *poor contrast*
118 Aurora
119 Century Schoolbook
121 Ionic 5

I
152 Basilia
153 Bauer Bodoni
168 Walbaum (Monotype)

I
196 Memphis
197 Rockwell
199 Stymie (ATF)

I *bracketed slab*
207 Consort
209 Clarendon (Linotype)
212 Egizio

I
259 Gill Sans
267 Univers 55
279 Helvetica

J *short tail, non-lining*
16 Cloister
60 Caslon 128
67 Imprint

J *medium length tail, non-lining*
31 Vendôme
52 Times Roman (Linotype)
99 Caslon 3

J *rounded tail, non-lining*
25 Lutetia
66 Granjon
148 Electra

J *poor contrast, lining*
119 Century Schoolbook
121 Ionic 5
146 Textype

J
168 Walbaum (Linotype)
171 Augustea
177 De Vinne

J
196 Memphis
197 Rockwell
199 Stymie (ATF)

J *short tail*
253 Erbar
266 Frutiger
282 Standard

J *full rounded tail*
267 Univers 55
275 Folio
279 Helvetica

K *single junction*
70 Old Style No. 7
76 Aster
92 Garamond (Stempel)

K *single junction*
35 Bembo
38 Plantin
88 Sabon

K *double junction*
115 Excelsior
119 Century Schoolbook
121 Ionic 5

K
153 Bauer Bodoni
163 Bodoni (Haas)
165 ITC Fenice

K
196 Memphis
198 Serifa 55
199 Stymie (ATF)

K
261 Grotesque 215
279 Helvetica
281 Standard

L
35 Bembo
38 Plantin
61 Caslon 540

L
79 Baskerville (Linotype)
123 Cheltenham
138 Melior

L *poor contrast*
115 Excelsior
119 Century Schoolbook
121 Ionic 5

L
171 Augustea
174 Caledonia
177 De Vinne

L
197 Rockwell
198 Serifa 55
199 Stymie (ATF)

L *narrow*
254 Futura
257 Spartan
264 Tempo

L *wider*
267 Univers 55
279 Helvetica
281 Standard

M
61 Caslon 540
67 Imprint
79 Baskerville (Linotype)

M
35 Bembo
39 Plantin
73 Ehrhardt

M
153 Bauer Bodoni
158 Fairfield
168 Walbaum (Linotype)

M
193 Glypha 55
196 Memphis
197 Rockwell

M
209 Clarendon (Linotype)
212 Egizio
213 Consort

M
275 Folio
279 Helvetica
281 Standard

N
61 Caslon 540
92 Garamond (Stempel)
105 Romulus

N *poor contrast*
56 Bookman
71 Olympian
138 Melior

N
153 Bauer Bodoni
156 Didot
158 Fairfield

'Common Earmarks'

The 'common earmarks' (or typical identifying features) are indicated either by the general appearance of letters or by 'marked' features. The general 'style' of typefaces with the same 'earmark' may vary. Example typefaces with their specimen numbers are listed against each letter.

'Common Earmarks'

The 'common earmarks' (or typical identifying features) are indicated either by the general appearance of letters or by 'marked' features. The general 'style' of typefaces with the same 'earmark' may vary. Example typefaces with their specimen numbers are listed against each letter.

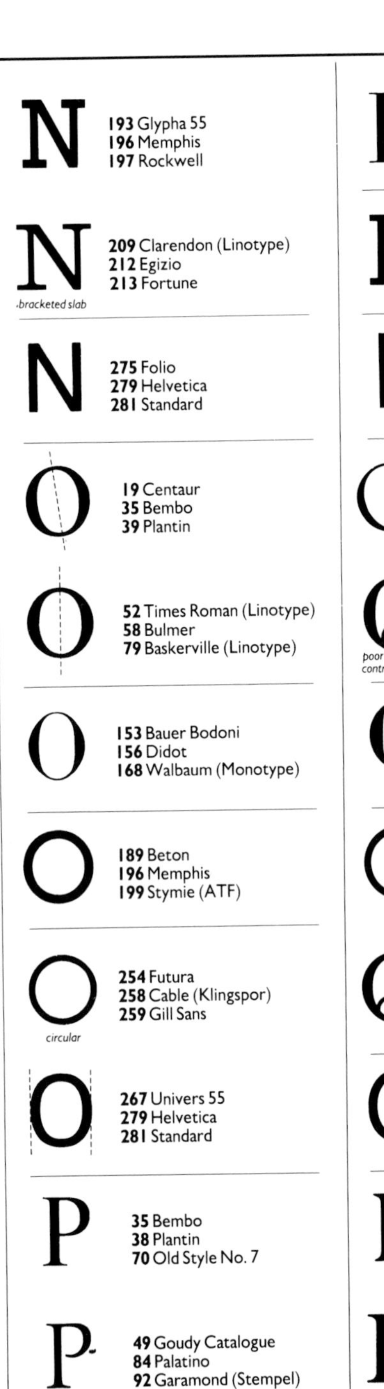

N		**193** Glypha 55; **196** Memphis; **197** Rockwell
N	bracketed slab	**209** Clarendon (Linotype); **212** Egizio; **213** Fortune
N		**275** Folio; **279** Helvetica; **281** Standard
O		**19** Centaur; **35** Bembo; **39** Plantin
O		**52** Times Roman (Linotype); **58** Bulmer; **79** Baskerville (Linotype)
O		**153** Bauer Bodoni; **156** Didot; **168** Walbaum (Monotype)
O		**189** Beton; **196** Memphis; **199** Stymie (ATF)
O	circular	**254** Futura; **258** Cable (Klingspor); **259** Gill Sans
O		**267** Univers 55; **279** Helvetica; **281** Standard
P		**35** Bembo; **38** Plantin; **70** Old Style No. 7
P		**49** Goudy Catalogue; **84** Palatino; **92** Garamond (Stempel)
P	poor contrast	**115** Excelsior; **119** Century Schoolbook; **137** Impressum
P		**153** Bauer Bodoni; **156** Didot; **158** Fairfield
P		**196** Memphis; **197** Rockwell; **198** Serifa 55
P		**259** Gill Sans; **260** Granby; **261** Grotesque 215
Q		**35** Bembo; **52** Times Roman (Linotype); **116** Perpetua
Q	poor contrast	**115** Excelsior; **119** Century Schoolbook; **121** Ionic 5
Q		**152** Basilia; **153** Bauer Bodoni; **174** Caledonia
Q		**189** Beton; **193** Glypha 55; **198** Serifa 55
Q		**209** Clarendon (Linotype); **212** Egizio; **213** Consort
Q		**278** Haas Unica; **279** Helvetica; **283** Video
R		**35** Bembo; **37** Goudy Old Style; **87** Quadriga Antiqua
R		**39** Plantin; **70** Old Style No. 7; **94** Garamond (Berthold)
R		**19** Centaur; **31** Vendôme; **75** Aldus
R	poor contrast	**115** Excelsior; **119** Century Schoolbook; **145** Primus Antiqua
R		**153** Bauer Bodoni; **156** Didot; **168** Walbaum (Monotype)
R		**188** A & S Gallantin; **196** Memphis; **198** Serifa 55
R		**254** Futura; **257** Spartan; **258** Cable (Klingspor)
R		**273** Akzidenz Grotesque; **281** Standard; **287** News Gothic
R		**267** Univers 55; **275** Folio; **279** Helvetica
S		**52** Times Roman (Linotype); **73** Ehrhardt; **80** Baskerville No. 2
S		**70** Old Style No. 7; **77** Baskerville (Berthold); **99** Caslon 3
S		**39** Plantin; **95** ITC Garamond; **130** Columbia
S	poor contrast	**115** Excelsior; **119** Century Schoolbook; **121** Ionic 5
S		**153** Bauer Bodoni; **156** Didot; **174** Caledonia
S		**196** Memphis; **197** Rockwell; **198** Stymie (ATF)
S	narrow	**254** Futura; **257** Spartan; **262** ITC Kabel
S	wider	**267** Univers 55; **279** Helvetica; **281** Standard
T		**35** Bembo; **69** Old Style No. 2; **107** Van Dijck
T		**52** Times Roman (Linotype); **76** Aster; **80** Baskerville No. 2
T	poor contrast	**118** Aurora; **119** Century Schoolbook; **121** Ionic 5
T		**153** Bauer Bodoni; **158** Fairfield; **161** Walbaum (Linotype)
T		**196** Memphis; **197** Rockwell; **198** Serifa 55
T		**154** Futura; **267** Univers 55; **279** Helvetica
U		**39** Plantin; **44** Trump Mediaeval; **92** Garamond (Stempel)
U	good contrast	**67** Imprint; **79** Baskerville (Linotype); **116** Perpetua
U	poor contrast	**118** Aurora; **119** Century Schoolbook; **121** Ionic 5
U		**153** Bauer Bodoni; **156** Didot; **168** Walbaum (Monotype)

U–a

U — **196** Memphis, **197** Rockwell, **198** Serifa 55

U — **254** Futura, **257** Spartan, **264** Tempo

U — **267** Univers 55, **275** Folio, **279** Helvetica

V — **52** Times Roman (Linotype), **61** Caslon 540, **69** Old Style No. 2

V (*poor contrast*) — **118** Aurora, **119** Century Schoolbook, **121** Ionic 5

V (*line serifs*) — **153** Bauer Bodoni, **156** Didot, **168** Walbaum (Monotype)

V (*bracketed serifs*) — **171** Augustea, **177** De Vinne, **186** Scotch 2 (Linotype)

V — **196** Memphis, **197** Rockwell, **198** Serifa 55

V — **254** Futura, **258** Cable (Klingspor), **259** Gill Sans

V — **261** Grotesque 215, **267** Univers 55, **279** Helvetica

W (*crossed centre strokes*) — **39** Plantin, **88** Sabon, **92** Garamond (Stempel)

W (*stepped centre strokes*) — **52** Times Roman (Linotype), **61** Caslon 540, **107** Van Dijck

W (*centre strokes meet at cap height*) — **67** Imprint, **69** Old Style No. 2, **74** Galliard

W (*no centre serif*) — **75** Aldus, **79** Baskerville (Linotype), **84** Palatino

W — **171** Augustea, **174** Caledonia, **185** Scotch 2 (Linotype)

W — **196** Memphis, **197** Rockwell, **202** Egyptian 173

W — **254** Futura, **263** Metro, **264** Tempo

W — **267** Univers 55, **277** ITC Franklin Gothic, **279** Helvetica

X — **35** Bembo, **39** Plantin, **92** Garamond (Stempel)

X (*poor contrast*) — **115** Excelsior, **119** Century Schoolbook, **121** Ionic 5

X — **158** Fairfield, **171** Augustea, **174** Caledonia

X — **196** Memphis, **197** Rockwell, **199** Stymie (ATF)

X (*narrow*) — **253** Erbar, **254** Futura, **264** Tempo

X (*wider*) — **267** Univers 55, **279** Helvetica, **281** Standard

Y — **67** Imprint, **92** Garamond (Stempel), **116** Perpetua

Y — **153** Bauer Bodoni, **158** Fairfield, **161** Walbaum (Linotype)

Y — **196** Memphis, **192** Rockwell, **198** Serifa 55

Y (*high junction*) — **253** Erbar, **254** Futura, **264** Tempo

Y (*lower junction*) — **275** Folio, **279** Helvetica, **281** Standard

Z — **60** Caslon 128, **70** Old Style No. 7, **88** Sabon

Z — **52** Times Roman (Linotype), **84** Palatino, **105** Romulus

Z — **161** Walbaum (Linotype), **171** Augustea, **174** Caledonia

Z — **196** Memphis, **197** Rockwell, **198** Serifa 55

Z — **254** Futura, **257** Spartan, **264** Tempo

Z — **267** Univers 55, **279** Helvetica, **287** News Gothic

& — **35** Bembo, **39** Plantin, **80** Baskerville No. 2

& — **97** Spectrum, **105** Romulus, **138** Melior

& — **52** Times Roman (Linotype), **76** Aster, **107** Van Dijck

& — **161** Walbaum (Linotype), **166** Modern (Linotype), **178** Madison

& — **193** Glypha 55, **197** Rockwell, **198** Serifa 55

& — **259** Gill Sans, **260** Granby, **267** Univers 55

& — **255** Neuzeit-Grotesk, **263** Metro, **268** Optima

& — **261** Grotesque 215, **277** ITC Franklin Gothic, **287** News Gothic

a — **20** Horley Old Style, **70** Old Style No. 7, **97** Spectrum

a — **52** Times Roman (Linotype), **100** Concorde, **131** French Round Face

a — **35** Bembo, **39** Plantin, **75** Aldus

a (*poor contrast*) — **114** Century Expanded, **119** Century Schoolbook, **121** Ionic 5

a — **153** Bauer Bodoni, **156** Didot, **186** Scotch 2 (Linotype)

'Common Earmarks'

The 'common earmarks' (or typical identifying features) are indicated either by the general appearance of letters or by 'marked' features. The general 'style' of typefaces with the same 'earmark' may vary. Example typefaces with their specimen numbers are listed against each letter.

'Common Earmarks'

The 'common earmarks' (or typical identifying features) are indicated either by the general appearance of letters or by 'marked' features. The general 'style' of typefaces with the same 'earmark' may vary. Example typefaces with their specimen numbers are listed against each letter.

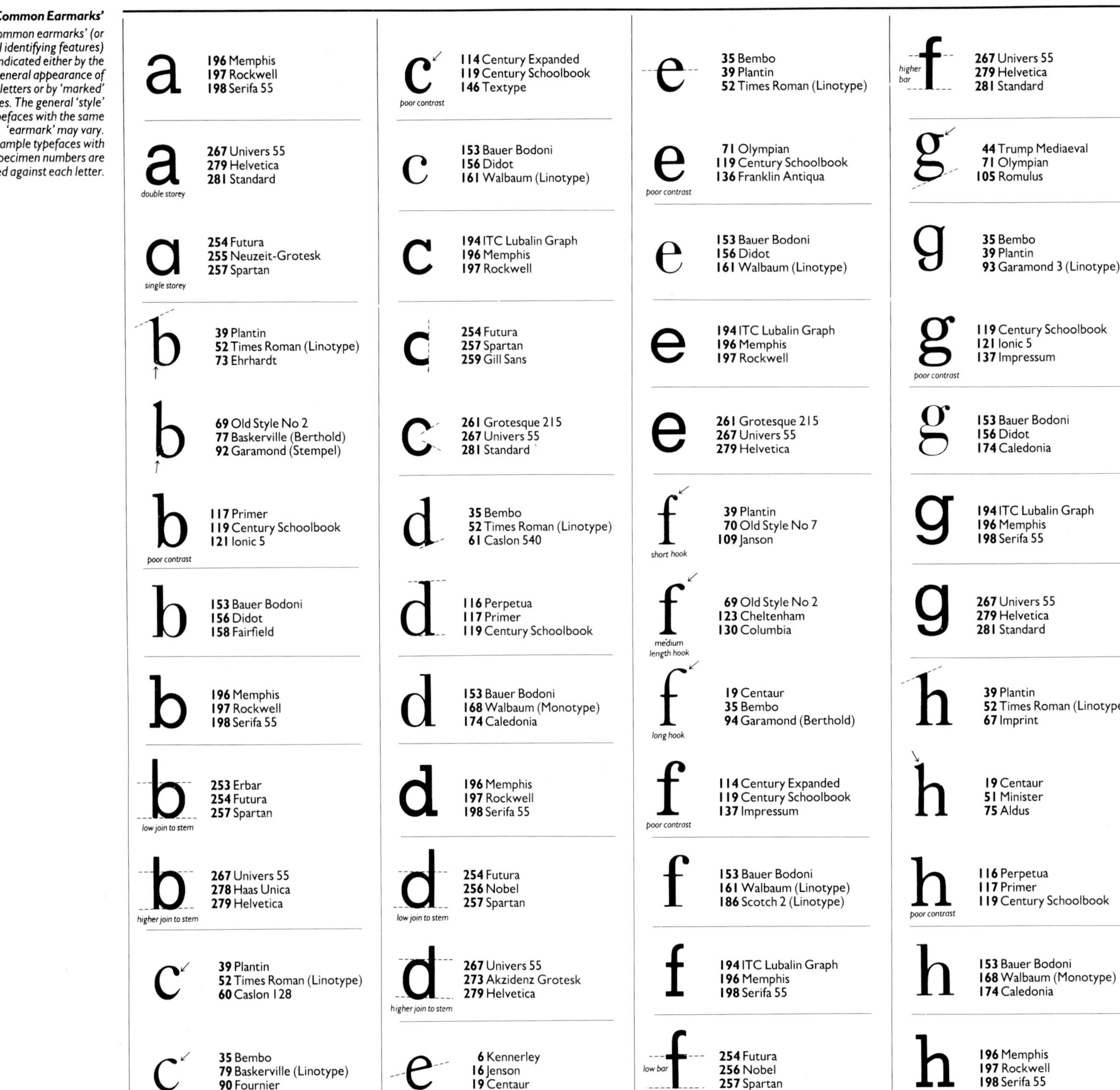

a		**196** Memphis **197** Rockwell **198** Serifa 55
a	double storey	**267** Univers 55 **279** Helvetica **281** Standard
a	single storey	**254** Futura **255** Neuzeit-Grotesk **257** Spartan
b		**39** Plantin **52** Times Roman (Linotype) **73** Ehrhardt
b		**69** Old Style No 2 **77** Baskerville (Berthold) **92** Garamond (Stempel)
b	poor contrast	**117** Primer **119** Century Schoolbook **121** Ionic 5
b		**153** Bauer Bodoni **156** Didot **158** Fairfield
b		**196** Memphis **197** Rockwell **198** Serifa 55
b	low join to stem	**253** Erbar **254** Futura **257** Spartan
b	higher join to stem	**267** Univers 55 **278** Haas Unica **279** Helvetica
c		**39** Plantin **52** Times Roman (Linotype) **60** Caslon 128
c		**35** Bembo **79** Baskerville (Linotype) **90** Fournier
c	poor contrast	**114** Century Expanded **119** Century Schoolbook **146** Textype
c		**153** Bauer Bodoni **156** Didot **161** Walbaum (Linotype)
c		**194** ITC Lubalin Graph **196** Memphis **197** Rockwell
c		**254** Futura **257** Spartan **259** Gill Sans
c		**261** Grotesque 215 **267** Univers 55 **281** Standard
d		**35** Bembo **52** Times Roman (Linotype) **61** Caslon 540
d		**116** Perpetua **117** Primer **119** Century Schoolbook
d		**153** Bauer Bodoni **168** Walbaum (Monotype) **174** Caledonia
d		**196** Memphis **197** Rockwell **198** Serifa 55
d	low join to stem	**254** Futura **256** Nobel **257** Spartan
d	higher join to stem	**267** Univers 55 **273** Akzidenz Grotesk **279** Helvetica
e		**6** Kennerley **16** Jenson **19** Centaur
e		**35** Bembo **39** Plantin **52** Times Roman (Linotype)
e	poor contrast	**71** Olympian **119** Century Schoolbook **136** Franklin Antiqua
e		**153** Bauer Bodoni **156** Didot **161** Walbaum (Linotype)
e		**194** ITC Lubalin Graph **196** Memphis **197** Rockwell
e		**261** Grotesque 215 **267** Univers 55 **279** Helvetica
f	short hook	**39** Plantin **70** Old Style No 7 **109** Janson
f	medium length hook	**69** Old Style No 2 **123** Cheltenham **130** Columbia
f	long hook	**19** Centaur **35** Bembo **94** Garamond (Berthold)
f	poor contrast	**114** Century Expanded **119** Century Schoolbook **137** Impressum
f		**153** Bauer Bodoni **161** Walbaum (Linotype) **186** Scotch 2 (Linotype)
f		**194** ITC Lubalin Graph **196** Memphis **198** Serifa 55
f	low bar	**254** Futura **256** Nobel **257** Spartan
f	higher bar	**267** Univers 55 **279** Helvetica **281** Standard
g		**44** Trump Mediaeval **71** Olympian **105** Romulus
g		**35** Bembo **39** Plantin **93** Garamond 3 (Linotype)
g	poor contrast	**119** Century Schoolbook **121** Ionic 5 **137** Impressum
g		**153** Bauer Bodoni **156** Didot **174** Caledonia
g		**194** ITC Lubalin Graph **196** Memphis **198** Serifa 55
g		**267** Univers 55 **279** Helvetica **281** Standard
h		**39** Plantin **52** Times Roman (Linotype) **67** Imprint
h		**19** Centaur **51** Minister **75** Aldus
h	poor contrast	**116** Perpetua **117** Primer **119** Century Schoolbook
h		**153** Bauer Bodoni **168** Walbaum (Monotype) **174** Caledonia
h		**196** Memphis **197** Rockwell **198** Serifa 55

'Common Earmarks'

The 'common earmarks' (or typical identifying features) are indicated either by the general appearance of letters or by 'marked' features. The general 'style' of typefaces with the same 'earmark' may vary. Example typefaces with their specimen numbers are listed against each letter.

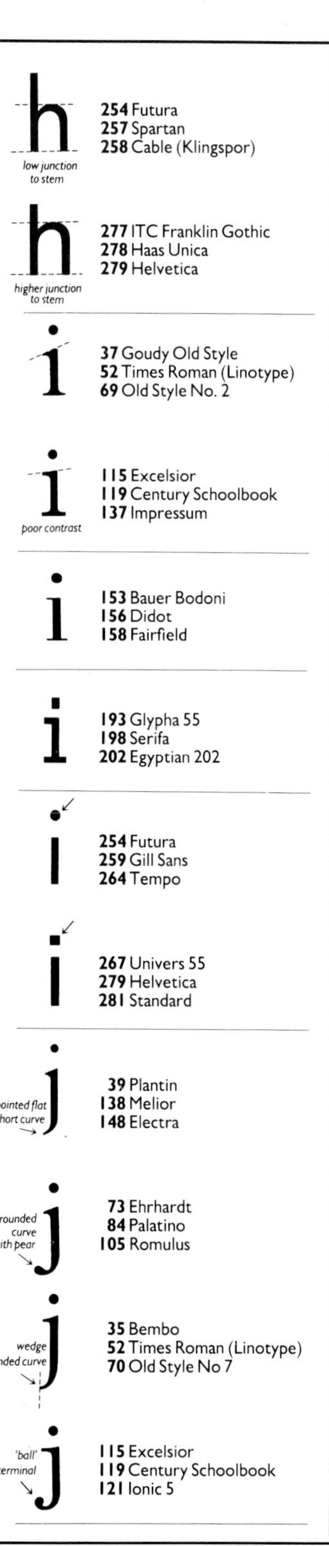

h — low junction to stem
254 Futura
257 Spartan
258 Cable (Klingspor)

h — higher junction to stem
277 ITC Franklin Gothic
278 Haas Unica
279 Helvetica

i
37 Goudy Old Style
52 Times Roman (Linotype)
69 Old Style No. 2

i — poor contrast
115 Excelsior
119 Century Schoolbook
137 Impressum

i
153 Bauer Bodoni
156 Didot
158 Fairfield

i
193 Glypha 55
198 Serifa
202 Egyptian 202

i
254 Futura
259 Gill Sans
264 Tempo

i
267 Univers 55
279 Helvetica
281 Standard

j — pointed flat short curve
39 Plantin
138 Melior
148 Electra

j — rounded curve with pear
73 Ehrhardt
84 Palatino
105 Romulus

j — wedge ended curve
35 Bembo
52 Times Roman (Linotype)
70 Old Style No 7

j — 'ball' terminal
115 Excelsior
119 Century Schoolbook
121 Ionic 5

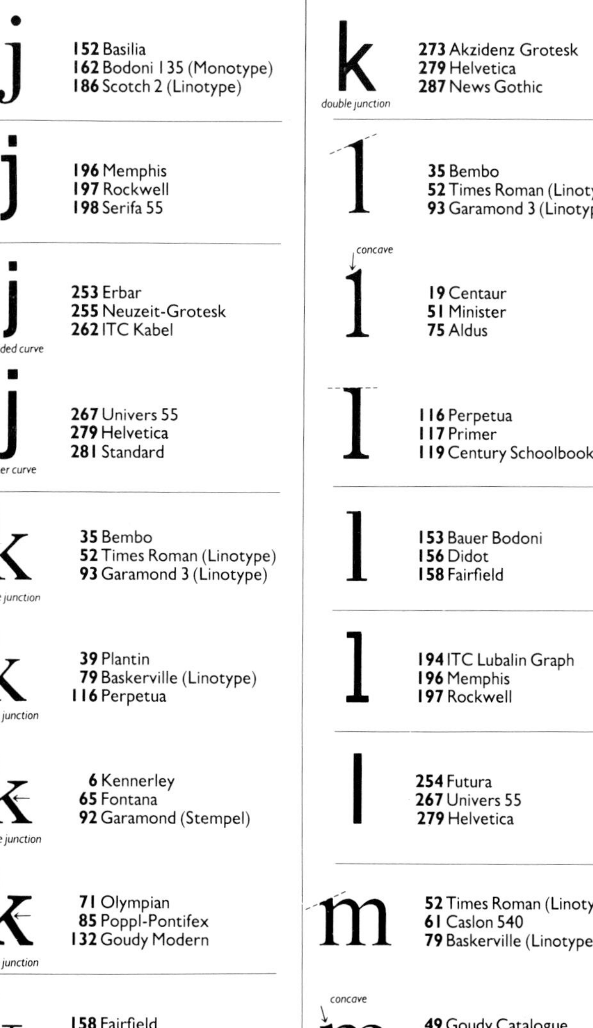

j
152 Basilia
162 Bodoni 135 (Monotype)
186 Scotch 2 (Linotype)

j
196 Memphis
197 Rockwell
198 Serifa 55

j — rounded curve
253 Erbar
255 Neuzeit-Grotesk
262 ITC Kabel

j — flatter curve
267 Univers 55
279 Helvetica
281 Standard

k — single junction
35 Bembo
52 Times Roman (Linotype)
93 Garamond 3 (Linotype)

k — single junction
39 Plantin
79 Baskerville (Linotype)
116 Perpetua

k — double junction
6 Kennerley
65 Fontana
92 Garamond (Stempel)

k — double junction
71 Olympian
85 Poppl-Pontifex
132 Goudy Modern

k
158 Fairfield
161 Walbaum (Linotype)
168 Walbaum (Monotype)

k
196 Memphis
197 Rockwell
198 Serifa 55

k — single junction
253 Erbar
254 Futura
258 Cable (Klingspor)

k — single junction
267 Univers 55
278 Haas Unica
283 Video

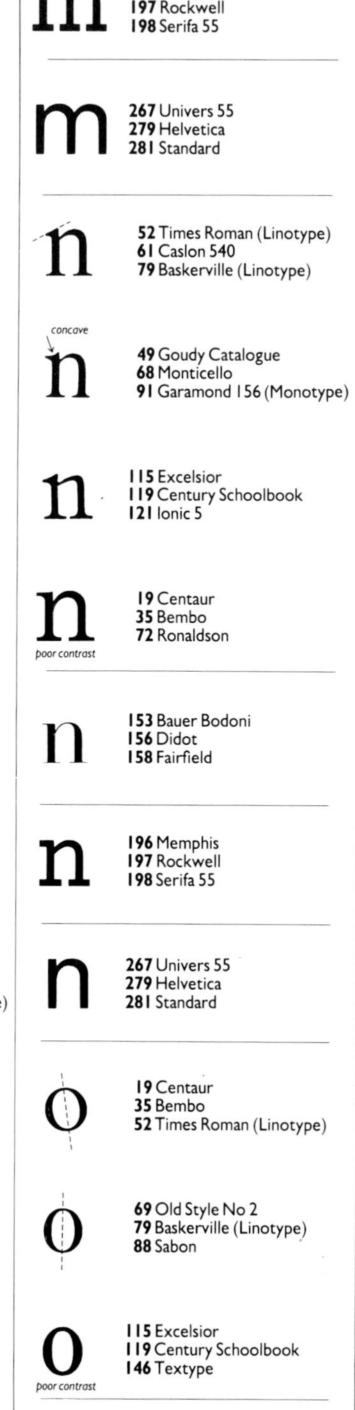

k — double junction
273 Akzidenz Grotesk
279 Helvetica
287 News Gothic

l
35 Bembo
52 Times Roman (Linotype)
93 Garamond 3 (Linotype)

l — concave
19 Centaur
51 Minister
75 Aldus

l
116 Perpetua
117 Primer
119 Century Schoolbook

l
153 Bauer Bodoni
156 Didot
158 Fairfield

l
194 ITC Lubalin Graph
196 Memphis
197 Rockwell

l
254 Futura
267 Univers 55
279 Helvetica

m
52 Times Roman (Linotype)
61 Caslon 540
79 Baskerville (Linotype)

m — concave
49 Goudy Catalogue
68 Monticello
91 Garamond 156 (Monotype)

m
19 Centaur
35 Bembo
72 Ronaldson

m — poor contrast
115 Excelsior
119 Century Schoolbook
121 Ionic 5

m
153 Bauer Bodoni
156 Didot
158 Fairfield

m
196 Memphis
197 Rockwell
198 Serifa 55

m
267 Univers 55
279 Helvetica
281 Standard

n
52 Times Roman (Linotype)
61 Caslon 540
79 Baskerville (Linotype)

n — concave
49 Goudy Catalogue
68 Monticello
91 Garamond 156 (Monotype)

n
115 Excelsior
119 Century Schoolbook
121 Ionic 5

n — poor contrast
19 Centaur
35 Bembo
72 Ronaldson

n
153 Bauer Bodoni
156 Didot
158 Fairfield

n
196 Memphis
197 Rockwell
198 Serifa 55

n
267 Univers 55
279 Helvetica
281 Standard

o
19 Centaur
35 Bembo
52 Times Roman (Linotype)

o
69 Old Style No 2
79 Baskerville (Linotype)
88 Sabon

o — poor contrast
115 Excelsior
119 Century Schoolbook
146 Textype

'Common Earmarks'

The 'common earmarks' (or typical identifying features) are indicated either by the general appearance of letters or by 'marked' features. The general 'style' of typefaces with the same 'earmark' may vary. Example typefaces with their specimen numbers are listed against each letter.

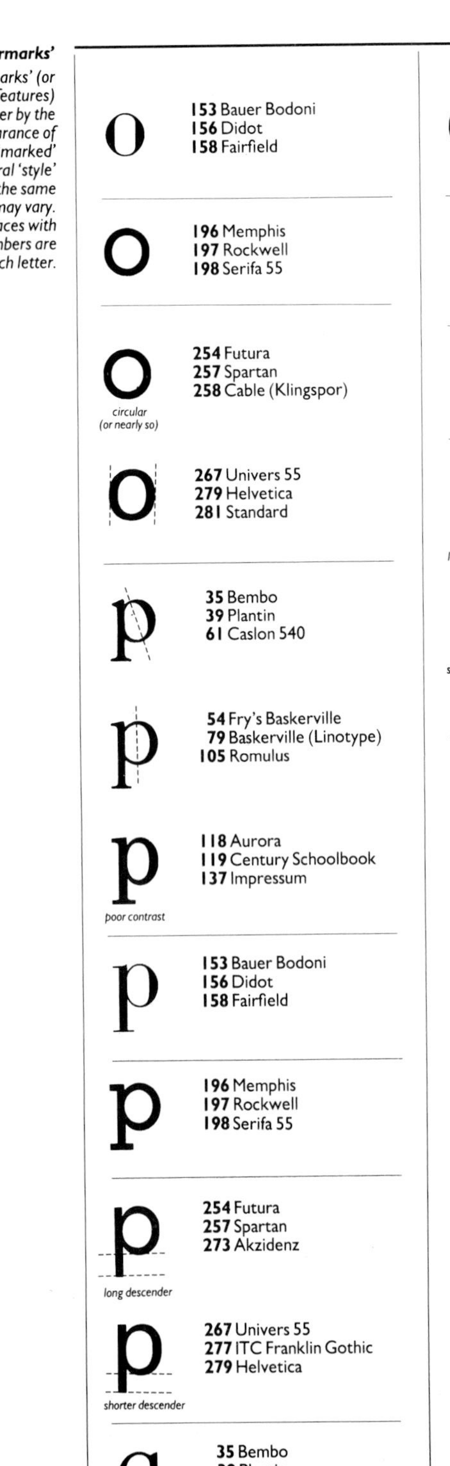

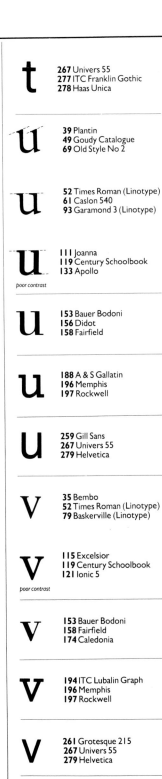

o
153 Bauer Bodoni
156 Didot
158 Fairfield

o
196 Memphis
197 Rockwell
198 Serifa 55

o — *circular (or nearly so)*
254 Futura
257 Spartan
258 Cable (Klingspor)

o
267 Univers 55
279 Helvetica
281 Standard

p
35 Bembo
39 Plantin
61 Caslon 540

p
54 Fry's Baskerville
79 Baskerville (Linotype)
105 Romulus

p — *poor contrast*
118 Aurora
119 Century Schoolbook
137 Impressum

p
153 Bauer Bodoni
156 Didot
158 Fairfield

p
196 Memphis
197 Rockwell
198 Serifa 55

p — *long descender*
254 Futura
257 Spartan
273 Akzidenz

p — *shorter descender*
267 Univers 55
277 ITC Franklin Gothic
279 Helvetica

q
35 Bembo
39 Plantin
61 Caslon 540

q
114 Century Expanded
119 Century Schoolbook
121 Ionic 5

q
153 Bauer Bodoni
156 Didot
158 Fairfield

q
194 ITC Lubalin Graph
197 Rockwell
199 Stymie (ATF)

q — *long descender*
254 Futura
257 Spartan
273 Akzidenz Grotesk

q — *shorter descender*
267 Univers 55
279 Helvetica
277 ITC Franklin Gothic

r
56 Bookman
88 Sabon
92 Garamond (Stempel)

r
52 Times Roman (Linotype)
92 Spectrum
105 Romulus

r — *poor contrast*
115 Excelsior
119 Century Schoolbook
121 Ionic 5

r
153 Bauer Bodoni
161 Walbaum (Linotype)
177 De Vinne

r
196 Memphis
197 Rockwell
198 Serifa 55

r
254 Futura
257 Spartan
259 Gill Sans

r
258 Cable (Klingspor)
261 Grotesque 215
267 Univers 55

s
52 Times Roman (Linotype)
73 Ehrhardt
80 Baskerville No 2

s
39 Plantin
95 ITC Garamond
130 Columbia

s
153 Bauer Bodoni
171 Augustea
172 Bell

s
196 Memphis
197 Rockwell
198 Serifa 55

s — *bracketed slab*
207 Consort
209 Clarendon (Linotype)
212 Egizio

s
254 Futura
257 Spartan
281 Standard

s
267 Univers 55
279 Helvetica
281 Standard

t
39 Plantin
52 Times Roman (Linotype)
92 Garamond (Stempel)

t — *definite concave head*
35 Bembo
70 Old Style No 7
98 Weiss

t
24 ITC Clearface
84 Palatino
138 Melior

t — *poor contrast*
115 Excelsior
119 Century Schoolbook
121 Ionic 5

t
171 Augustea
174 Caledonia
186 Scotch 2 (Linotype)

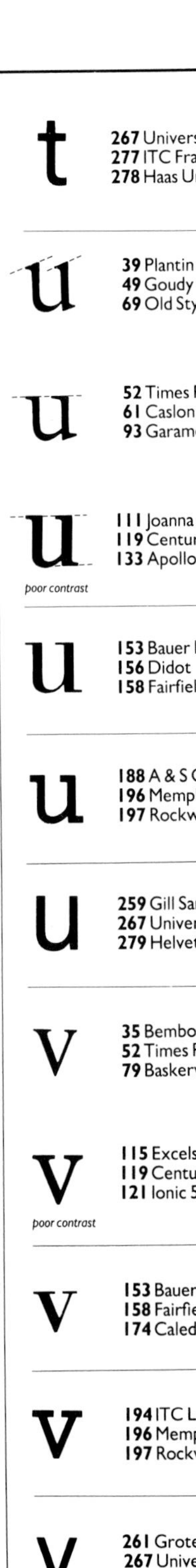

t
267 Univers 55
277 ITC Franklin Gothic
278 Haas Unica

u
39 Plantin
49 Goudy Catalogue
69 Old Style No 2

u
52 Times Roman (Linotype)
61 Caslon 540
93 Garamond 3 (Linotype)

u — *poor contrast*
111 Joanna
119 Century Schoolbook
133 Apollo

u
153 Bauer Bodoni
156 Didot
158 Fairfield

u
188 A & S Gallatin
196 Memphis
197 Rockwell

u
259 Gill Sans
267 Univers 55
279 Helvetica

v
35 Bembo
52 Times Roman (Linotype)
79 Baskerville (Linotype)

v — *poor contrast*
115 Excelsior
119 Century Schoolbook
121 Ionic 5

v
153 Bauer Bodoni
158 Fairfield
174 Caledonia

v
194 ITC Lubalin Graph
196 Memphis
197 Rockwell

v
261 Grotesque 215
267 Univers 55
279 Helvetica

centre strokes meet at centre
- **35** Bembo
- **39** Plantin
- **61** Caslon 540

W *stepped centre strokes*
- **52** Times Roman (Linotype)
- **73** Ehrhardt
- **91** Garamond 156 (Monotype)

W *no centre serif*
- **15** Cloister
- **77** Baskerville (Berthold)
- **123** Cheltenham

W
- **188** A & S Gallatin
- **196** Memphis
- **197** Rockwell

W
- **254** Futura
- **259** Gill Sans
- **264** Tempo

W
- **261** Grotesque 215
- **267** Univers 55
- **279** Helvetica

X
- **35** Bembo
- **78** Baskerville 169 (Monotype)
- **93** Garamond 3 (Linotype)

X
- **153** Bauer Bodoni
- **161** Walbaum (Linotype)
- **174** Caledonia

X
- **196** Memphis
- **197** Rockwell
- **198** Serifa 55

X *narrow*
- **273** Akzidenz Grotesk
- **281** Standard
- **287** News Gothic

X *wider*
- **259** Gill Sans
- **267** Univers 55
- **279** Helvetica

y *ounded tail with pear*
- **35** Bembo
- **52** Times Roman (Linotype)
- **94** Garamond (Berthold)

y *short tail*
- **25** Lutetia
- **59** Caslon Old Face No. 2
- **79** Baskerville (Linotype)

y *rounded tail with ball*
- **114** Century Expanded
- **119** Century Schoolbook
- **149** Iridium

y
- **153** Bauer Bodoni
- **161** Walbaum (Linotype)
- **171** Augustea

y
- **261** Grotesque 215
- **273** Akzidenz Grotesque
- **279** Helvetica

z
- **19** Centaur
- **69** Old Style No 2
- **72** Ronaldson

z
- **52** Times Roman (Linotype)
- **79** Baskerville (Linotype)
- **90** Fournier

z
- **153** Bauer Bodoni
- **171** Augustea
- **174** Caledonia

z
- **193** Glypha 55
- **196** Memphis
- **197** Rockwell

z
- **254** Futura
- **257** Spartan
- **259** Gill Sans

z
- **216** Grotesque 215
- **267** Univers 55
- **279** Helvetica

1
- **52** Times Roman (Linotype)
- **56** Bookman
- **73** Ehrhardt

1
- **35** Bembo
- **75** Aldus
- **117** Primer

I *non-lining*
- **40** Poliphilus
- **78** Baskerville 169 (Monotype)
- **91** Garamond 156 (Monotype)

1
- **153** Bauer Bodoni
- **161** Walbaum (Linotype)
- **181** Paganini

1
- **194** ITC Lubalin Graph
- **196** Memphis
- **197** Rockwell

1
- **253** Erbar
- **267** Univers 55
- **277** Franklin Gothic

1 *concave*
- **273** Akzidenz Grotesk
- **279** Helvetica
- **281** Standard

2
- **35** Bembo
- **52** Times Roman (Linotype)
- **39** Plantin

2
- **24** ITC Clearface
- **119** Century Schoolbook
- **121** Ionic 5

2 *non-lining*
- **19** Centaur
- **59** Caslon 128
- **107** Van Dijck

2
- **153** Bauer Bodoni
- **175** ITC Century
- **176** Century Nova

2
- **196** Memphis
- **197** Rockwell
- **198** Serifa 55

2
- **254** Futura
- **259** Gill Sans
- **264** Tempo

2
- **267** Univers 55
- **273** Akzidenz Grotesk
- **281** Standard

3
- **39** Plantin
- **52** Times Roman (Linotype)
- **67** Imprint

3
- **24** ITC Clearface
- **119** Century Schoolbook
- **146** Textype

3 *non-lining*
- **69** Old Style No 2
- **91** Garamond 156 (Monotype)
- **132** Goudy Modern

3
- **152** Basilia
- **153** Bauer Bodoni
- **156** Didot

3
- **196** Memphis
- **197** Rockwell
- **198** Serifa 55

3
- **258** Cable (Klingspor)
- **279** ITC Franklin Gothic
- **287** News Gothic

3
- **254** Futura
- **267** Univers 55
- **279** Helvetica

4
- **35** Bembo
- **39** Plantin
- **52** Times Roman (Linotype)

4
- **56** Bookman
- **64** Concorde Nova
- **86** Times Europa

4
- **115** Excelsior
- **119** Century Schoolbook
- **121** Ionic 5

4 *non-lining*
- **40** Poliphilus
- **60** Caslon 128
- **65** Fontana

4
- **194** ITC Lubalin Graph
- **197** Rockwell
- **199** Stymie (ATF)

'Common Earmarks'

The 'common earmarks' (or typical identifying features) are indicated either by the general appearance of letters or by 'marked' features. The general 'style' of typefaces with the same 'earmark' may vary. Example typefaces with their specimen numbers are listed against each letter.

'Common Earmarks'

The 'common earmarks' (or typical identifying features) are indicated either by the general appearance of letters or by 'marked' features. The general 'style' of typefaces with the same 'earmark' may vary. Example typefaces with their specimen numbers are listed against each letter.

4
261 Grotesque 215
267 Univers 55
279 Helvetica

5
39 Plantin
52 Times Roman (Linotype)
67 Imprint

5
75 Aldus
94 Garamond (Berthold)
105 Romulus

5
79 Baskerville (Linotype)
114 Century Expanded
119 Century Schoolbook

5 *non-lining*
19 Centaur
48 Emerson
89 Barbou

5
156 Didot
171 Augustea
186 Scotch 2 (Linotype)

5
188 A & S Gallantin
197 Rockwell
199 Stymie (ATF)

5
254 Futura
257 Spartan
260 Granby

5
267 Univers 55
279 Helvetica
281 Standard

6
35 Bembo
39 Plantin
52 Times Roman (Linotype)

6 *poor contrast*
57 ITC Bookman
119 Century Schoolbook
121 Ionic 5

6 *non-lining*
25 Lutetia
65 Fontana
107 Van Dijck

6
171 Augustea
174 Caledonia
186 Scotch 2 (Linotype)

6
196 Memphis
197 Rockwell
198 Serifa 55

6
254 Futura
258 Cable (Klingspor)
259 Gill Sans

6
267 Univers 55
279 Helvetica
281 Standard

7 *full serif*
35 Bembo
39 Plantin
52 Times Roman (Linotype)

7 *half serif*
61 Caslon 540
67 Imprint
79 Baskerville (Linotype)

7 *half serif*
118 Aurora
119 Century Schoolbook
145 Primus Antiqua

7 *non-lining*
4 Pastonchi
91 Garamond 156 (Monotype)
97 Spectrum

7
171 Augustea
175 ITC Century
177 De Vinne

7
188 A & S Gallatin
197 Rockwell
199 Stymie (ATF)

7 *curve*
207 Consort
209 Clarendon (Linotype)
212 Egizio

7
255 Neuzeit-Grotesk
257 Spartan
260 Granby

7
275 Folio
277 ITC Franklin Gothic
279 Helvetica

8 *diagonal crossover*
16 Jenson
35 Bembo
39 Plantin

8 *bowls touching (no crossover)*
80 Baskerville No 2
119 Century Schoolbook
138 Melior

8 *non-lining*
25 Lutetia
40 Poliphilus
60 Caslon 128

8
174 Caledonia
177 De Vinne
186 Scotch 2 (Linotype)

8
196 Memphis
197 Rockwell
198 Serifa 55

8 *narrow*
254 Futura
257 Spartan
259 Gill Sans

8 *wider*
267 Univers 55
279 Helvetica
281 Standard

9
35 Bembo
39 Plantin
52 Times Roman (Linotype)

9
57 ITC Bookman
119 Century Schoolbook
121 Ionic 5

9 *non-lining*
25 Lutetia
65 Fontana
107 Van Dijck

9
171 Augustea
174 Caledonia
186 Scotch 2 (Linotype)

9
196 Memphis
197 Rockwell
198 Serifa 55

9
254 Futura
258 Cable (Klingspor)
259 Gill Sans

9
267 Univers 55
279 Helvetica
281 Standard

0
35 Bembo
52 Times Roman (Linotype)
77 Baskerville (Berthold)

0 *poor contrast*
56 Bookman
119 Century Schoolbook
121 Ionic 5

0 *non-lining*
69 Old Style No 2
72 Ronaldson
78 Baskerville 169 (Monotype)

0
153 Bauer Bodoni
161 Walbaum (Linotype)
174 Caledonia

0
193 Glypha 55
197 Rockwell
188 A & S Gallatin

0 *narrow*
254 Futura
257 Spartan
262 ITC Kabel

0 *wider*
277 ITC Franklin Gothic
279 Helvetica
281 Standard

'Special Earmarks'

The 'special earmarks' (or distinctive identifying features) are indicated on each letter. The general 'style' of typefaces with the same 'earmark' may vary. The figures refer to specimen numbers.

For foot serif 'earmarks' of A refer to those of H as they are generally the same. Other 'earmarks' are as follows:

(general)

wide
99, **112**, 123-4, 127

narrow
29, 43, **64**, 93

bowing
1, 12, **30**, 42

(top)

27, 60, 63

35, **38**-41, 61-2, 74, 76, 99, 123-4, 132, 147

36, 46, 126-7, 129

32, 44, 56-7, **71**, 73, 85, 101-2, 106, 121, 125, 128, 136, 138, 141, 145-6

28, 82

51

33

23-4, 27, 59, 66, **72**, 92, 94, 150

110

143

107

sheared
8, **128**

A16
1-3, 9, 12, 29, 42, 140, 142

(bar)

high
6, 14, 20, 47, **65**, 81, 95, 97, 128

low
12, 29, 36, 78, 98-9, 123-4, **126**-7, 129, 142

74

28

142

wide
164, **184**

narrow
160, 176

155

high bar
182

low bar
170, **176**-7, 183

189, **194**-5

half serifs
A27
190, 192

long serifs
201, 207

220, **225**, 227-8, 236, 238

230

231

no serif
223-4, 229, 232, **234-5**

226

218-9, **233**, 257

slightly rounded
239-40

221

'nick' on bar
240

wide
246, 249, 290, 292

narrow
284-9

bowing
269

272

296, **299**

high bar
256, **258**, 262, 295

low bar
246, 249, 253, 284-5, 290, 292, 294, 298, 300-1, 303

297

296

270

(general)

wide
7, 56-7, 131

narrow
4, 8, **47**

(top)

concave
B11
2, 3, 12, **14**, 17, 48-9, 102

B12
26, 40, 42, 108

squashed
B13
125, 136, 138, 140, 150

concave back
113

(bar)

low bar
B4
36, 73, 89

high bar
3, **5**, 14, 42

2

12-3, 22, **104**

9, **28**, 30, 128

29

73, 147

(serifs)

long
27, **46**, 56-7, 59, 72, 86, 92, 115, 146

short
5, 7, 13, 22, 28-30, **82**, 98, 123-4, 126-7, 129

no bottom serif
134

wide
164, **184**

narrow
155, **176**

NB. *Bold figures indicate the specimen illustrated above.*

'Special Earmarks'

The 'special earmarks' (or distinctive identifying features) are indicated on each letter. The general 'style' of typefaces with the same 'earmark' may vary. The figures refer to specimen numbers.

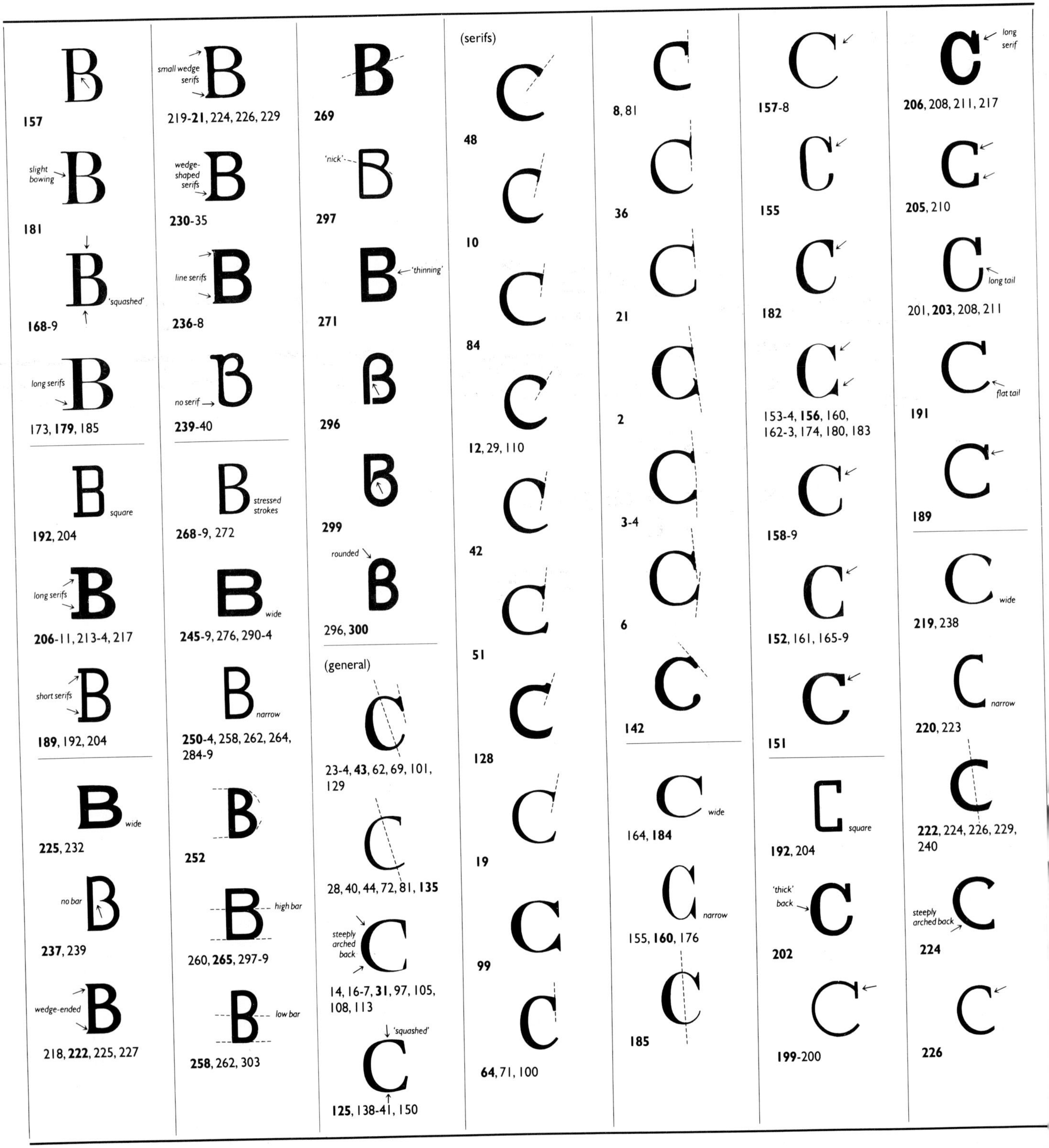

B

157

slight bowing

181

'squashed'

168-9

long serifs

173, **179**, 185

---

square

192, 204

long serifs

206-11, 213-4, 217

short serifs

189, 192, 204

---

wide

225, 232

no bar

237, 239

wedge-ended

218, **222**, 225, 227

small wedge serifs

219-**21**, 224, 226, 229

wedge-shaped serifs

230-35

line serifs

236-8

no serif

239-40

---

stressed strokes

268-9, 272

wide

245-9, 276, 290-4

narrow

250-4, 258, 262, 264, 284-9

252

high bar

260, **265**, 297-9

low bar

258, 262, 303

269

'nick'

297

'thinning'

271

296

299

rounded

296, **300**

(general)

C

23-4, **43**, 62, 69, 101, 129

28, 40, 44, 72, 81, **135**

steeply arched back

14, 16-7, **31**, 97, 105, 108, 113

'squashed'

125, 138-41, 150

(serifs)

48

10

84

12, 29, 110

42

51

128

19

99

64, 71, 100

8, 81

36

21

2

3-4

6

142

---

wide

164, **184**

narrow

155, **160**, 176

185

157-8

155

182

153-4, **156**, 160, 162-3, 174, 180, 183

158-9

152, 161, 165-9

151

---

square

192, 204

'thick' back

202

199-200

long serif

206, 208, 211, 217

205, 210

long tail

201, **203**, 208, 211

flat tail

191

189

---

wide

219, 238

narrow

220, 223

222, 224, 226, 229, 240

steeply arched back

224

226

NB. *Bold figures indicate the specimen illustrated above.*

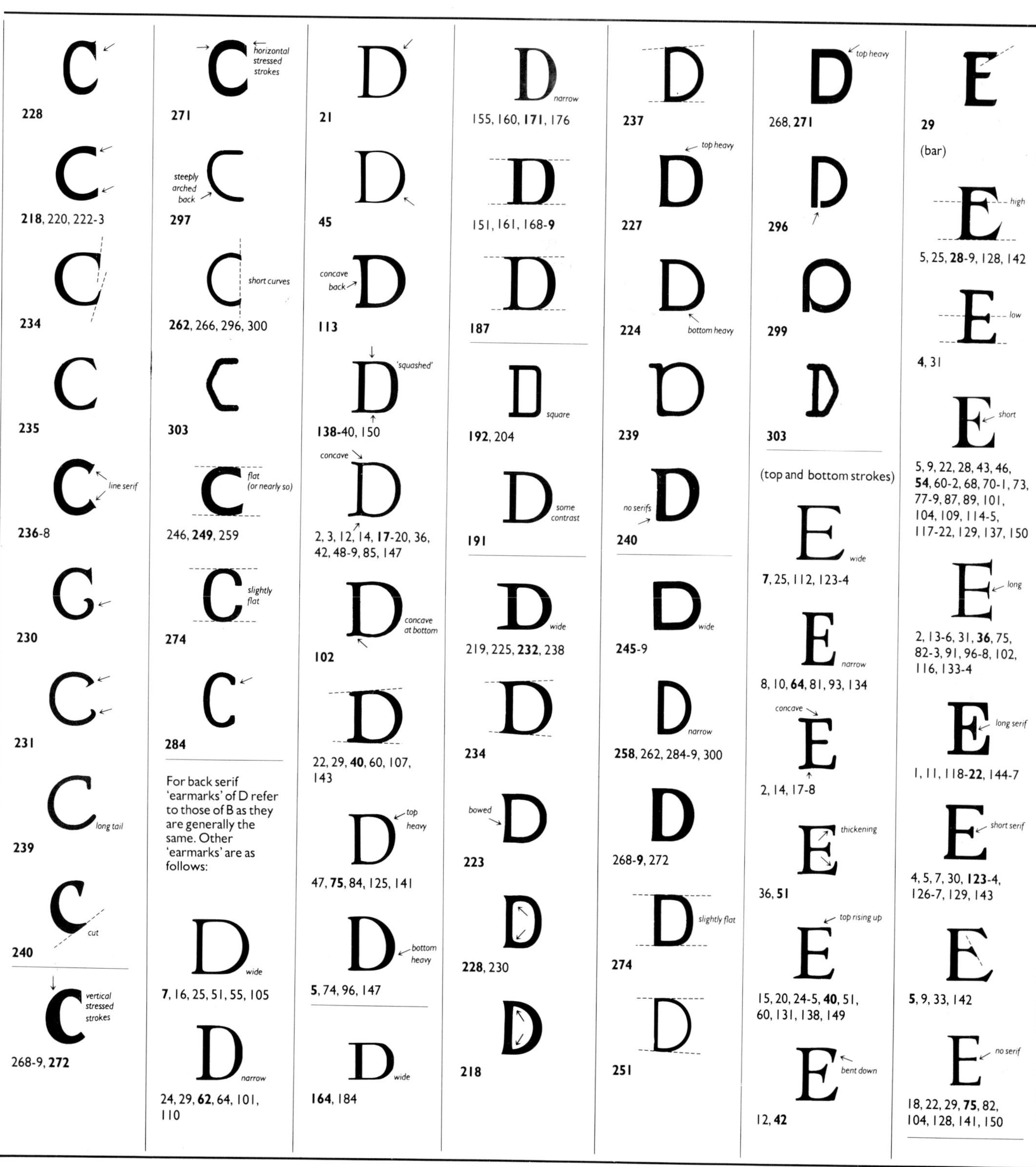
228
218, 220, 222-3
234
235
line serif
236-8
230
231
long tail
239
cut
240
vertical stressed strokes
268-9, 272
horizontal stressed strokes
271
steeply arched back
297
short curves
262, 266, 296, 300
303
flat (or nearly so)
246, 249, 259
slightly flat
274
284
For back serif 'earmarks' of D refer to those of B as they are generally the same. Other 'earmarks' are as follows:
wide
7, 16, 25, 51, 55, 105
narrow
24, 29, 62, 64, 101, 110
21
45
concave back
113
'squashed'
138-40, 150
concave
2, 3, 12, 14, 17-20, 36, 42, 48-9, 85, 147
concave at bottom
102
22, 29, 40, 60, 107, 143
top heavy
47, 75, 84, 125, 141
bottom heavy
5, 74, 96, 147
wide
164, 184
narrow
155, 160, 171, 176
151, 161, 168-9
187
square
192, 204
some contrast
191
wide
219, 225, 232, 238
234
bowed
223
228, 230
218
237
top heavy
227
bottom heavy
224
239
no serifs
240
wide
245-9
narrow
258, 262, 284-9, 300
268-9, 272
slightly flat
274
251
top heavy
268, 271
296
299
303
(top and bottom strokes)
wide
7, 25, 112, 123-4
narrow
8, 10, 64, 81, 93, 134
concave
2, 14, 17-8
thickening
36, 51
top rising up
15, 20, 24-5, 40, 51, 60, 131, 138, 149
bent down
12, 42
29
(bar)
high
5, 25, 28-9, 128, 142
low
4, 31
short
5, 9, 22, 28, 43, 46, 54, 60-2, 68, 70-1, 73, 77-9, 87, 89, 101, 104, 109, 114-5, 117-22, 129, 137, 150
long
2, 13-6, 31, 36, 75, 82-3, 91, 96-8, 102, 116, 133-4
long serif
1, 11, 118-22, 144-7
short serif
4, 5, 7, 30, 123-4, 126-7, 129, 143
5, 9, 33, 142
no serif
18, 22, 29, 75, 82, 104, 128, 141, 150

'Special Earmarks'

The 'special earmarks' (or distinctive identifying features) are indicated on each letter. The general 'style' of typefaces with the same 'earmark' may vary. The figures refer to specimen numbers.

***NB.** Bold figures indicate the specimen illustrated above.*

'Special Earmarks'

The 'special earmarks' (or distinctive identifying features) are indicated on each letter. The general 'style' of typefaces with the same 'earmark' may vary. The figures refer to specimen numbers.

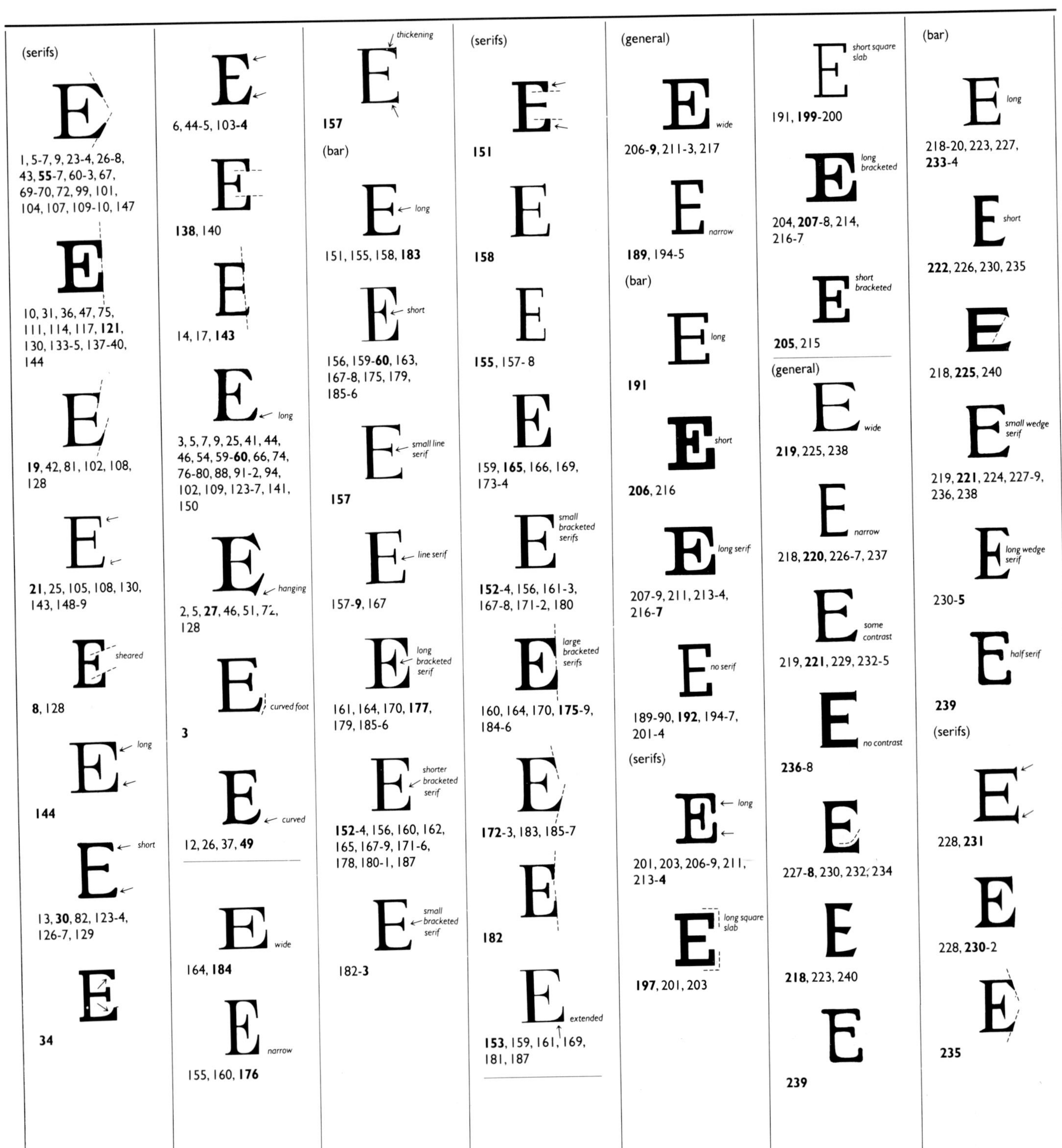
(serifs)
1, 5-7, 9, 23-4, 26-8, 43, 55-7, 60-3, 67, 69-70, 72, 99, 101, 104, 107, 109-10, 147
10, 31, 36, 47, 75, 111, 114, 117, 121, 130, 133-5, 137-40, 144
19, 42, 81, 102, 108, 128
21, 25, 105, 108, 130, 143, 148-9
sheared
8, 128
long
144
short
13, 30, 82, 123-4, 126-7, 129
34
6, 44-5, 103-4
138, 140
14, 17, 143
long
3, 5, 7, 9, 25, 41, 44, 46, 54, 59-60, 66, 74, 76-80, 88, 91-2, 94, 102, 109, 123-7, 141, 150
hanging
2, 5, 27, 46, 51, 72, 128
curved foot
3
curved
12, 26, 37, 49
wide
164, 184
narrow
155, 160, 176
thickening
157
(bar)
long
151, 155, 158, 183
short
156, 159-60, 163, 167-8, 175, 179, 185-6
small line serif
157
line serif
157-9, 167
long bracketed serif
161, 164, 170, 177, 179, 185-6
shorter bracketed serif
152-4, 156, 160, 162, 165, 167-9, 171-6, 178, 180-1, 187
small bracketed serif
182-3
(serifs)
151
158
155, 157-8
159, 165, 166, 169, 173-4
small bracketed serifs
152-4, 156, 161-3, 167-8, 171-2, 180
large bracketed serifs
160, 164, 170, 175-9, 184-6
172-3, 183, 185-7
182
extended
153, 159, 161, 169, 181, 187
(general)
wide
206-9, 211-3, 217
narrow
189, 194-5
(bar)
long
191
short
206, 216
long serif
207-9, 211, 213-4, 216-7
no serif
189-90, 192, 194-7, 201-4
(serifs)
long
201, 203, 206-9, 211, 213-4
long square slab
197, 201, 203
short square slab
191, 199-200
long bracketed
204, 207-8, 214, 216-7
short bracketed
205, 215
(general)
wide
219, 225, 238
narrow
218, 220, 226-7, 237
some contrast
219, 221, 229, 232-5
no contrast
236-8
227-8, 230, 232, 234
218, 223, 240
239
(bar)
long
218-20, 223, 227, 233-4
short
222, 226, 230, 235
218, 225, 240
small wedge serif
219, 221, 224, 227-9, 236, 238
long wedge serif
230-5
half serif
239
(serifs)
228, 231
228, 230-2
235

***NB.** Bold figures indicate the specimen illustrated above.*

'Special Earmarks'

The 'special earmarks' (or distinctive identifying features) are indicated on each letter. The general 'style' of typefaces with the same 'earmark' may vary. The figures refer to specimen numbers.

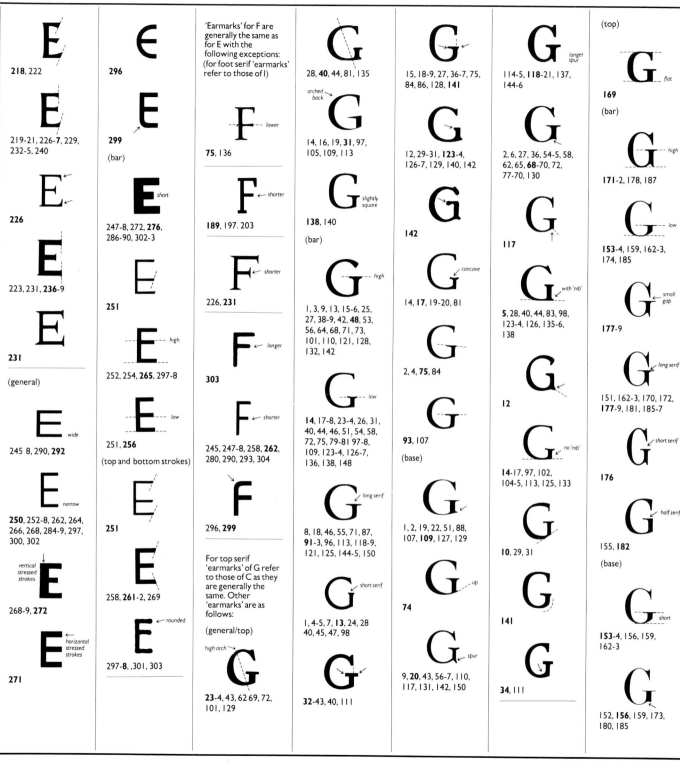

218, 222

219-21, 226-**7**, 229, 232-5, 240

226

223, 231, **236**-9

231

(general)

wide

245 8, 290, **292**

narrow

250, 252-8, 262, 264, 266, 268, 284-9, 297, 300, 302

vertical stressed strokes

268-9, **272**

horizontal stressed strokes

271

296

299

(bar)

short

247-8, 272, **276**, 286-90, 302-3

251

high

252, 254, **265**, 297-8

low

251, **256**

(top and bottom strokes)

251

258, **261**-2, 269

rounded

297-**8**, ,301, 303

'Earmarks' for F are generally the same as for E with the following exceptions: (for foot serif 'earmarks' refer to those of I)

lower

75, 136

shorter

189, 197. 203

shorter

226, **231**

longer

303

shorter

245, 247-8, 258, **262**, 280, 290, 293, 304

296, **299**

For top serif 'earmarks' of G refer to those of C as they are generally the same. Other 'earmarks' are as follows:

(general/top)

high arch

23-4, 43, 62 69, 72, 101, 129

28, **40**, 44, 81, 135

arched back

14, 16, 19, **31**, 97, 105, 109, 113

slightly square

138, 140

(bar)

high

1, 3, 9, 13, 15-6, 25, 27, 38-9, 42, **48**, 53, 56, 64, 68, 71, 73, 101, 110, 121, 128, 132, 142

low

14, 17-8, 23-4, 26, 31, 40, 44, 46, 51, 54, 58, 72, 75, 79-81 97-8, 109, 123-4, 126-7, 136, 138, 148

long serif

8, 18, 46, 55, 71, 87, **91**-3, 96, 113, 118-9, 121, 125, 144-5, 150

short serif

1, 4-5, 7, **13**, 24, 28 40, 45, 47, 98

32-43, 40, 111

15, 18-9, 27, 36-7, 75, 84, 86, 128, **141**

12, 29-31, **123**-4, 126-7, 129, 140, 142

142

concave

14, **17**, 19-20, 81

2, 4, **75**, 84

93, 107

(base)

1, 2, 19, 22, 51, 88, 107, **109**, 127, 129

up

74

spur

9, **20**, 43, 56-7, 110, 117, 131, 142, 150

longer spur

114-5, **118**-21, 137, 144-6

2, 6, 27, 36, 54-5, 58, 62, 65, **68**-70, 72, 77-70, 130

117

with 'nib'

5, 28, 40, 44, 83, 98, 123-4, 126, 135-6, 138

12

no 'nib'

14-17, 97, 102, 104-5, 113, 125, 133

10, 29, 31

141

34, 111

(top)

flat

169

(bar)

high

171-2, 178, 187

low

153-4, 159, 162-3, 174, 185

small gap

177-9

long serif

151, 162-3, 170, 172, **177**-9, 181, 185-7

short serif

176

half serif

155, **182**

(base)

short

153-4, 156, 159, 162-3

152, **156**, 159, 173, 180, 185

***NB.** Bold figures indicate the specimen illustrated above.*

'Special Earmarks'

The 'special earmarks' (or distinctive identifying features) are indicated on each letter. The general 'style' of typefaces with the same 'earmark' may vary. The figures refer to specimen numbers.

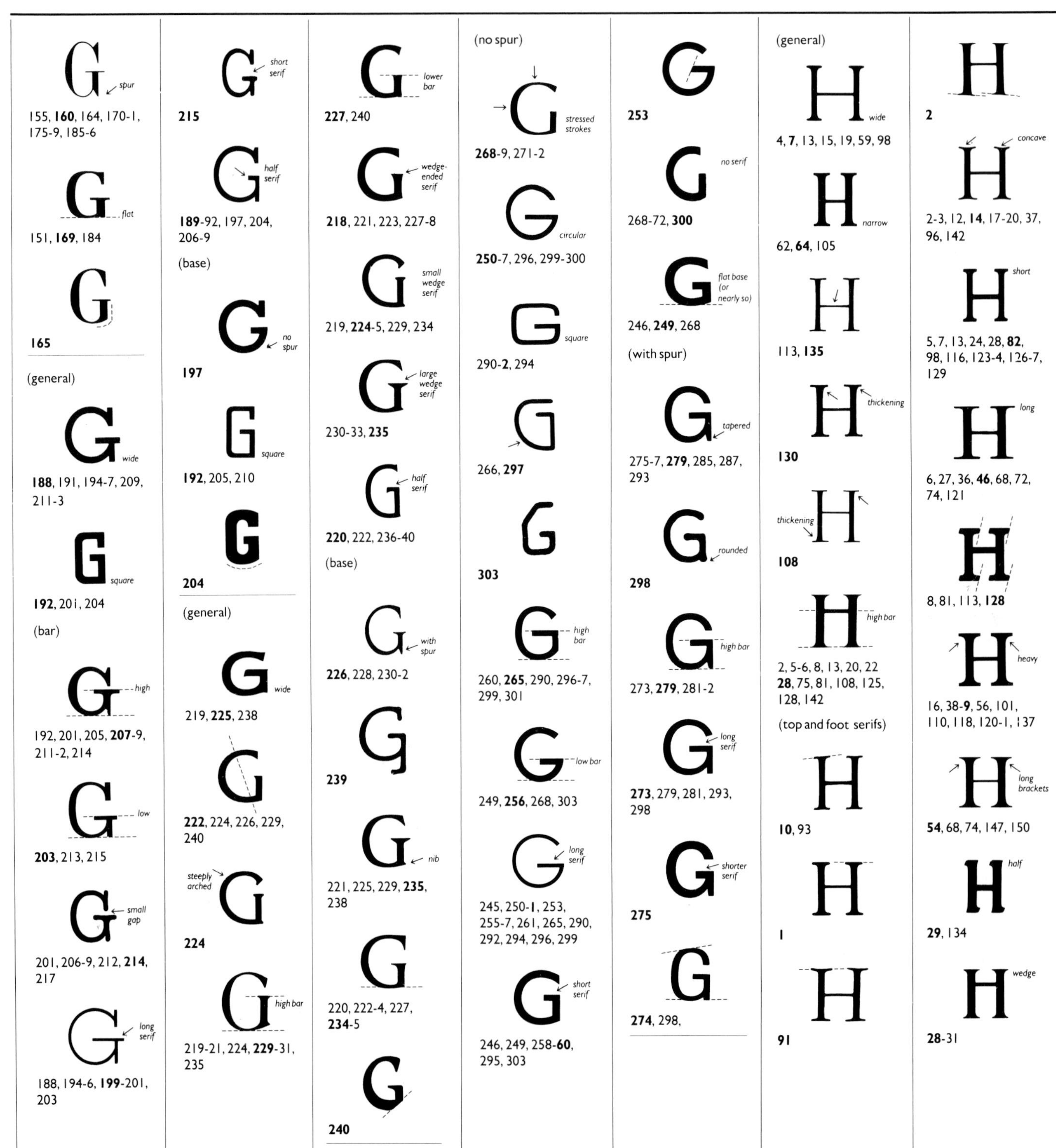
spur
155, 160, 164, 170-1, 175-9, 185-6
flat
151, 169, 184
165
(general)
wide
188, 191, 194-7, 209, 211-3
square
192, 201, 204
(bar)
high
192, 201, 205, 207-9, 211-2, 214
low
203, 213, 215
small gap
201, 206-9, 212, 214, 217
long serif
188, 194-6, 199-201, 203
short serif
215
half serif
189-92, 197, 204, 206-9
(base)
no spur
197
square
192, 205, 210
204
(general)
wide
219, 225, 238
222, 224, 226, 229, 240
steeply arched
224
high bar
219-21, 224, 229-31, 235
lower bar
227, 240
wedge-ended serif
218, 221, 223, 227-8
small wedge serif
219, 224-5, 229, 234
large wedge serif
230-33, 235
half serif
220, 222, 236-40
(base)
with spur
226, 228, 230-2
239
nib
221, 225, 229, 235, 238
220, 222-4, 227, 234-5
240
(no spur)
stressed strokes
268-9, 271-2
circular
250-7, 296, 299-300
square
290-2, 294
266, 297
303
high bar
260, 265, 290, 296-7, 299, 301
low bar
249, 256, 268, 303
long serif
245, 250-1, 253, 255-7, 261, 265, 290, 292, 294, 296, 299
short serif
246, 249, 258-60, 295, 303
253
no serif
268-72, 300
flat base (or nearly so)
246, 249, 268
(with spur)
tapered
275-7, 279, 285, 287, 293
rounded
298
high bar
273, 279, 281-2
long serif
273, 279, 281, 293, 298
shorter serif
275
274, 298,
(general)
wide
4, 7, 13, 15, 19, 59, 98
narrow
62, 64, 105
113, 135
thickening
130
thickening
108
high bar
2, 5-6, 8, 13, 20, 22, 28, 75, 81, 108, 125, 128, 142
(top and foot serifs)
10, 93
1
91
2
concave
2-3, 12, 14, 17-20, 37, 96, 142
short
5, 7, 13, 24, 28, 82, 98, 116, 123-4, 126-7, 129
long
6, 27, 36, 46, 68, 72, 74, 121
8, 81, 113, 128
heavy
16, 38-9, 56, 101, 110, 118, 120-1, 137
long brackets
54, 68, 74, 147, 150
half
29, 134
wedge
28-31

NB. *Bold figures indicate the specimen illustrated above.*

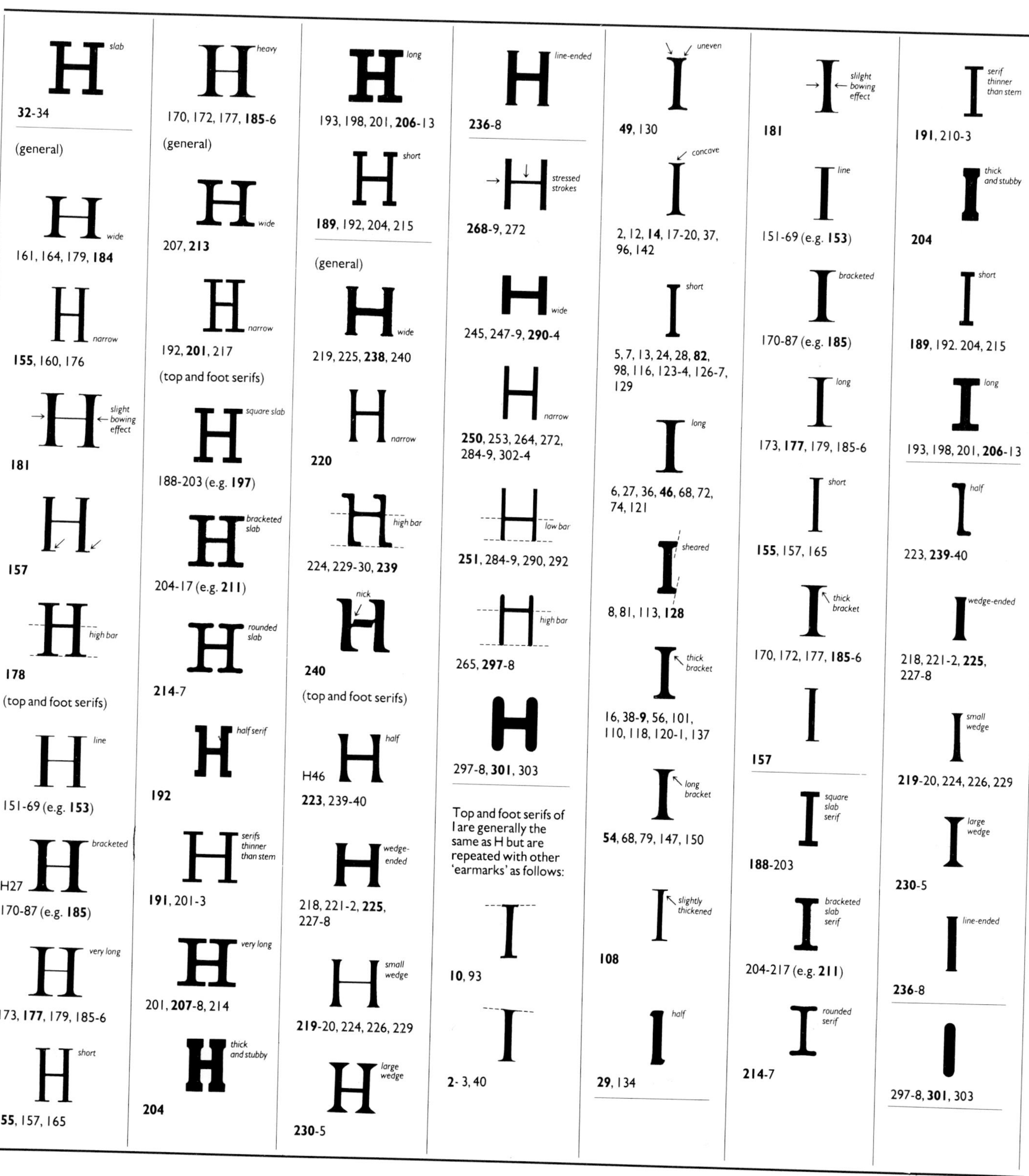
slab
32-34
(general)
wide
161, 164, 179, 184
narrow
155, 160, 176
slight bowing effect
181
157
high bar
178
(top and foot serifs)
line
151-69 (e.g. 153)
bracketed
H27
170-87 (e.g. 185)
very long
173, 177, 179, 185-6
short
155, 157, 165
heavy
170, 172, 177, 185-6
(general)
wide
207, 213
narrow
192, 201, 217
(top and foot serifs)
square slab
188-203 (e.g. 197)
bracketed slab
204-17 (e.g. 211)
rounded slab
214-7
half serif
192
serifs thinner than stem
191, 201-3
very long
201, 207-8, 214
thick and stubby
204
long
193, 198, 201, 206-13
short
189, 192, 204, 215
(general)
wide
219, 225, 238, 240
narrow
220
high bar
224, 229-30, 239
nick
240
(top and foot serifs)
half
H46
223, 239-40
wedge-ended
218, 221-2, 225, 227-8
small wedge
219-20, 224, 226, 229
large wedge
230-5
line-ended
236-8
stressed strokes
268-9, 272
wide
245, 247-9, 290-4
narrow
250, 253, 264, 272, 284-9, 302-4
low bar
251, 284-9, 290, 292
high bar
265, 297-8
297-8, 301, 303
Top and foot serifs of I are generally the same as H but are repeated with other 'earmarks' as follows:
10, 93
2-3, 40
uneven
49, 130
concave
2, 12, 14, 17-20, 37, 96, 142
short
5, 7, 13, 24, 28, 82, 98, 116, 123-4, 126-7, 129
long
6, 27, 36, 46, 68, 72, 74, 121
sheared
8, 81, 113, 128
thick bracket
16, 38-9, 56, 101, 110, 118, 120-1, 137
long bracket
54, 68, 79, 147, 150
slightly thickened
108
half
29, 134
slight bowing effect
181
line
151-69 (e.g. 153)
bracketed
170-87 (e.g. 185)
long
173, 177, 179, 185-6
short
155, 157, 165
thick bracket
170, 172, 177, 185-6
157
square slab serif
188-203
bracketed slab serif
204-217 (e.g. 211)
rounded serif
214-7
serif thinner than stem
191, 210-3
thick and stubby
204
short
189, 192. 204, 215
long
193, 198, 201, 206-13
half
223, 239-40
wedge-ended
218, 221-2, 225, 227-8
small wedge
219-20, 224, 226, 229
large wedge
230-5
line-ended
236-8
297-8, 301, 303

'Special Earmarks'

The 'special earmarks' (or distinctive identifying features) are indicated on each letter. The general 'style' of typefaces with the same 'earmark' may vary. The figures refer to specimen numbers.

***NB.** Bold figures indicate the specimen illustrated above.*

'Special Earmarks'

The 'special earmarks' (or distinctive identifying features) are indicated on each letter. The general 'style' of typefaces with the same 'earmark' may vary. The figures refer to specimen numbers.

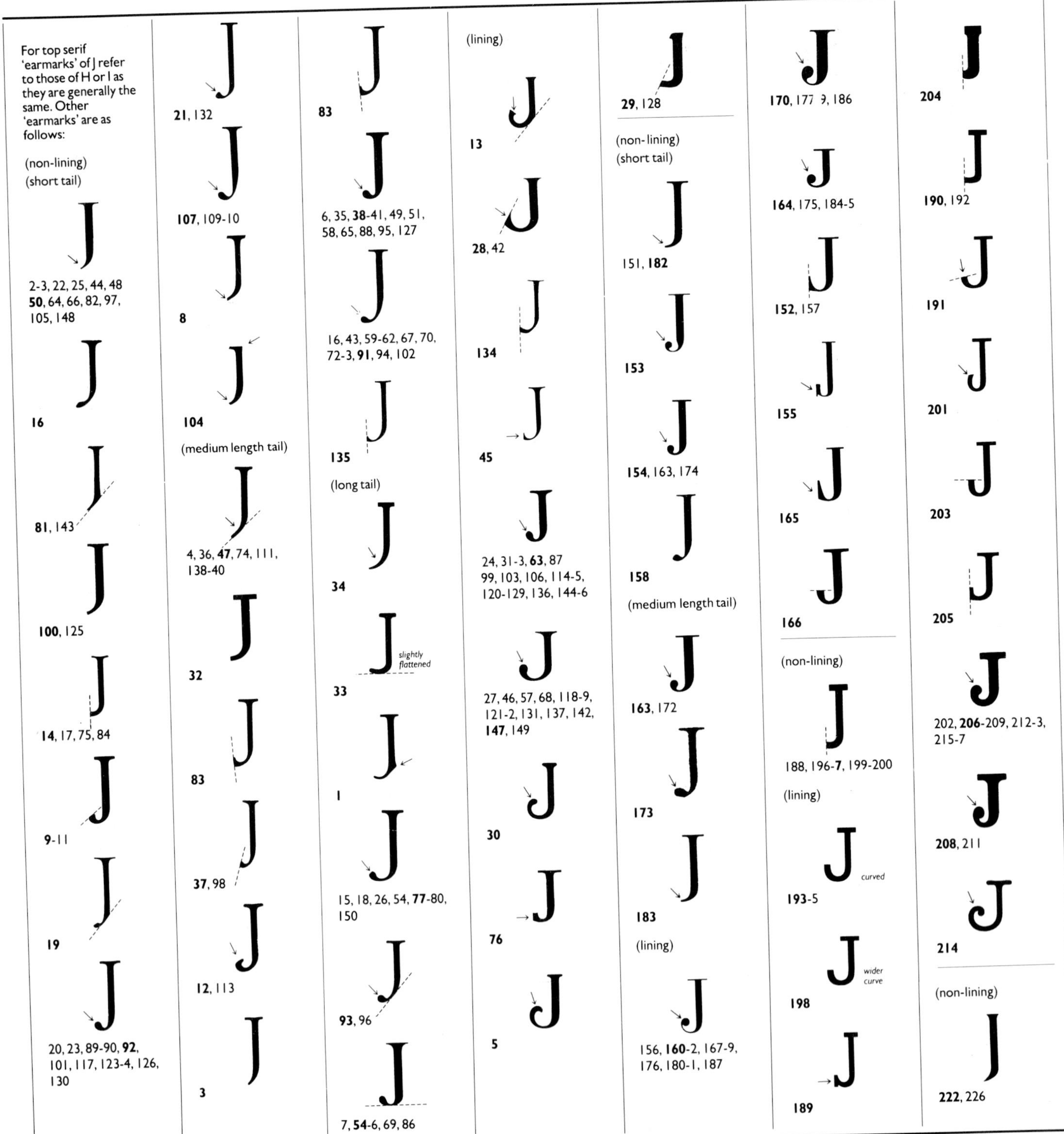

For top serif 'earmarks' of J refer to those of H or I as they are generally the same. Other 'earmarks' are as follows:
(non-lining)
(short tail)
2-3, 22, 25, 44, 48 50, 64, 66, 82, 97, 105, 148
16
81, 143
100, 125
14, 17, 75, 84
9-11
19
20, 23, 89-90, 92, 101, 117, 123-4, 126, 130
21, 132
107, 109-10
8
104
(medium length tail)
4, 36, 47, 74, 111, 138-40
32
83
37, 98
12, 113
3
83
6, 35, 38-41, 49, 51, 58, 65, 88, 95, 127
16, 43, 59-62, 67, 70, 72-3, 91, 94, 102
135
(long tail)
34
slightly flattened
33
1
15, 18, 26, 54, 77-80, 150
93, 96
7, 54-6, 69, 86
(lining)
13
28, 42
134
45
24, 31-3, 63, 87 99, 103, 106, 114-5, 120-129, 136, 144-6
27, 46, 57, 68, 118-9, 121-2, 131, 137, 142, 147, 149
30
76
5
29, 128
(non-lining)
(short tail)
151, 182
153
154, 163, 174
158
(medium length tail)
163, 172
173
183
(lining)
156, 160-2, 167-9, 176, 180-1, 187
170, 177-9, 186
164, 175, 184-5
152, 157
155
165
166
(non-lining)
188, 196-7, 199-200
(lining)
curved
193-5
wider curve
198
189
204
190, 192
191
201
203
205
202, 206-209, 212-3, 215-7
208, 211
214
(non-lining)
222, 226

***NB.** Bold figures indicate the specimen illustrated above.*

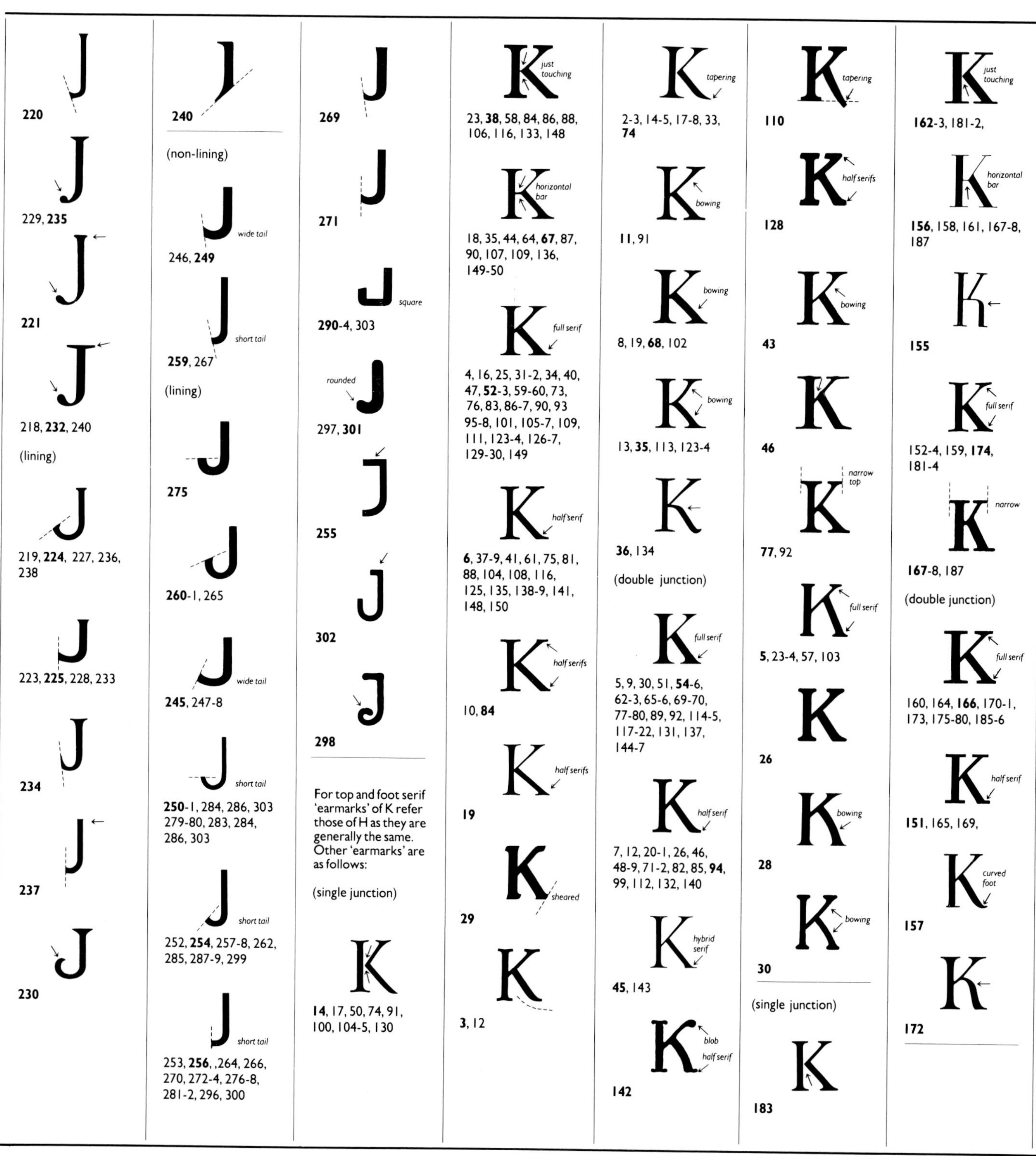
220
229, 235
221
218, 232, 240
(lining)
219, 224, 227, 236, 238
223, 225, 228, 233
234
237
230
240
(non-lining)
wide tail
246, 249
short tail
259, 267
(lining)
275
260-1, 265
wide tail
245, 247-8
short tail
250-1, 284, 286, 303
279-80, 283, 284, 286, 303
short tail
252, 254, 257-8, 262, 285, 287-9, 299
short tail
253, 256, ,264, 266, 270, 272-4, 276-8, 281-2, 296, 300
269
271
square
290-4, 303
rounded
297, 301
255
302
298
For top and foot serif 'earmarks' of K refer those of H as they are generally the same. Other 'earmarks' are as follows:
(single junction)
14, 17, 50, 74, 91, 100, 104-5, 130
just touching
23, 38, 58, 84, 86, 88, 106, 116, 133, 148
horizontal bar
18, 35, 44, 64, 67, 87, 90, 107, 109, 136, 149-50
full serif
4, 16, 25, 31-2, 34, 40, 47, 52-3, 59-60, 73, 76, 83, 86-7, 90, 93 95-8, 101, 105-7, 109, 111, 123-4, 126-7, 129-30, 149
half serif
6, 37-9, 41, 61, 75, 81, 88, 104, 108, 116, 125, 135, 138-9, 141, 148, 150
half serifs
10, 84
half serifs
19
sheared
29
3, 12
tapering
2-3, 14-5, 17-8, 33, 74
bowing
11, 91
bowing
8, 19, 68, 102
bowing
13, 35, 113, 123-4
36, 134
(double junction)
full serif
5, 9, 30, 51, 54-6, 62-3, 65-6, 69-70, 77-80, 89, 92, 114-5, 117-22, 131, 137, 144-7
half serif
7, 12, 20-1, 26, 46, 48-9, 71-2, 82, 85, 94, 99, 112, 132, 140
hybrid serif
45, 143
blob
half serif
142
tapering
110
half serifs
128
bowing
43
46
narrow top
77, 92
full serif
5, 23-4, 57, 103
26
bowing
28
bowing
30
(single junction)
183
just touching
162-3, 181-2,
horizontal bar
156, 158, 161, 167-8, 187
155
full serif
152-4, 159, 174, 181-4
narrow
167-8, 187
(double junction)
full serif
160, 164, 166, 170-1, 173, 175-80, 185-6
half serif
151, 165, 169,
curved foot
157
172

'Special Earmarks'

The 'special earmarks' (or distinctive identifying features) are indicated on each letter. The general 'style' of typefaces with the same 'earmark' may vary. The figures refer to specimen numbers.

NB. *Bold figures indicate the specimen illustrated above.*

K–L

'Special Earmarks'
The 'special earmarks' (or distinctive identifying features) are indicated on each letter. The general 'style' of typefaces with the same 'earmark' may vary. The figures refer to specimen numbers.

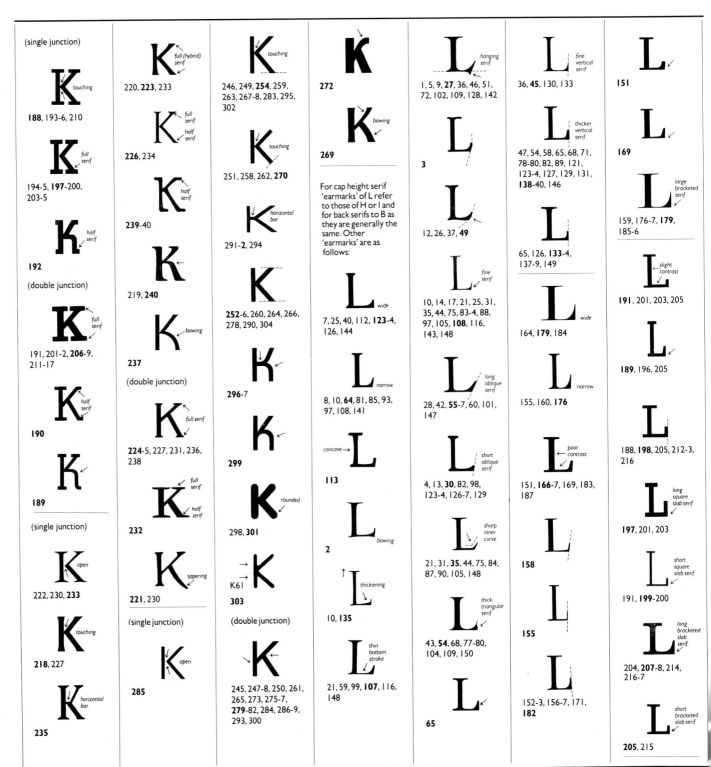

(single junction)

K — touching
188, 193-6, 210

K — full serif
194-5, **197**-200, 203-5

K — half serif
192

(double junction)

K — full serif
191, 201-2, **206**-9, 211-17

K — half serif
190

K
189

(single junction)

K — open
222, 230, **233**

K — touching
218, 227

K — horizontal bar
235

K — full (hybrid) serif
220, **223**, 233

K — full serif, half serif
226, 234

K — half serif
239-40

K
219, **240**

K — bowing
237

(double junction)

K — full serif
224-5, 227, 231, 236, 238

K — full serif, half serif
232

K — tapering
221, 230

(single junction)

K — open
285

K — touching
246, 249, **254**, 259, 263, 267-8, 283, 295, 302

K — touching
251, 258, 262, **270**

K — horizontal bar
291-**2**, 294

K
252-6, 260, 264, 266, 278, 290, 304

K
296-7

K
299

K — rounded
298, **301**

K61 K
303

(double junction)

K
245, 247-8, 250, 261, 265, 273, 275-7, **279**-82, 284, 286-9, 293, 300

K
272

K — bowing
269

For cap height serif 'earmarks' of L refer to those of H or I and for back serifs to B as they are generally the same. Other 'earmarks' are as follows:

L — wide
7, 25, 40, 112, **123**-4, 126, 144

L — narrow
8, 10, **64**, 81, 85, 93, 97, 108, 141

L — concave
113

L — bowing
2

L — thickening
10, **135**

L — thin bottom stroke
21, 59, 99, **107**, 116, 148

L — hanging serif
1, 5, 9, **27**, 36, 46, 51, 72, 102, 109, 128, 142

L
3

L
12, 26, 37, **49**

L — fine serif
10, 14, 17, 21, 25, 31, 35, 44, 75, 83-4, 88, 97, 105, **108**, 116, 143, 148

L — long oblique serif
28, 42, **55**-7, 60, 101, 147

L — short oblique serif
4, 13, **30**, 82, 98, 123-4, 126-7, 129

L — sharp inner curve
21, 31, **35**, 44, 75, 84, 87, 90, 105, 148

L — thick triangular serif
43, **54**, 68, 77-80, 104, 109, 150

L
65

L — fine vertical serif
36, **45**, 130, 133

L — thicker vertical serif
47, 54, 58, 65, 68, 71, 78-80, 82, 89, 121, 123-4, 127, 129, 131, **138**-40, 146

L
65, 126, **133**-4, 137-9, 149

L — wide
164, **179**, 184

L — narrow
155, 160, **176**

L — poor contrast
151, **166**-7, 169, 183, 187

L
158

L
155

L
152-3, 156-7, 171, **182**

L
151

L
169

L — large bracketed serif
159, 176-7, **179**, 185-6

L — slight contrast
191, 201, 203, 205

L
189, 196, 205

L
188, **198**, 205, 212-3, 216

L — long square slab serif
197, 201, 203

L — short square slab serif
191, **199**-200

L — long bracketed slab serif
204, **207**-8, 214, 216-7

L — short bracketed slab serif
205, 215

NB. *Bold figures indicate the specimen illustrated above.*

L wide
219, 225, 238

L narrow
218, **220**, 226-7, 237

L some contrast
219, 221, **229**, 232-5

L no contrast
236-8

L
227-**8**, 230, 232, 234

L deeply cut
218, 223, 240

L
239

L small hanging serif
228, **231**

L long oblique serif
228, 230-**2**

L triangular shape serif
235

L
218, **222**

L
219-21, 226-**7**,
229-30, 232-5, 240

L
226

L
223, 231, **236**-9

L
231

L
228

L wide
245-8, **290**, 292

L narrow
250, **252**-8, 262, 264,
266, 268, 284-9,
297-300, 302

L slight stress
268-9, 272

L
296

L
251, 258, **262**, 269

L rounded
297, 298, **301**, 303

For foot serif 'earmarks' of M refer to those of H as they are generally the same. Other 'earmarks' are as follows:

(parallel strokes or nearly so)

M full serif
3, 15, 32, 34

M full serif
28, 30, 142-3

M half serif, full serif
2

M half serif, pointed base
8, 16, 19-21, 25, 37,
41-3, 47-55, 58, 60-3,
65-7, 70-1, 75, **78**-80,
83-4, 86-91, 97,
99-103, 105-7,
117-22, 125-7,
129-32, 136-40,
144-6, 148-9

M half serif, flat base
33, 140-**1**

M wide
7, 16, 48, 156-7, 59,
68, 107, 111-2, 115,
123-4, 139, 145, 150

M narrow
43, 63, 69, 114

M
12

M thinning at junction
72, 114-5, 117, 144,
146

M thickening
81

M
23-4, 104

M
27

(splayed strokes)

M full serif
1, **5**

M half serif
4, 6, 9, 11, 26, 31, 35,
38-40, 44, 66, 73-4,
85, 110, 116, 125,
133, 147

M
13, 36, 46, 128

M
95, **147**

M
113, 143

M
108

M
29

M
109

M no serifs
134

M pointed strokes
10, 98, **135**

M centre point above base line
14, 17

(parallel strokes)

M full serifs
157

M half serifs
152-4, 156, 158, 163,
165, 167-8, 170,
173-5, 178-9, 185-6

M thick stem
151, **166**-7, 183

M flat base
169

M thinning at junction
177

M wide
161, 164, 166, 169,
172, 183-4, 187

M narrow
160, 162, 171, 176,
180

(splayed strokes)

M full serifs
155

M half serifs
159, **181**-2

M flat base
182

(parallel strokes)

M pointed
188-9, 193-**7**, 202,
204-9

M flat
190, 193, **198**, 203,
205, 210

M
191-2, 196, **199**-200

M thinning at junction
208

M some contrast
191

M wide
211, **213**-4

M narrow
201, 215-7

'Special Earmarks'

The 'special earmarks' (or distinctive identifying features) are indicated on each letter. The general 'style' of typefaces with the same 'earmark' may vary. The figures refer to specimen numbers.

NB. *Bold figures indicate the specimen illustrated above.*

'Special Earmarks'

The 'special earmarks' (or distinctive identifying features) are indicated on each letter. The general 'style' of typefaces with the same 'earmark' may vary. The figures refer to specimen numbers.

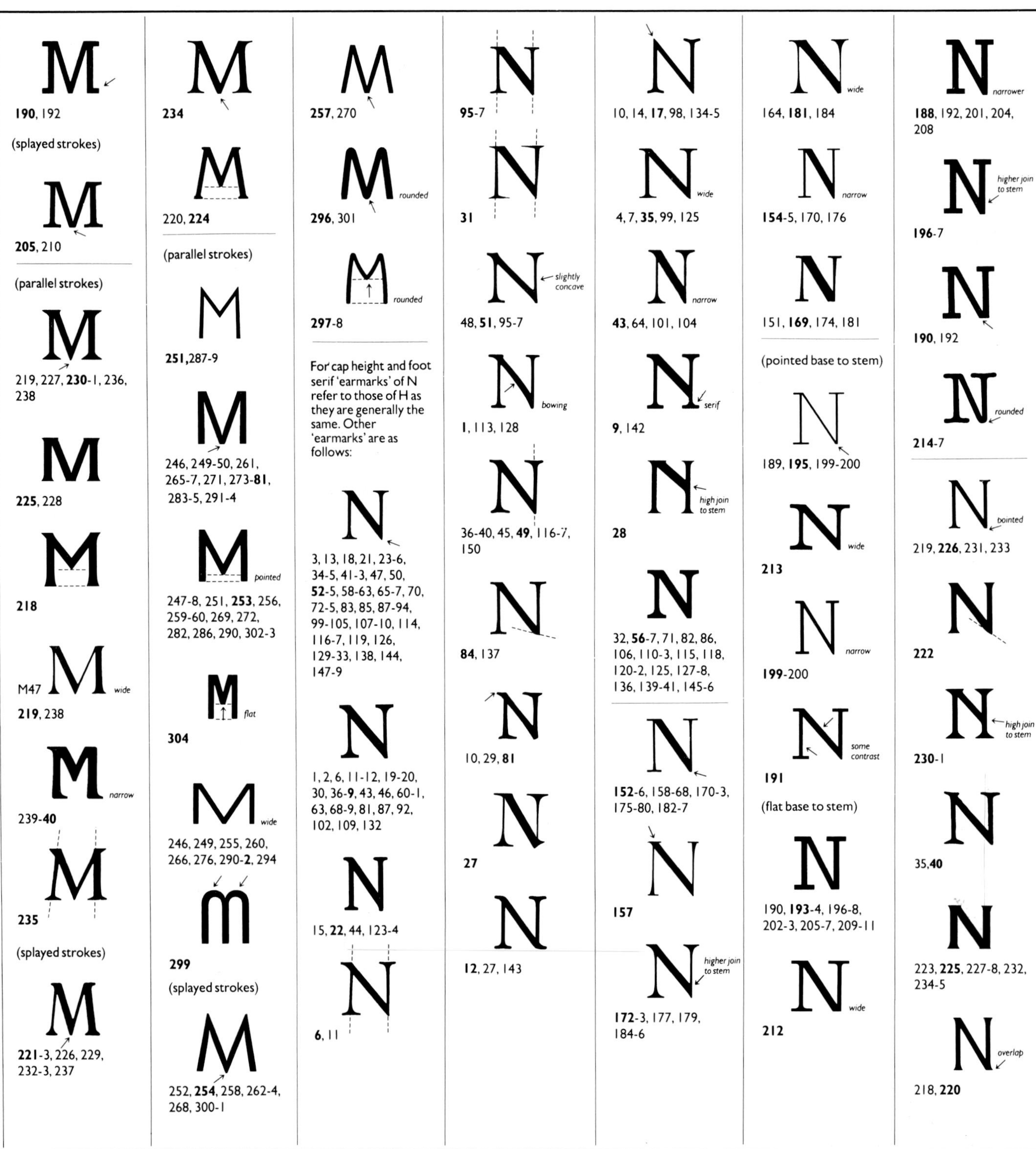
190, 192
(splayed strokes)
205, 210
(parallel strokes)
219, 227, **230**-1, 236, 238
225, 228
218
M47
wide
219, 238
narrow
239-**40**
235
(splayed strokes)
221-3, 226, 229, 232-3, 237
234
220, **224**
(parallel strokes)
251,287-9
246, 249-50, 261, 265-7, 271, 273-**81**, 283-5, 291-4
pointed
247-8, 251, **253**, 256, 259-60, 269, 272, 282, 286, 290, 302-3
flat
304
wide
246, 249, 255, 260, 266, 276, 290-**2**, 294
299
(splayed strokes)
252, **254**, 258, 262-4, 268, 300-1
257, 270
rounded
296, 301
rounded
297-8
For cap height and foot serif 'earmarks' of N refer to those of H as they are generally the same. Other 'earmarks' are as follows:
3, 13, 18, 21, 23-6, 34-5, 41-3, 47, 50, **52**-5, 58-63, 65-7, 70, 72-5, 83, 85, 87-94, 99-105, 107-10, 114, 116-7, 119, 126, 129-33, 138, 144, 147-9
1, 2, 6, 11-12, 19-20, 30, 36-**9**, 43, 46, 60-1, 63, 68-9, 81, 87, 92, 102, 109, 132
15, **22**, 44, 123-4
6, 11
95-7
31
slightly concave
48, **51**, 95-7
bowing
1, 113, 128
36-40, 45, **49**, 116-7, 150
84, 137
10, 29, **81**
27
12, 27, 143
10, 14, **17**, 98, 134-5
wide
4, 7, **35**, 99, 125
narrow
43, 64, 101, 104
serif
9, 142
high join to stem
28
32, **56**-7, 71, 82, 86, 106, 110-3, 115, 118, 120-2, 125, 127-8, 136, 139-41, 145-6
152-6, 158-68, 170-3, 175-80, 182-7
157
higher join to stem
172-3, 177, 179, 184-6
wide
164, **181**, 184
narrow
154-5, 170, 176
151, **169**, 174, 181
(pointed base to stem)
189, **195**, 199-200
wide
213
narrow
199-200
some contrast
191
(flat base to stem)
190, **193**-4, 196-8, 202-3, 205-7, 209-11
wide
212
narrower
188, 192, 201, 204, 208
higher join to stem
196-7
190, 192
rounded
214-7
pointed
219, **226**, 231, 233
222
high join to stem
230-1
35,**40**
223, **225**, 227-8, 232, 234-5
overlap
218, **220**

***NB.** Bold figures indicate the specimen illustrated above.*

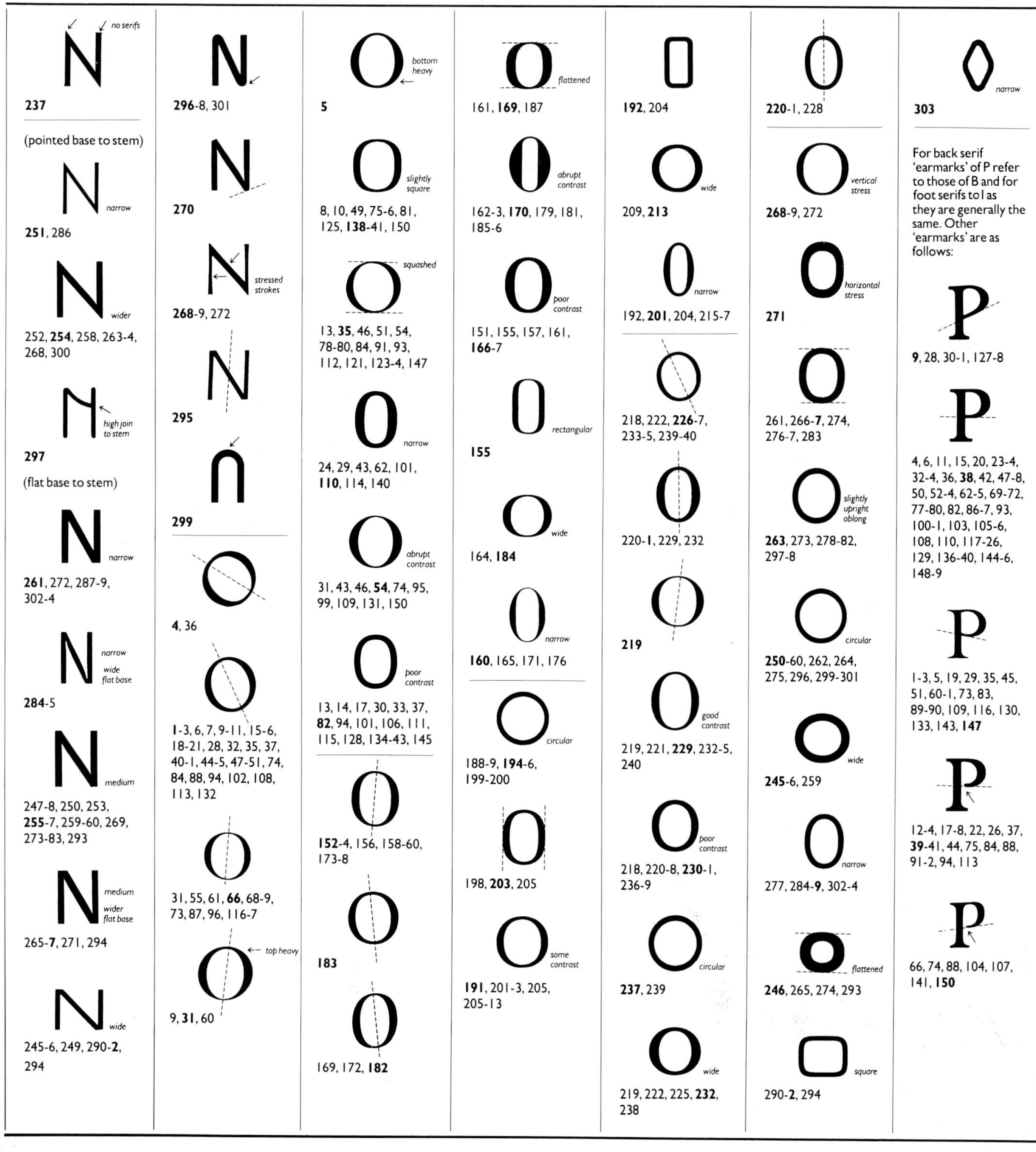
no serifs
237
(pointed base to stem)
narrow
251, 286
wider
252, **254**, 258, 263-4, 268, 300
high join to stem
297
(flat base to stem)
narrow
261, 272, 287-9, 302-4
narrow
wide
flat base
284-5
medium
247-8, 250, 253, **255**-7, 259-60, 269, 273-83, 293
medium
wider
flat base
265-**7**, 271, 294
wide
245-6, 249, 290-**2**, 294
296-8, 301
270
stressed strokes
268-9, 272
295
299
4, 36
1-3, 6, 7, 9-11, 15-6, 18-21, 28, 32, 35, 37, 40-1, 44-5, 47-51, 74, 84, 88, 94, 102, 108, 113, 132
31, 55, 61, **66**, 68-9, 73, 87, 96, 116-7
top heavy
9, **31**, 60
bottom heavy
5
slightly square
8, 10, 49, 75-6, 81, 125, **138**-41, 150
squashed
13, **35**, 46, 51, 54, 78-80, 84, 91, 93, 112, 121, 123-4, 147
narrow
24, 29, 43, 62, 101, **110**, 114, 140
abrupt contrast
31, 43, 46, **54**, 74, 95, 99, 109, 131, 150
poor contrast
13, 14, 17, 30, 33, 37, **82**, 94, 101, 106, 111, 115, 128, 134-43, 145
152-4, 156, 158-60, 173-8
183
169, 172, **182**
flattened
161, **169**, 187
abrupt contrast
162-3, **170**, 179, 181, 185-6
poor contrast
151, 155, 157, 161, **166**-7
rectangular
155
wide
164, **184**
narrow
160, 165, 171, 176
circular
188-9, **194**-6, 199-200
198, **203**, 205
some contrast
191, 201-3, 205, 205-13
192, 204
wide
209, **213**
narrow
192, **201**, 204, 215-7
218, 222, **226**-7, 233-5, 239-40
220-**1**, 229, 232
219
good contrast
219, 221, **229**, 232-5, 240
poor contrast
218, 220-8, **230**-1, 236-9
circular
237, 239
wide
219, 222, 225, **232**, 238
220-1, 228
vertical stress
268-9, 272
horizontal stress
271
261, 266-**7**, 274, 276-7, 283
slightly upright oblong
263, 273, 278-82, 297-8
circular
250-60, 262, 264, 275, 296, 299-301
wide
245-6, 259
narrow
277, 284-**9**, 302-4
flattened
246, 265, 274, 293
square
290-**2**, 294
narrow
303
For back serif 'earmarks' of P refer to those of B and for foot serifs to I as they are generally the same. Other 'earmarks' are as follows:
9, 28, 30-1, 127-8
4, 6, 11, 15, 20, 23-4, 32-4, 36, **38**, 42, 47-8, 50, 52-4, 62-5, 69-72, 77-80, 82, 86-7, 93, 100-1, 103, 105-6, 108, 110, 117-26, 129, 136-40, 144-6, 148-9
1-3, 5, 19, 29, 35, 45, 51, 60-1, 73, 83, 89-90, 109, 116, 130, 133, 143, **147**
12-4, 17-8, 22, 26, 37, **39**-41, 44, 75, 84, 88, 91-2, 94, 113
66, 74, 88, 104, 107, 141, **150**

'Special Earmarks'

The 'special earmarks' (or distinctive identifying features) are indicated on each letter. The general 'style' of typefaces with the same 'earmark' may vary. The figures refer to specimen numbers.

NB. *Bold figures indicate the specimen illustrated above.*

'Special Earmarks'

The 'special earmarks' (or distinctive identifying features) are indicated on each letter. The general 'style' of typefaces with the same 'earmark' may vary. The figures refer to specimen numbers.

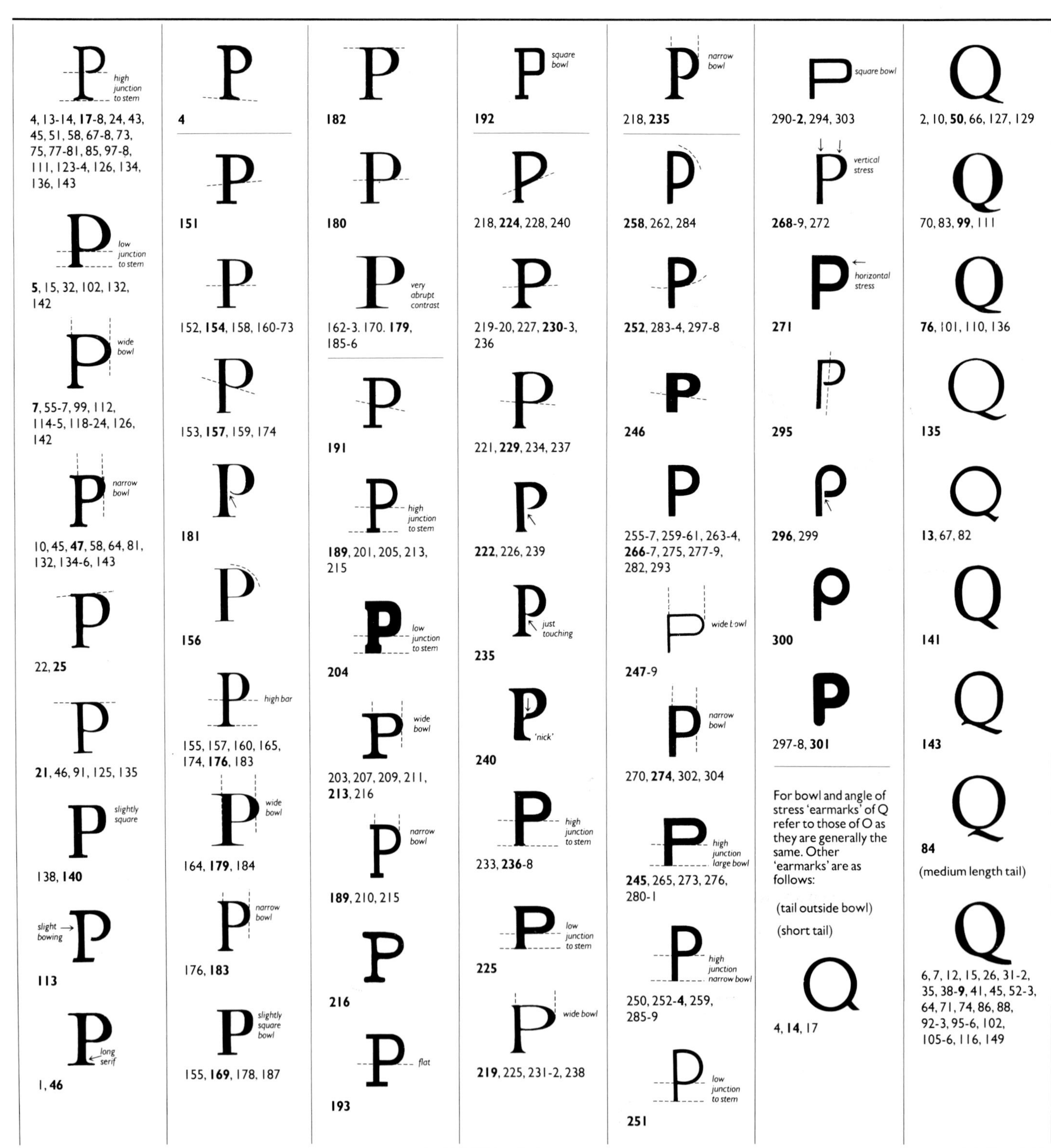
high junction to stem
4, 13-14, 17-8, 24, 43, 45, 51, 58, 67-8, 73, 75, 77-81, 85, 97-8, 111, 123-4, 126, 134, 136, 143
low junction to stem
5, 15, 32, 102, 132, 142
wide bowl
7, 55-7, 99, 112, 114-5, 118-24, 126, 142
narrow bowl
10, 45, 47, 58, 64, 81, 132, 134-6, 143
22, 25
21, 46, 91, 125, 135
slightly square
138, 140
slight bowing
113
long serif
1, 46
4
151
152, 154, 158, 160-73
153, 157, 159, 174
181
156
high bar
155, 157, 160, 165, 174, 176, 183
wide bowl
164, 179, 184
narrow bowl
176, 183
slightly square bowl
155, 169, 178, 187
182
180
very abrupt contrast
162-3. 170. 179, 185-6
191
high junction to stem
189, 201, 205, 213, 215
low junction to stem
204
wide bowl
203, 207, 209, 211, 213, 216
narrow bowl
189, 210, 215
216
flat
193
square bowl
192
218, 224, 228, 240
219-20, 227, 230-3, 236
221, 229, 234, 237
222, 226, 239
just touching
235
'nick'
240
high junction to stem
233, 236-8
low junction to stem
225
wide bowl
219, 225, 231-2, 238
narrow bowl
218, 235
258, 262, 284
252, 283-4, 297-8
246
255-7, 259-61, 263-4, 266-7, 275, 277-9, 282, 293
wide bowl
247-9
narrow bowl
270, 274, 302, 304
high junction large bowl
245, 265, 273, 276, 280-1
high junction narrow bowl
250, 252-4, 259, 285-9
low junction to stem
251
square bowl
290-2, 294, 303
vertical stress
268-9, 272
horizontal stress
271
295
296, 299
300
297-8, 301
For bowl and angle of stress 'earmarks' of Q refer to those of O as they are generally the same. Other 'earmarks' are as follows:
(tail outside bowl)
(short tail)
4, 14, 17
2, 10, 50, 66, 127, 129
70, 83, 99, 111
76, 101, 110, 136
135
13, 67, 82
141
143
84
(medium length tail)
6, 7, 12, 15, 26, 31-2, 35, 38-9, 41, 45, 52-3, 64, 71, 74, 86, 88, 92-3, 95-6, 102, 105-6, 116, 149

***NB.** Bold figures indicate the specimen illustrated above.*

42, 47, 90, 103, 109, **123**-4, 126

34, 46, 89, 98, **100**, 112

91

113

11, 29, **37**, 49, 140

27, 150

131

36, 75

43, 69, **72**

22

1, 51

148

8, 81, 130

147

(long tail)

21, 25, 40, **65**, 87, 96, 107

73, **108**, 132

97

94

77-80, 85

(tail extends into bowl)

(short tail)

3, 23-4, 142

48

33, 128

5

30

44

104

(medium length tail)

68

114-5, 117-21, 137, 144-6

122

9

28

134

125

138

139

(tail outside bowl)

154, 157

153, 155, 165, 167-8

160

152, 161, **174**-4, 180-1, 187

162-3

159, 166, 173, **183**

156, 187

158

172

169

182

(tail extends into bowl)

151

171

164, 170, **175**-9, 185-6

184

(tail outside bowl)

189, 193, 198, 210

192

201

203-4

197

190

205

206

199-200, 202

(tail extends into bowl)

188, 196

191

194-5

207-**9**, 211-7

(tail outside bowl)

218

226

239

227

220

'Special Earmarks'

The 'special earmarks' (or distinctive identifying features) are indicated on each letter. The general 'style' of typefaces with the same 'earmark' may vary. The figures refer to specimen numbers.

NB. *Bold figures indicate the specimen illustrated above.*

'Special Earmarks'

The 'special earmarks' (or distinctive identifying features) are indicated on each letter. The general 'style' of typefaces with the same 'earmark' may vary. The figures refer to specimen numbers.

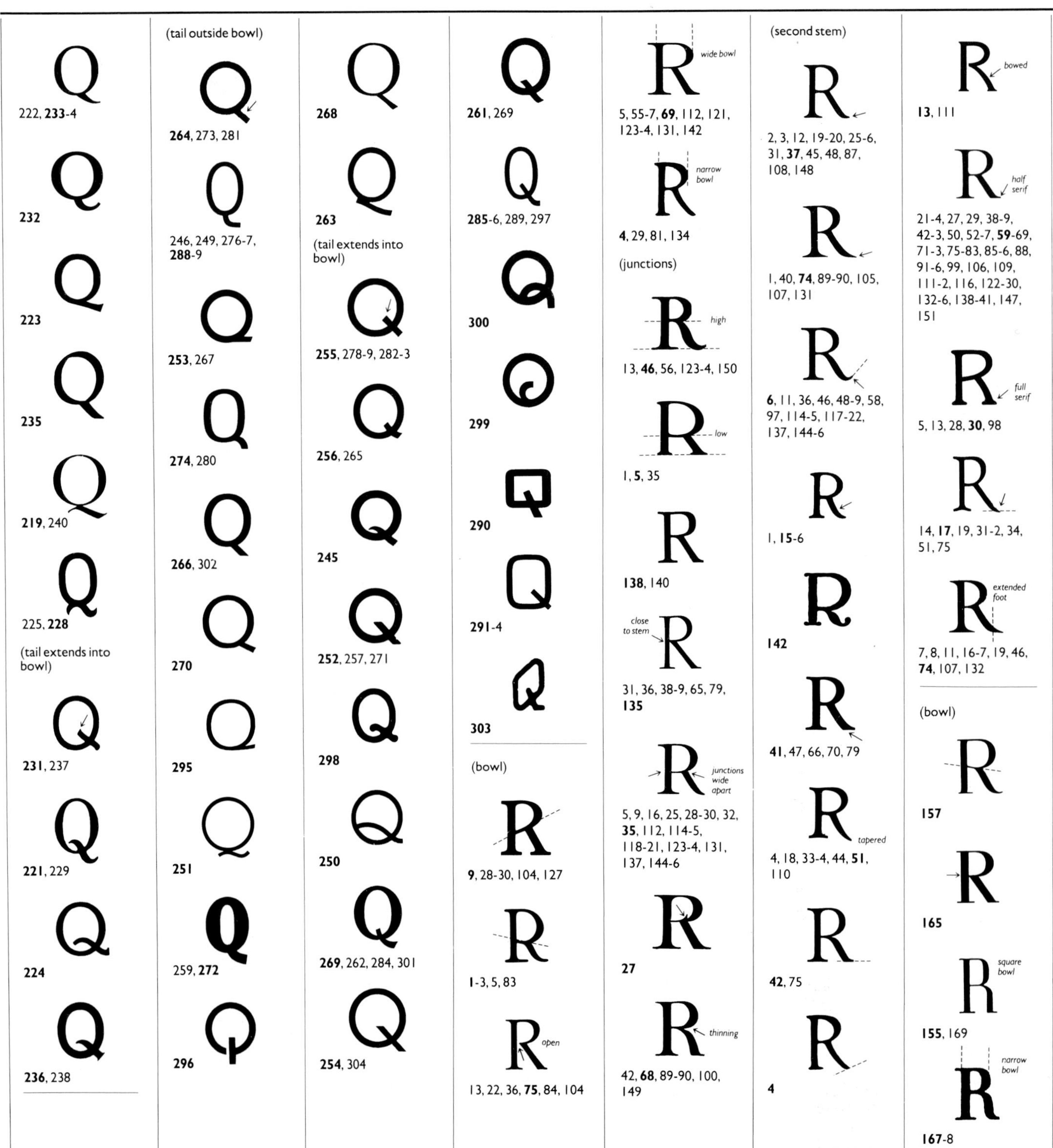
222, **233**-4
232
223
235
219, 240
225, **228**
(tail extends into bowl)
231, 237
221, 229
224
236, 238
(tail outside bowl)
264, 273, 281
246, 249, 276-7, **288**-9
253, 267
274, 280
266, 302
270
295
251
259, **272**
296
268
263
(tail extends into bowl)
255, 278-9, 282-3
256, 265
245
252, 257, 271
298
250
269, 262, 284, 301
254, 304
261, 269
285-6, 289, 297
300
299
290
291-4
303
(bowl)
9, 28-30, 104, 127
1-3, 5, 83
open
13, 22, 36, **75**, 84, 104
wide bowl
5, 55-7, **69**, 112, 121, 123-4, 131, 142
narrow bowl
4, 29, 81, 134
(junctions)
high
13, **46**, 56, 123-4, 150
low
1, **5**, 35
138, 140
close to stem
31, 36, 38-9, 65, 79, **135**
junctions wide apart
5, 9, 16, 25, 28-30, 32, **35**, 112, 114-5, 118-21, 123-4, 131, 137, 144-6
27
thinning
42, **68**, 89-90, 100, 149
(second stem)
2, 3, 12, 19-20, 25-6, 31, **37**, 45, 48, 87, 108, 148
1, 40, **74**, 89-90, 105, 107, 131
6, 11, 36, 46, 48-9, 58, 97, 114-5, 117-22, 137, 144-6
1, **15**-6
142
41, 47, 66, 70, 79
tapered
4, 18, 33-4, 44, **51**, 110
42, 75
4
bowed
13, 111
half serif
21-4, 27, 29, 38-9, **42**-3, 50, 52-7, **59**-69, 71-3, 75-83, 85-6, 88, 91-6, 99, 106, 109, 111-2, 116, 122-30, 132-6, 138-41, 147, 151
full serif
5, 13, 28, **30**, 98
14, **17**, 19, 31-2, 34, 51, 75
extended foot
7, 8, 11, 16-7, 19, 46, **74**, 107, 132
(bowl)
157
165
square bowl
155, 169
narrow bowl
167-8

***NB.** Bold figures indicate the specimen illustrated above.*

(second stem)

half serif

151, 173

straight stem half serif

157

152-155, 158, 161, 172, 174, 180, 182-3, 184, 187

153-4, 156, 159-60, 62-4, 171, 175-6, 181

(bowl)

wide bowl

170, **177**-9, 85-6

194-5

narrow bowl

203

(second stem)

straight

197

curved stem

188, **190**, 192-5, 198, 204

199-200

189, 202-3, **205**, 215-7

201, 206-**209**, 211-214

bowing

216

(bowl)

218

open

222, **226**, 230, 237, 239

'nick'

240

wide

219, 221, 225, **229**, 231-2, 238

narrow

218, **235**

(junctions)

high junction to stem

220

low junction to stem

221, **234**

close to stem

218, **223**

wide apart

219, 225, 238

(second stem)

218, 222-**4**, 226-7

219-20, 225, **228**

tapered

221, 229

tapered & curved

236

half serif

224, 226, 231-**3**, 239-40

234-5

237

full serif

220, **236**, 238

(bowl)

258, 262

263-4, 269

297

open

250-1, 295-6

299

wide bowl

250, **271**, 280

narrow bowl

253, 259, 262, 264, 284, 302

(junctions)

high

265, 276, 297, 303

low

251, 298

2nd junction close to stem

252-8, 262, 264, 268, 271-2, 298-301

wide apart

245-8, 261, **267**, 273-5, 278-9, 291-4

(second stem)

245, 247-8, 250, 252-7, 260, 265, 268-9, 272-3, 276-**7** 280-90, 295, 300, 302, 304

251. 258. **270**, 299

301, 304

246, 249, 259, 266-7, 274-5, 278-**9**, 291-4 296

298

bowing

269, **297**

(general)

vertical stress

268-9, 272

horizontal stress

271

296, 299-**300**

For 'earmarks' for capital S refer to those of lower case s as they are generally the same. Exceptions are as follows:

(top and bottom serifs)

4

12

13

19

23-**4**, 142

34

49

90

59-60, 63, **67**, 99

61, 148

123-4, 126, 129

134

143

(top serif only)

29

15, 40

86-7

'Special Earmarks'

The 'special earmarks' (or distinctive identifying features) are indicated on each letter. The general 'style' of typefaces with the same 'earmark' may vary. The figures refer to specimen numbers.

NB. *Bold figures indicate the specimen illustrated above.*

'Special Earmarks'

The 'special earmarks' (or distinctive identifying features) are indicated on each letter. The general 'style' of typefaces with the same 'earmark' may vary. The figures refer to specimen numbers.

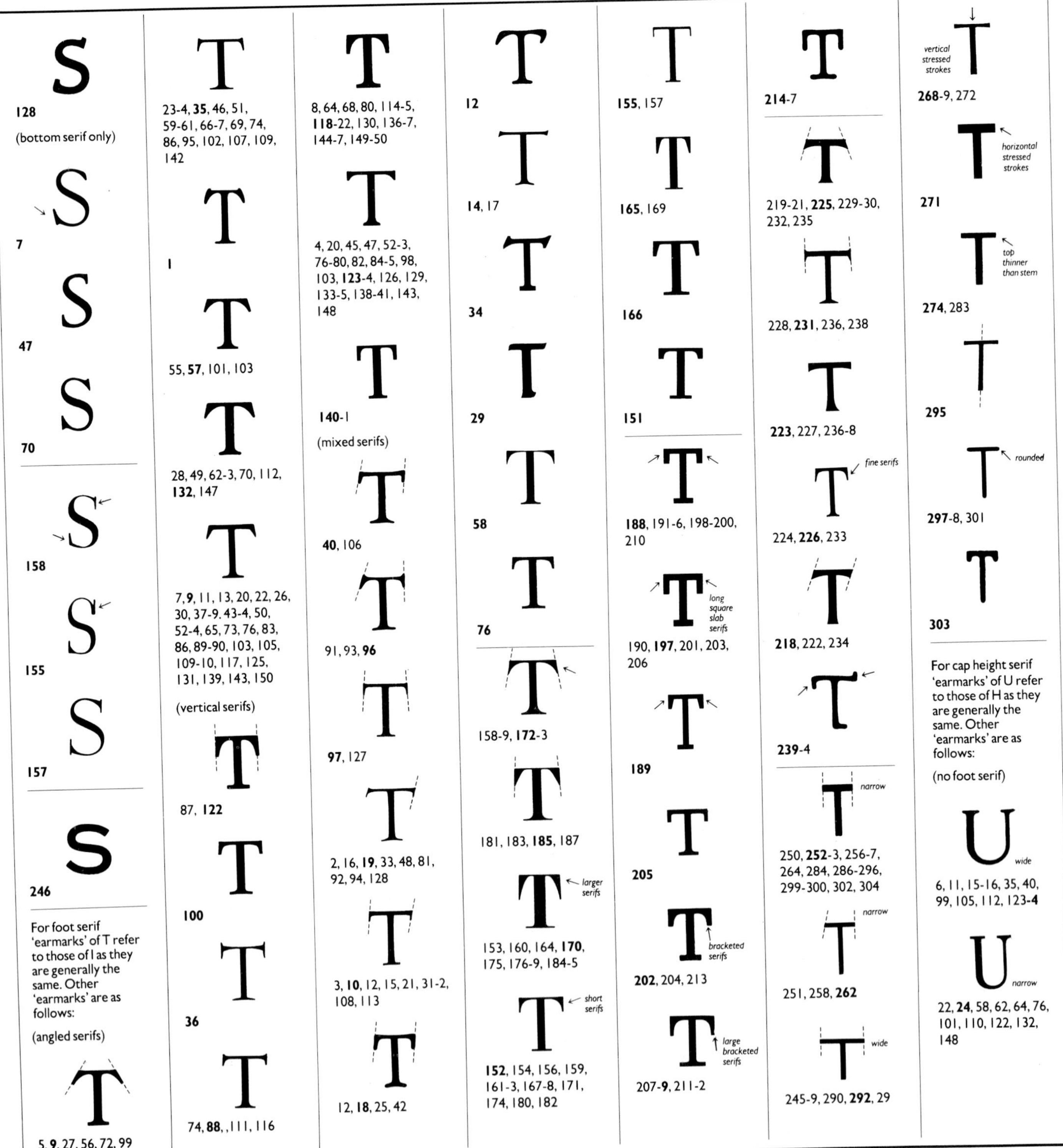

S
128
(bottom serif only)
S
7
S
47
S
70
S
158
S
155
S
157
S
246
For foot serif 'earmarks' of T refer to those of I as they are generally the same. Other 'earmarks' are as follows:
(angled serifs)
T
5, 9, 27, 56, 72, 99
T
23-4, 35, 46, 51, 59-61, 66-7, 69, 74, 86, 95, 102, 107, 109, 142
T
1
T
55, 57, 101, 103
T
28, 49, 62-3, 70, 112, 132, 147
T
7, 9, 11, 13, 20, 22, 26, 30, 37-9. 43-4, 50, 52-4, 65, 73, 76, 83, 86, 89-90, 103, 105, 109-10, 117, 125, 131, 139, 143, 150
(vertical serifs)
T
87, 122
T
100
T
36
T
74, 88, ,111, 116
T
8, 64, 68, 80, 114-5, 118-22, 130, 136-7, 144-7, 149-50
T
4, 20, 45, 47, 52-3, 76-80, 82, 84-5, 98, 103, 123-4, 126, 129, 133-5, 138-41, 143, 148
T
140-1
(mixed serifs)
T
40, 106
T
91, 93, 96
T
97, 127
T
2, 16, 19, 33, 48, 81, 92, 94, 128
T
3, 10, 12, 15, 21, 31-2, 108, 113
T
12, 18, 25, 42
T
12
T
14, 17
T
34
T
29
T
58
T
76
T
158-9, 172-3
T
181, 183, 185, 187
T
larger serifs
153, 160, 164, 170, 175, 176-9, 184-5
T
short serifs
152, 154, 156, 159, 161-3, 167-8, 171, 174, 180, 182
T
155, 157
T
165, 169
T
166
T
151
T
188, 191-6, 198-200, 210
T
long square slab serifs
190, 197, 201, 203, 206
T
189
T
205
T
bracketed serifs
202, 204, 213
T
large bracketed serifs
207-9, 211-2
T
214-7
T
219-21, 225, 229-30, 232, 235
T
228, 231, 236, 238
T
223, 227, 236-8
T
fine serifs
224, 226, 233
T
218, 222, 234
T
239-4
T
narrow
250, 252-3, 256-7, 264, 284, 286-296, 299-300, 302, 304
T
narrow
251, 258, 262
T
wide
245-9, 290, 292, 29
vertical stressed strokes
T
268-9, 272
T
horizontal stressed strokes
271
T
top thinner than stem
274, 283
T
295
T
rounded
297-8, 301
T
303
For cap height serif 'earmarks' of U refer to those of H as they are generally the same. Other 'earmarks' are as follows:
(no foot serif)
U
wide
6, 11, 15-16, 35, 40, 99, 105, 112, 123-4
U
narrow
22, 24, 58, 62, 64, 76, 101, 110, 122, 132, 148

NB. *Bold figures indicate the specimen illustrated above.*

long serifs
27, **46**, 56, 65, 71, 74, 101, 114, 121

short serifs
7, 13, 30, 37, 45, 82, 98, 108, 123-4, 126-7, 129-30, 148

good contrast
21, 27, 31, 43, 54, **58**, 60, 95, 99, 131

poor contrast
4, 8, 13-14, 17-18, 22, **26**, 28, 30-4, 44, 56-7, 71, 106, 110, 113, 115, 127-8, 133, 137, 141, 145-6

no contrast
13, 32-4, 82

68, 71, 73

slightly flattened base
11, 19, **40**, 57, 105, 132, 138, 140

thicker stem
111

thickening
2

thickening
113, 134-5, 150

sheared
8, **128**

147

59-**60**, 102, 104, 107-8

14, **17**, 19, 31, 87

5, 9, 28, 46

bowing
28, **30**, 134

(with foot serif)

full
1, 25

half
48, 81, 116

3

10, 98

high join to stem
143

wide
161, 164, **184**

narrow
154, **160**, 165, 170-1, 176, 182

long serifs
177-9

short serifs
155, 157, **180**

poor contrast
151, 183

abrupt contrast
162-3, **170**, 179, 185-6

thickening
157

flattened base
161, 167-8, **182**, 187

158

thicker second stem
183

slight bowing
181

155

wide
213

narrow
192, **194**-5, 201, 203-4, 215, 217

long serifs
201, 206-9, 211, 213-4, 217

shorter serifs
189, **203**-4, 215

some contrast
201, 207, **209**, 211-3

poor contrast
188

very
189, 191, 201-3, **207**-13

half serif
216

192

204

218, 220, 223, 225, **227**-8

219, **221**, 224, 226, 229

wide
219, 225, 238

narrow
220, 226, 228, 237, 239

some contrast
219, 221, 229, 232-**3**, 235

long serifs
230, **232**

thicker second stem
231

223

slightly flattened base
219

240

218

222

224

239

wide
245-8, 290-2, 294

narrow
250, 252-3, 262, 272, 284-9, 296, 299-300, 302, 304

slightly flattened base
245, **265**, 274, 283, 291, 293

290, **292**, 294, 303

269, **297**

thicker stem
276-**7**

vertical stress
268-9, 272

horizontal stress
271

295

298, **301**

258, 298

'Special Earmarks'

The 'special earmarks' (or distinctive identifying features) are indicated on each letter. The general 'style' of typefaces with the same 'earmark' may vary. The figures refer to specimen numbers.

***NB.** Bold figures indicate the specimen illustrated above.*

'Special Earmarks'

The 'special earmarks' (or distinctive identifying features) are indicated on each letter. The general 'style' of typefaces with the same 'earmark' may vary. The figures refer to specimen numbers.

For 'earmarks' of capital V refer to those of lower case v as they are generally the same but with the following exceptions:
slightly narrower
3
straight (not bowed)
49, 51
full (horizontal) serifs
14, 19, 23-4, 113, 125, 142-3
half serifs
104
pointed base
6, 34, 64
'kink'
60
narrower
162
narrower
189
overlap
272
pointed
300
For cap height 'earmarks' of W refer to those of H as they are generally the same. Other 'earmarks' are as follows:
(centre strokes meet at cap height)
10, 12, 17, 43, 54-5, 58-60, 62-3, 66-9, 74, 114-6, 18-20, 122, 129, 144, 150
wide
13
33, 44, 56-7, 64-5, 70-3, 121, 145-6
bowing
30, 42
bowing
113
stepped
27
high
18, 45, 75, 77-80, 83-4, 139, 149
long pointed
135
46, 134
8, 82, 85-6, 112, 137
133, 136, 138, 140-1
81
wedge serifs
28
(crossed centre strokes)
4, 9, 15-16, 31, 34, 37, 39-41, 87-98, 127, 131
low crossing
14, 36
98
wide
96
half serifs
32
serifs touching
123-4, 126
serifs touching
142
bowed
1
flat base
35, 38
(stepped centre strokes)
high junction
2, 3, 5, 11, 19-21, 47, 50-3, 61, 99, 106-7, 109, 111, 117, 130-1, 148
medium
6, 22, 25, 49, 61-3, 105, 108, 110, 132, 147
low
29
wide gap
6, 132, 143
slight bowing
11, 26
half serifs
104
bowing
29
flat
48, 100, 125
stepped
23-4
143
(centre strokes meet at cap height)
wide
172
narrow
176
155-6, 161, 167-8, 170, 173-4, 176, 179-80, 184-7
no serif
wide
164
152, 159
151, 166, 169, 182
(crossed centre strokes)
153-4, 160-162
(stepped centre strokes)
narrow
160
high junction
157-8, 165, 170-1, 175, 177-8, 180, 183
(centre strokes meet at cap height)
188, 196-7, 202, 206-9, 211
narrow
201, 215-7
213
flatter
189, 191, 194-5, 199-200, 203
190, 193, 198, 204-5
half serifs
192
210
214
stepped
212
(centre strokes meet at cap height)
230-1
220, 225, 227-8, 236, 238
223
222

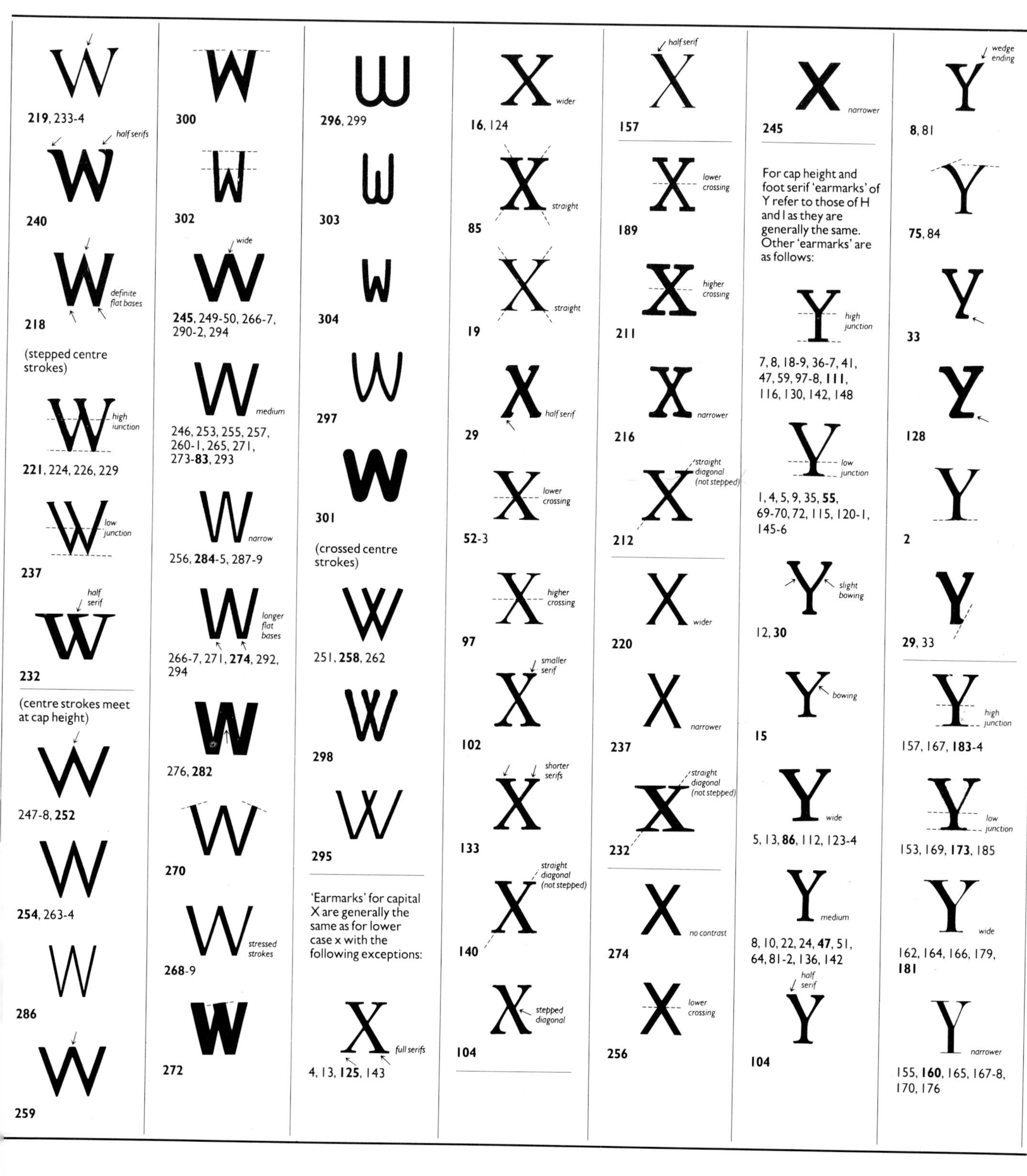
219, 233-4
half serifs
240
definite flat bases
218
(stepped centre strokes)
high junction
221, 224, 226, 229
low junction
237
half serif
232
(centre strokes meet at cap height)
247-8, 252
254, 263-4
286
259
300
302
wide
245, 249-50, 266-7, 290-2, 294
medium
246, 253, 255, 257, 260-1, 265, 271, 273-83, 293
narrow
256, 284-5, 287-9
longer flat bases
266-7, 271, 274, 292, 294
276, 282
270
stressed strokes
268-9
272
296, 299
303
304
297
301
(crossed centre strokes)
251, 258, 262
298
295
'Earmarks' for capital X are generally the same as for lower case x with the following exceptions:
full serifs
4, 13, 125, 143
wider
16, 124
straight
85
straight
19
half serif
29
lower crossing
52-3
higher crossing
97
smaller serif
102
shorter serifs
133
straight diagonal (not stepped)
140
stepped diagonal
104
half serif
157
lower crossing
189
higher crossing
211
narrower
216
straight diagonal (not stepped)
212
wider
220
narrower
237
straight diagonal (not stepped)
232
no contrast
274
lower crossing
256
narrower
245
For cap height and foot serif 'earmarks' of Y refer to those of H and I as they are generally the same. Other 'earmarks' are as follows:
high junction
7, 8, 18-9, 36-7, 41, 47, 59, 97-8, 111, 116, 130, 142, 148
low junction
1, 4, 5, 9, 35, 55, 69-70, 72, 115, 120-1, 145-6
slight bowing
12, 30
bowing
15
wide
5, 13, 86, 112, 123-4
medium
8, 10, 22, 24, 47, 51, 64, 81-2, 136, 142
half serif
104
wedge ending
8, 81
75, 84
33
128
2
29, 33
high junction
157, 167, 183-4
low junction
153, 169, 173, 185
wide
162, 164, 166, 179, 181
narrower
155, 160, 165, 167-8, 170, 176

'Special Earmarks'

The 'special earmarks' (or distinctive identifying features) are indicated on each letter. The general 'style' of typefaces with the same 'earmark' may vary. The figures refer to specimen numbers.

'Special Earmarks'

The 'special earmarks' (or distinctive identifying features) are indicated on each letter. The general 'style' of typefaces with the same 'earmark' may vary. The figures refer to specimen numbers.

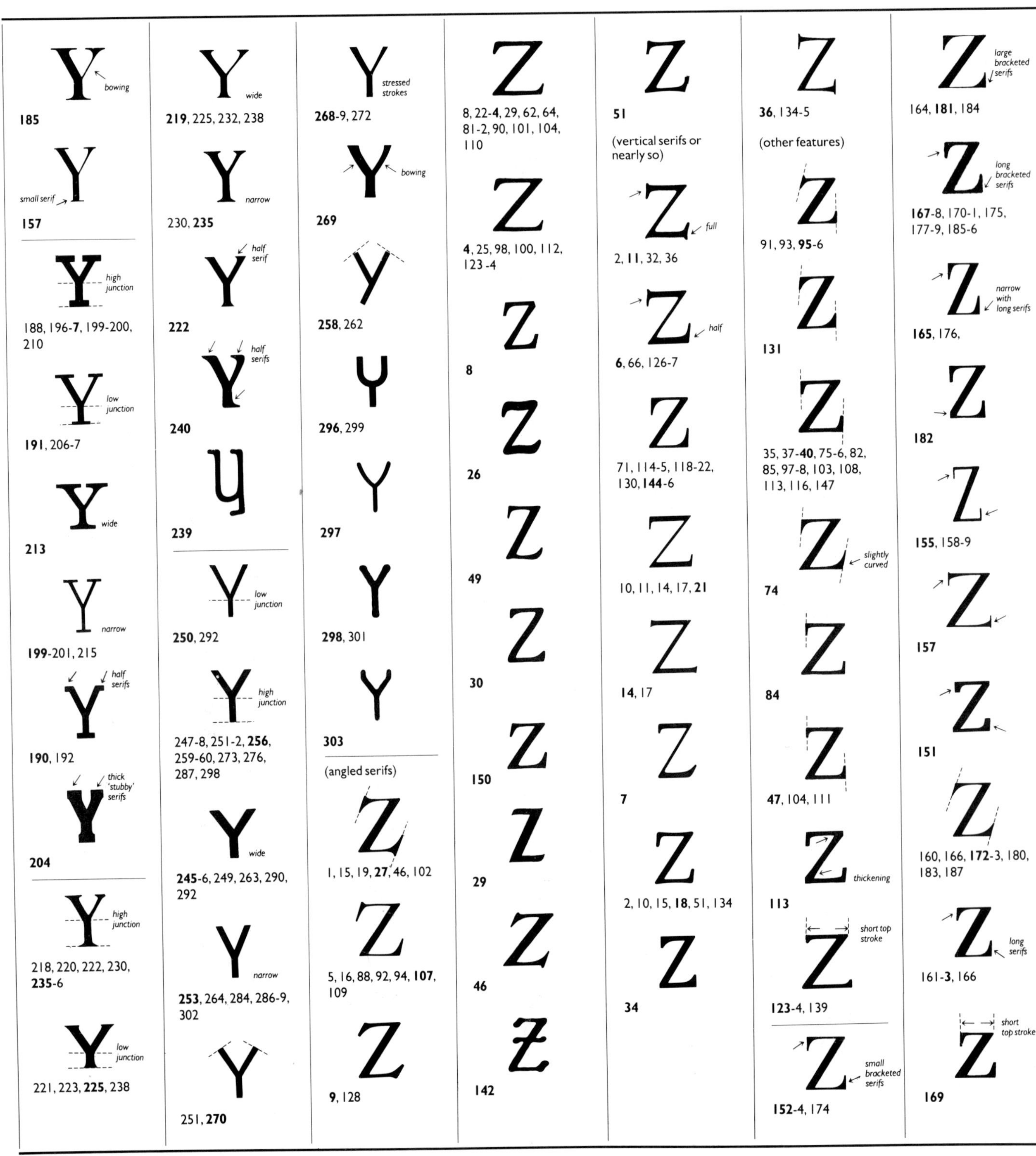
bowing
185
small serif
157
high junction
188, 196-7, 199-200, 210
low junction
191, 206-7
wide
213
narrow
199-201, 215
half serifs
190, 192
thick 'stubby' serifs
204
high junction
218, 220, 222, 230, 235-6
low junction
221, 223, 225, 238
wide
219, 225, 232, 238
narrow
230, 235
half serif
222
half serifs
240
239
low junction
250, 292
high junction
247-8, 251-2, 256, 259-60, 273, 276, 287, 298
wide
245-6, 249, 263, 290, 292
narrow
253, 264, 284, 286-9, 302
251, 270
stressed strokes
268-9, 272
bowing
269
258, 262
296, 299
297
298, 301
303
(angled serifs)
1, 15, 19, 27, 46, 102
5, 16, 88, 92, 94, 107, 109
9, 128
8, 22-4, 29, 62, 64, 81-2, 90, 101, 104, 110
4, 25, 98, 100, 112, 123-4
8
26
49
30
150
29
46
142
51
(vertical serifs or nearly so)
full
2, 11, 32, 36
half
6, 66, 126-7
71, 114-5, 118-22, 130, 144-6
10, 11, 14, 17, 21
14, 17
7
2, 10, 15, 18, 51, 134
34
36, 134-5
(other features)
91, 93, 95-6
131
35, 37-40, 75-6, 82, 85, 97-8, 103, 108, 113, 116, 147
slightly curved
74
84
47, 104, 111
thickening
113
short top stroke
123-4, 139
small bracketed serifs
152-4, 174
large bracketed serifs
164, 181, 184
long bracketed serifs
167-8, 170-1, 175, 177-9, 185-6
narrow with long serifs
165, 176,
182
155, 158-9
157
151
160, 166, 172-3, 180, 183, 187
long serifs
161-3, 166
short top stroke
169

'Special Earmarks'

The 'special earmarks' (or distinctive identifying features) are indicated on each letter. The general 'style' of typefaces with the same 'earmark' may vary. The figures refer to specimen numbers.

Z — slightly extended bottom — **187**

Z — **189**, 210

Z — 191, **207**-9

Z — short serifs — **194**-5

Z — longer serifs — **201**, 203, 207-8, 214

Z — **218**, 220, 225

Z — **223**, 227

Z — **228**

Z — wedge serifs — **219**, 221, 226, 229, 232, 234-5, 240

Z — **224**

Z — 230, **233**

Z — no contrast — **236**-8

Z — full serif — **231**

Z — wide top stroke — **232**

Z — **239**

Z — 245, **251**-9, 262-4, 300, 302

Z — **253**

Z — **248**, 270

Z — stressed strokes — **268**

Z — **298**, 301, 303

Z — curved — **269**, 297

Z — **296**, 299

(closed bowls)

& — **96**

& — 1, 12, 19-20, 27, 42, 45-6, 57, 71, 89-90, **97**-8, 105, 126, 133, 138, 147, 149

& — **64**, 100

& — **113**

& — **127**

& — **44**

& — **1**

& — **123**-4, 126

& — **50**, 52-3, 76, 101, 107, 112, 114, 119-22, 129, 131

& — **68**

& — 58, 62, 69, **79**

& — **56**

& — **142**

& — 10, **74**-5, 116, 139, 147

& — **141**

& — **14**, 17-8, ,33, 77

& — **82**

& — **2**

& — **125**

& — **5**

(open bowls)

& — 21, **23**-4, 49, 51, 132

& — 22, **37**, 140

& — 29, **32**

& — **9**

& — **104**, 110

& — 8, **81**

& — **128**

& — **36**, 130

& — 6, **150**

& — 2, **108**

& — **3**

& — **4**

& — **134**

& — **135**

& — **13**

& — **143**

& — 151-2, **159**, 165, 174, 184-4

& — 154, **162**-3. 165, 181-2

& — 156, 164, 167, 170, **173**, 186

& — 161, 166, 170-1, **175**-80, 185, 187

& — 153, **160**

& — **169**

& — **158**, 172

& — open — **157**

& — **189**, 193, 196, 198

& — **197**

& — **191**

& — **190**

'Special Earmarks'

The 'special earmarks' (or distinctive identifying features) are indicated on each letter. The general 'style' of typefaces with the same 'earmark' may vary. The figures refer to specimen numbers.

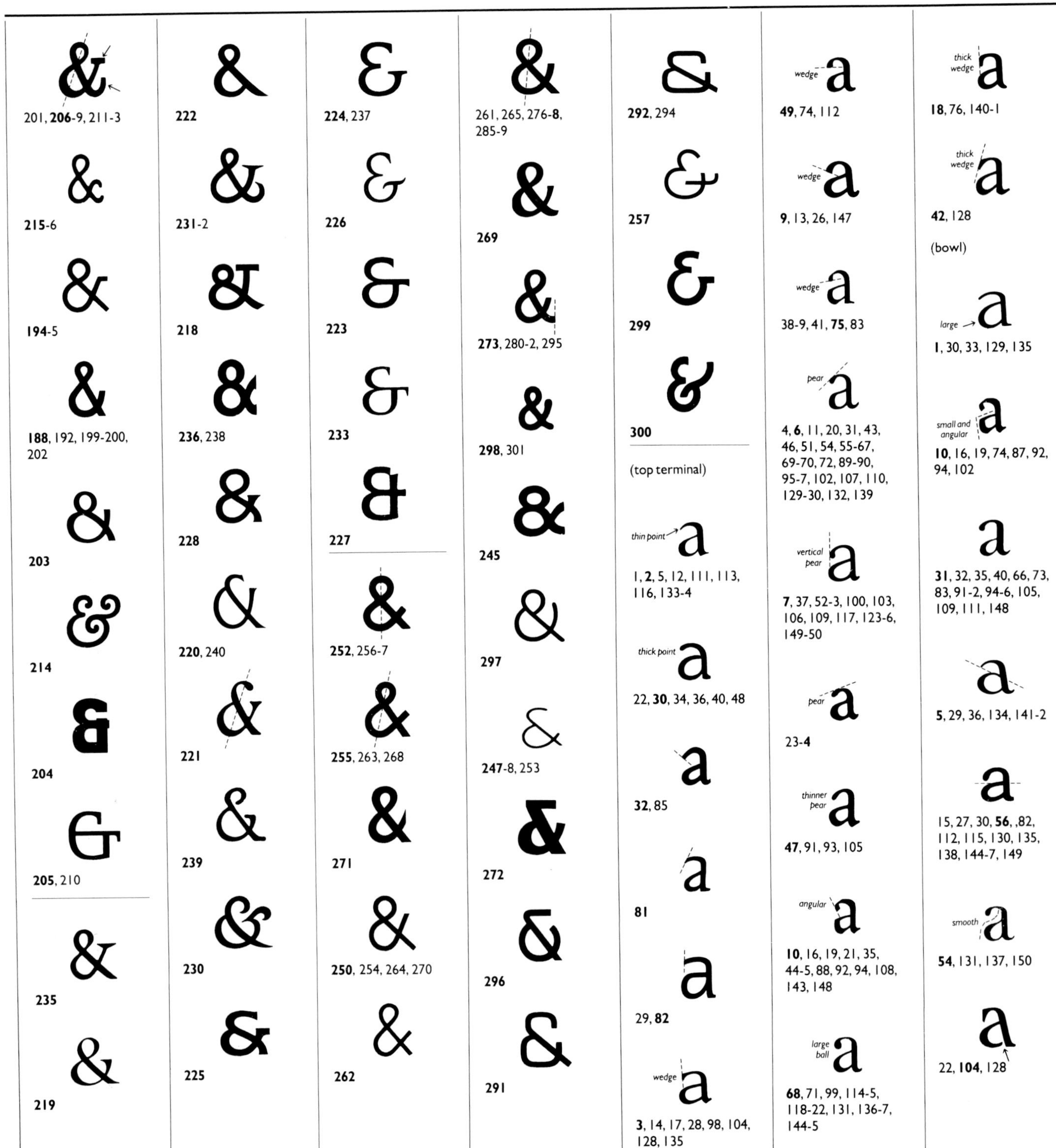
201, 206-9, 211-3
215-6
194-5
188, 192, 199-200, 202
203
214
204
205, 210
235
219
222
231-2
218
236, 238
228
220, 240
221
239
230
225
224, 237
226
223
233
227
252, 256-7
255, 263, 268
271
250, 254, 264, 270
262
261, 265, 276-8, 285-9
269
273, 280-2, 295
298, 301
245
297
247-8, 253
272
296
291
292, 294
257
299
300
(top terminal)
thin point
1, 2, 5, 12, 111, 113, 116, 133-4
thick point
22, 30, 34, 36, 40, 48
32, 85
81
29, 82
wedge
3, 14, 17, 28, 98, 104, 128, 135
wedge
49, 74, 112
wedge
9, 13, 26, 147
wedge
38-9, 41, 75, 83
pear
4, 6, 11, 20, 31, 43, 46, 51, 54, 55-67, 69-70, 72, 89-90, 95-7, 102, 107, 110, 129-30, 132, 139
vertical pear
7, 37, 52-3, 100, 103, 106, 109, 117, 123-6, 149-50
pear
23-4
thinner pear
47, 91, 93, 105
angular
10, 16, 19, 21, 35, 44-5, 88, 92, 94, 108, 143, 148
large ball
68, 71, 99, 114-5, 118-22, 131, 136-7, 144-5
thick wedge
18, 76, 140-1
thick wedge
42, 128
(bowl)
large
1, 30, 33, 129, 135
small and angular
10, 16, 19, 74, 87, 92, 94, 102
31, 32, 35, 40, 66, 73, 83, 91-2, 94-6, 105, 109, 111, 148
5, 29, 36, 134, 141-2
15, 27, 30, 56, ,82, 112, 115, 130, 135, 138, 144-7, 149
smooth
54, 131, 137, 150
22, 104, 128

***NB.** Bold figures indicate the specimen illustrated above.*

'Special Earmarks'

The 'special earmarks' (or distinctive identifying features) are indicated on each letter. The general 'style' of typefaces with the same 'earmark' may vary. The figures refer to specimen numbers.

(back)

5, 13, 104, 123-4, 129

23-4, 29-30

40, **44**, 47, 73, 87, 91-6

wide opening

8, **14**, 17, 23-4, 48, 77-81, 98, 135, 143

(foot serif)

thin

1, 75, 84, 125, 131, 134-5

thicker

81, 113, **133**, 136, 138, 140-3, 150

short and thick

8, 12, 22, 29-30, 56 71, 82, 104, 112, 126, 128

pointed

28

short

2-3, 10, 15, 37, 45, 47, 66, 76, 98, 102, 108, 142, 148

short and heavy

44

longer

19, 42, 97, 108, 147

14, 17-8, 21, 37, 46, 111, 129

short and rounded

4, 7, 15, 23-4, 26, 32-3, 38-9, 41, 48, 50-2, 60-4, 66-8, 74, 78, 89-90, 100, 106, 115, 118-9, 120, 124, 128, 130, 139, 144, 146

long and rounded

5, **6**, 9, 11, 13, 16, 20, 25, 27, 31, 34-6, 43, 53-4, 65, 69-70, 72, 77-80, 83, 85, 91-2 99, 101, 103, 107, 109-10, 114, 117, 121, 127, 132, 149

35-6, **40**, 42, 49, 55, 58-9, 73, 76, 83, 87-8, 93-7, 105, 115-6

86, 122

long curled up

70, 78, 114, **137**

(top terminal)

151, 182

157, **165**

155, **166**

ball

160, 162-4, 170-1, 175-81, 184-6

pear

152-4, **156**, 167-9, 172-4

thin pear

158-9, 161, **172**, 187

pointed

183

(bowl)

155, **157**, 159

153, 161-3, 187

smooth

156, 160, 164, 169, 178-81

(foot serif)

angled and flat

151-2, 155, 165, **183**

161, 167-8, 171, 180, 182, 187

158

curled up

160, 164, 170, 173, 175-9, **185**-6

(double storey)

188-9, 191, 197, 203

190, 204, 206-9, 211

192, **198**, 201-2, 205, 210, 215

212-4, 216-7

189, 204-5

188, 191

188-**93**, 197-8, 203-5

201, 206-9, 211-5, 217

(single storey)

194-6

199-200

(double storey)

wide

219, 225

218, 222, 225, 235, 240

227, 231

223-4, 226, 228, 234

pear

229, 232

curl

230

curl

231

pointed

233

smooth

222, **226**, 228, 230

239

(single storey)

237

(double storey)

square

291-2, 297

245-6, **249**, 251, 253, 256, 261, 264-5, 270, 282, 285-9

259, 262, 266, 268-9, 271-2, 295

267, 273-81, 283, 291-3, 304

284

251, **253**, 262, 264

smooth

245, **261**, 265, 268, 271, 275, 279, 295

large top

271

small top

270

259, **270**

NB. *Bold figures indicate the specimen illustrated above.*

'Special Earmarks'

The 'special earmarks' (or distinctive identifying features) are indicated on each letter. The general 'style' of typefaces with the same 'earmark' may vary. The figures refer to specimen numbers.

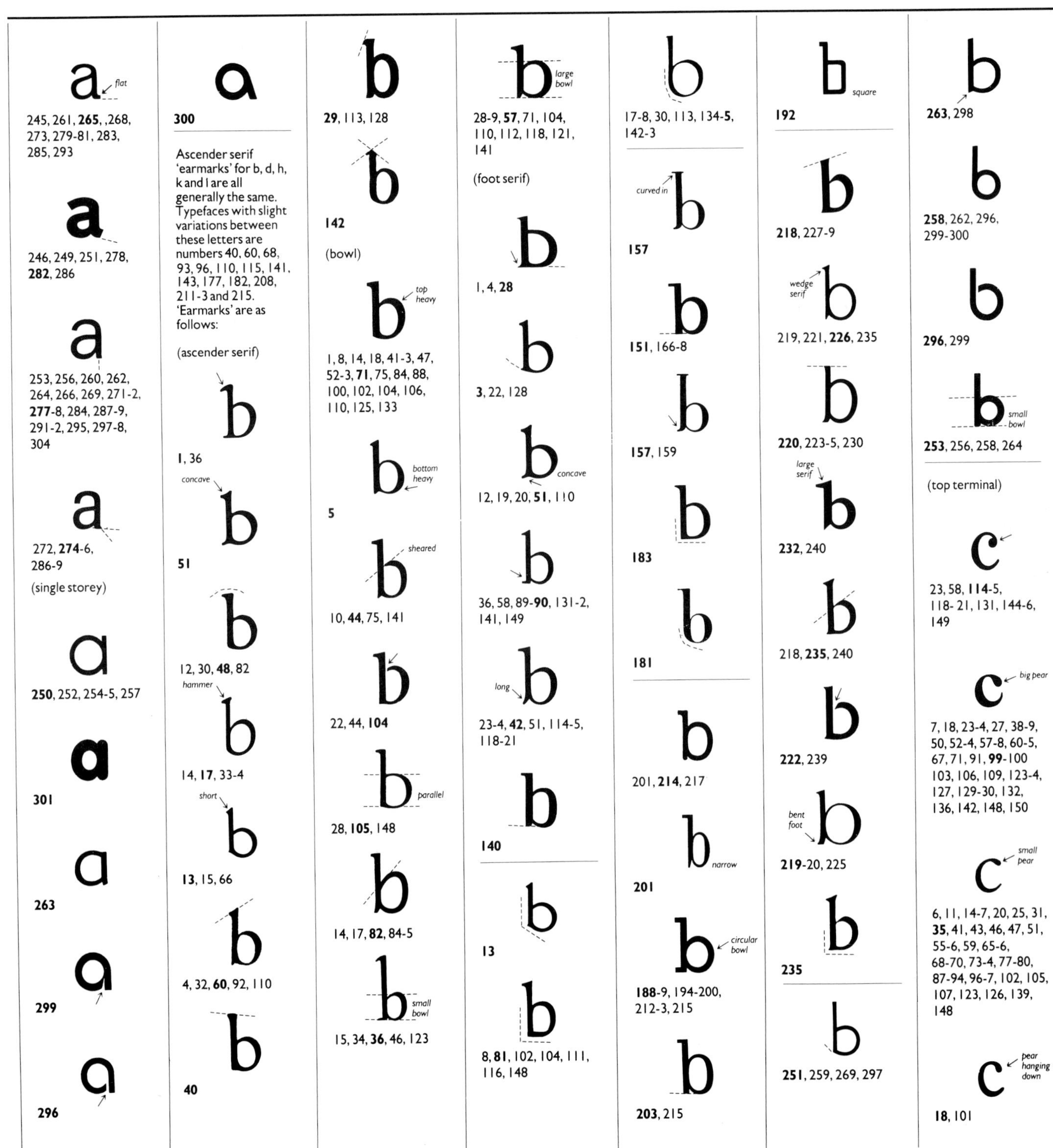
flat
245, 261, **265**, ,268, 273, 279-81, 283, 285, 293
246, 249, 251, 278, **282**, 286
253, 256, 260, 262, 264, 266, 269, 271-2, **277**-8, 284, 287-9, 291-2, 295, 297-8, 304
272, **274**-6, 286-9
(single storey)
250, 252, 254-5, 257
301
263
299
296
300
Ascender serif 'earmarks' for b, d, h, k and l are all generally the same. Typefaces with slight variations between these letters are numbers 40, 60, 68, 93, 96, 110, 115, 141, 143, 177, 182, 208, 211-3 and 215. 'Earmarks' are as follows:
(ascender serif)
1, 36
concave
51
12, 30, **48**, 82
hammer
14, **17**, 33-4
short
13, 15, 66
4, 32, **60**, 92, 110
40
29, 113, 128
142
(bowl)
top heavy
1, 8, 14, 18, 41-3, 47, 52-3, **71**, 75, 84, 88, 100, 102, 104, 106, 110, 125, 133
bottom heavy
5
sheared
10, **44**, 75, 141
22, 44, **104**
parallel
28, **105**, 148
14, 17, **82**, 84-5
small bowl
15, 34, **36**, 46, 123
large bowl
28-9, **57**, 71, 104, 110, 112, 118, 121, 141
(foot serif)
1, 4, **28**
3, 22, 128
concave
12, 19, 20, **51**, 110
36, 58, 89-**90**, 131-2, 141, 149
long
23-4, **42**, 51, 114-5, 118-21
140
13
8, **81**, 102, 104, 111, 116, 148
17-8, 30, 113, 134-**5**, 142-3
curved in
157
151, 166-8
157, 159
183
181
201, **214**, 217
narrow
201
circular bowl
188-9, 194-200, 212-3, 215
203, 215
square
192
218, 227-9
wedge serif
219, 221, **226**, 235
220, 223-5, 230
large serif
232, 240
218, **235**, 240
222, 239
bent foot
219-20, 225
235
251, 259, 269, 297
263, 298
258, 262, 296, 299-300
296, 299
small bowl
253, 256, 258, 264
(top terminal)
23, 58, **114**-5, 118-21, 131, 144-6, 149
big pear
7, 18, 23-4, 27, 38-9, 50, 52-4, 57-8, 60-5, 67, 71, 91, **99**-100, 103, 106, 109, 123-4, 127, 129-30, 132, 136, 142, 148, 150
small pear
6, 11, 14-7, 20, 25, 31, **35**, 41, 43, 46, 47, 51, 55-6, 59, 65-6, 68-70, 73-4, 77-80, 87-94, 96-7, 102, 105, 107, 123, 126, 139, 148
pear hanging down
18, 101

NB. *Bold figures indicate the specimen illustrated above.*

'Special Earmarks'

The 'special earmarks' (or distinctive identifying features) are indicated on each letter. The general 'style' of typefaces with the same 'earmark' may vary. The figures refer to specimen numbers.

1, 22, 28

2, 3, 5, 10, 12-3, **26**, 29, 42, 49, 128, 143

117

4, 16, **19**, 32, 34, 48, 83, 108

81, 147

86, **125** (rounded wedge)

33, **37**, 45, 82, 95, 98, 134-5

36, **111**, 116, 137

75, 84-5, 104, 112-3, 133, 138, 140-1 (hook)

74, **76**, 138, 140-1 (square pear)

28, **138**, 140-2 (identical serifs)

44 (general)

8, 18, 23-4, 29, **64**, 75, 93, 104, 134 (narrow)

2, 4, 6, 21, **43**, 45, 70, 72, 83

23, 26, 31, 35, 41, 87 **93**, 102, 113

153-4, 160, 162-4, 170-1, 175-81, 184-6 (ball)

152, 156, 167-9, 174, 187 (pear)

158-9, 161, 172-3 (thin pear)

157, 183 (serif)

165-6 (spiked serif)

151, 182 (square)

155

155, 165, **176** (narrow)

188, 191, **196**-7, 199

190, 193-4, 198

189 (half serif)

201-3 (narrow opening)

205, 210

206-9, 211-7 (ball)

218, 220, 222-3, 225-8

219, 233-4

221, **229** (narrow)

235 (flat top)

224, 231, 240 (hook)

230-1 (curl)

250, 265, 267, 273-5, 278-280, 283, 291-3, 304

246, 249, 252, **254**, 257-60, 263-4, 266, 269, 271, 295-6

245, 247-8, 251, 253, **255**-6, 261-2, 270, 276-7, 282, 285-9, 299-300

281

268 (slight contrast)

271 (top heavy, slight contrast)

272 (bottom heavy)

284 (small serifs)

297

298

For ascender serif and bowl 'earmarks' of d refer to those of b as they are generally the same. Other 'earmarks' are as follows:

(foot serif)

1, 28, 111, 116 (flat)

4, 8-10, 12, 22, 27, 33, 56-7, **62**, 64, 75, 78, 80-2, 84, 87, 89-90, 104, 110, 112-5, 118-149

6, 7, 11, 14-9, 21, 26, 31-2, 34-5, **37**-44, 47, 49, 52-5, 58-61, 63, 65-72, 74, 76, 83, 85-6, 88, 91-7, 99-103, 105-7, 146, 148

2, 3, 5, 13, **20**, 23-5, 45-6, 48, 50-1, 73, 77, 79, 98, 108-9, 117, 150

30

36 (rounded)

42 (angular)

157, 159

171-2, 182-3

169 (wide bowl)

208-213

218-30

231-5, 240

246 (tapered)

269

272

271 (top heavy)

251, 259, 297

299-**300**

NB. Bold figures indicate the specimen illustrated above.

'Special Earmarks'

The 'special earmarks' (or distinctive identifying features) are indicated on each letter. The general 'style' of typefaces with the same 'earmark' may vary. The figures refer to specimen numbers.

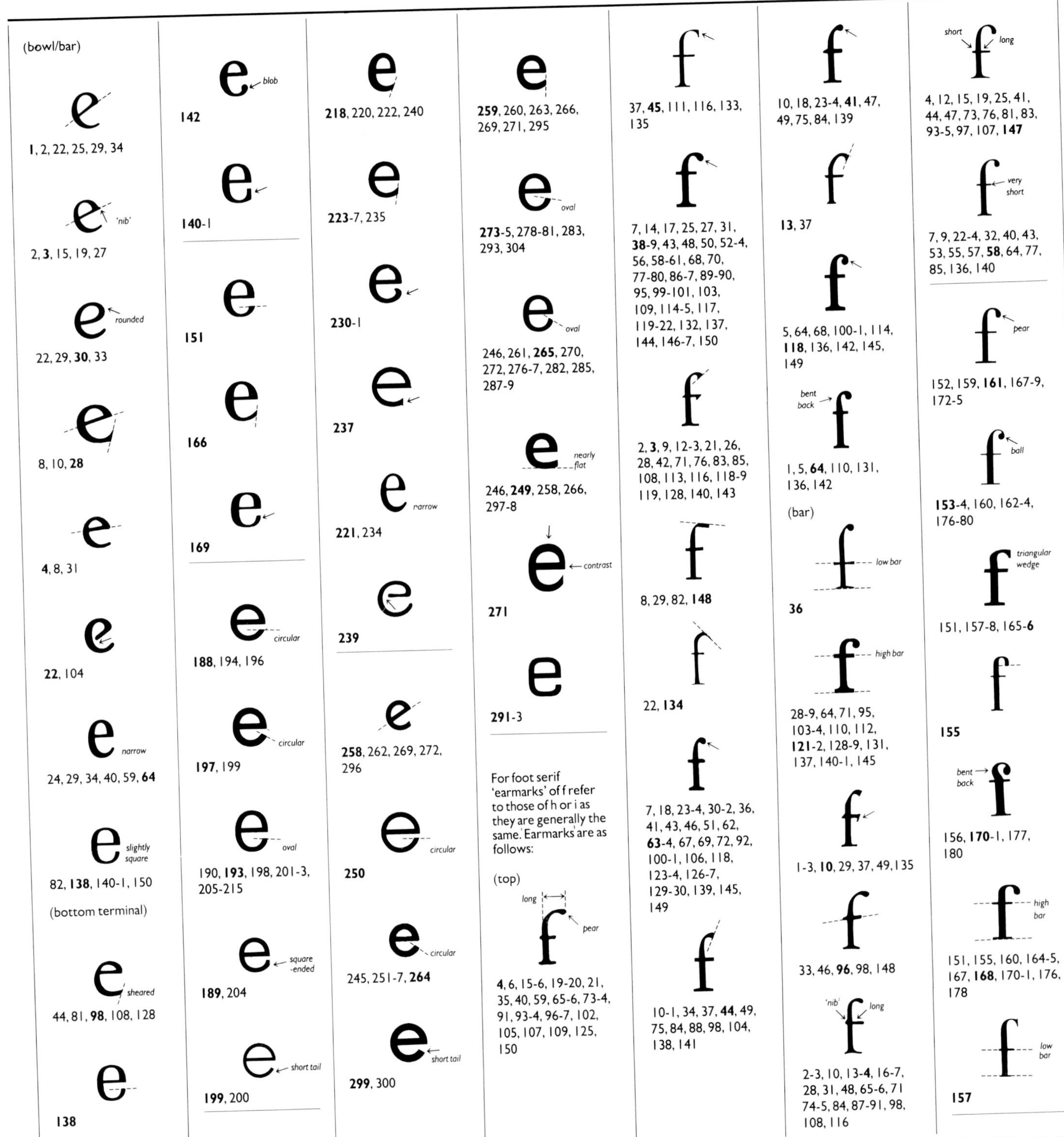
(bowl/bar)
1, 2, 22, 25, 29, 34
'nib'
2, 3, 15, 19, 27
rounded
22, 29, 30, 33
8, 10, 28
4, 8, 31
22, 104
narrow
24, 29, 34, 40, 59, 64
slightly square
82, 138, 140-1, 150
(bottom terminal)
sheared
44, 81, 98, 108, 128
138
blob
142
140-1
151
166
169
circular
188, 194, 196
circular
197, 199
oval
190, 193, 198, 201-3, 205-215
square -ended
189, 204
short tail
199, 200
218, 220, 222, 240
223-7, 235
230-1
237
narrow
221, 234
239
258, 262, 269, 272, 296
circular
250
circular
245, 251-7, 264
short tail
299, 300
259, 260, 263, 266, 269, 271, 295
oval
273-5, 278-81, 283, 293, 304
oval
246, 261, 265, 270, 272, 276-7, 282, 285, 287-9
nearly flat
246, 249, 258, 266, 297-8
contrast
271
291-3
For foot serif 'earmarks' of f refer to those of h or i as they are generally the same. Earmarks are as follows:
(top)
long
pear
4, 6, 15-6, 19-20, 21, 35, 40, 59, 65-6, 73-4, 91, 93-4, 96-7, 102, 105, 107, 109, 125, 150
37, 45, 111, 116, 133, 135
7, 14, 17, 25, 27, 31, 38-9, 43, 48, 50, 52-4, 56, 58-61, 68, 70, 77-80, 86-7, 89-90, 95, 99-101, 103, 109, 114-5, 117, 119-22, 132, 137, 144, 146-7, 150
2, 3, 9, 12-3, 21, 26, 28, 42, 71, 76, 83, 85, 108, 113, 116, 118-9, 119, 128, 140, 143
8, 29, 82, 148
22, 134
7, 18, 23-4, 30-2, 36, 41, 43, 46, 51, 62, 63-4, 67, 69, 72, 92, 100-1, 106, 118, 123-4, 126-7, 129-30, 139, 145, 149
10-1, 34, 37, 44, 49, 75, 84, 88, 98, 104, 138, 141
10, 18, 23-4, 41, 47, 49, 75, 84, 139
13, 37
5, 64, 68, 100-1, 114, 118, 136, 142, 145, 149
bent back
1, 5, 64, 110, 131, 136, 142
(bar)
low bar
36
high bar
28-9, 64, 71, 95, 103-4, 110, 112, 121-2, 128-9, 131, 137, 140-1, 145
1-3, 10, 29, 37, 49, 135
33, 46, 96, 98, 148
'nib'
long
2-3, 10, 13-4, 16-7, 28, 31, 48, 65-6, 71 74-5, 84, 87-91, 98, 108, 116
short
long
4, 12, 15, 19, 25, 41, 44, 47, 73, 76, 81, 83, 93-5, 97, 107, 147
very short
7, 9, 22-4, 32, 40, 43, 53, 55, 57, 58, 64, 77, 85, 136, 140
pear
152, 159, 161, 167-9, 172-5
ball
153-4, 160, 162-4, 176-80
triangular wedge
151, 157-8, 165-6
155
bent back
156, 170-1, 177, 180
high bar
151, 155, 160, 164-5, 167, 168, 170-1, 176, 178
low bar
157

NB. *Bold figures indicate the specimen illustrated above.*

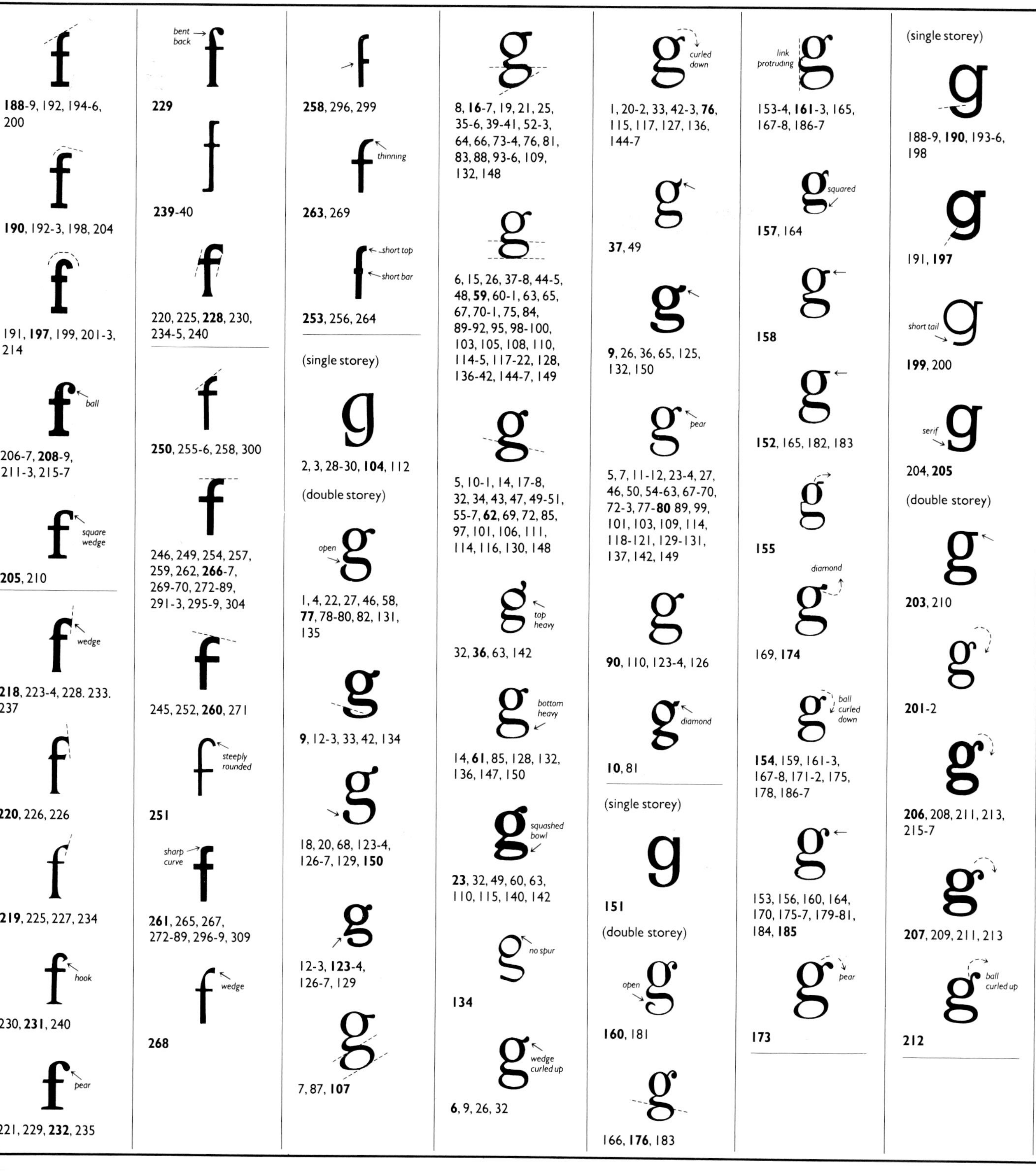
188-9, 192, 194-6, 200
190, 192-3, 198, 204
191, **197**, 199, 201-3, 214
ball
206-7, **208**-9, 211-3, 215-7
square wedge
205, 210
wedge
218, 223-4, 228. 233. 237
220, 226, 226
219, 225, 227, 234
hook
230, **231**, 240
pear
221, 229, **232**, 235
bent back
229
239-40
220, 225, **228**, 230, 234-5, 240
250, 255-6, 258, 300
246, 249, 254, 257, 259, 262, **266**-7, 269-70, 272-89, 291-3, 295-9, 304
245, 252, **260**, 271
steeply rounded
251
sharp curve
261, 265, 267, 272-89, 296-9, 309
wedge
268
258, 296, 299
thinning
263, 269
short top
short bar
253, 256, 264
(single storey)
2, 3, 28-30, **104**, 112
(double storey)
open
1, 4, 22, 27, 46, 58, **77**, 78-80, 82, 131, 135
9, 12-3, 33, 42, 134
18, 20, 68, 123-4, 126-7, 129, **150**
12-3, **123**-4, 126-7, 129
7, 87, **107**
8, **16**-7, 19, 21, 25, 35-6, 39-41, 52-3, 64, 66, 73-4, 76, 81, 83, 88, 93-6, 109, 132, 148
6, 15, 26, 37-8, 44-5, 48, **59**, 60-1, 63, 65, 67, 70-1, 75, 84, 89-92, 95, 98-100, 103, 105, 108, 110, 114-5, 117-22, 128, 136-42, 144-7, 149
5, 10-1, 14, 17-8, 32, 34, 43, 47, 49-51, 55-7, **62**, 69, 72, 85, 97, 101, 106, 111, 114, 116, 130, 148
top heavy
32, **36**, 63, 142
bottom heavy
14, **61**, 85, 128, 132, 136, 147, 150
squashed bowl
23, 32, 49, 60, 63, 110, 115, 140, 142
no spur
134
wedge curled up
6, 9, 26, 32
curled down
1, 20-2, 33, 42-3, **76**, 115, 117, 127, 136, 144-7
37, 49
9, 26, 36, 65, 125, 132, 150
pear
5, 7, 11-12, 23-4, 27, 46, 50, 54-63, 67-70, 72-3, 77-**80** 89, 99, 101, 103, 109, 114, 118-121, 129-131, 137, 142, 149
90, 110, 123-4, 126
diamond
10, 81
(single storey)
151
(double storey)
open
160, 181
166, **176**, 183
link protruding
153-4, **161**-3, 165, 167-8, 186-7
squared
157, 164
158
152, 165, 182, 183
155
diamond
169, **174**
ball curled down
154, 159, 161-3, 167-8, 171-2, 175, 178, 186-7
153, 156, 160, 164, 170, 175-7, 179-81, 184, **185**
pear
173
(single storey)
188-9, **190**, 193-6, 198
191, **197**
short tail
199, 200
serif
204, **205**
(double storey)
203, 210
201-2
206, 208, 211, 213, 215-7
207, 209, 211, 213
ball curled up
212

'Special Earmarks'

The 'special earmarks' (or distinctive identifying features) are indicated on each letter. The general 'style' of typefaces with the same 'earmark' may vary. The figures refer to specimen numbers.

***NB.** Bold figures indicate the specimen illustrated above.*

'Special Earmarks'

The 'special earmarks' (or distinctive identifying features) are indicated on each letter. The general 'style' of typefaces with the same 'earmark' may vary. The figures refer to specimen numbers.

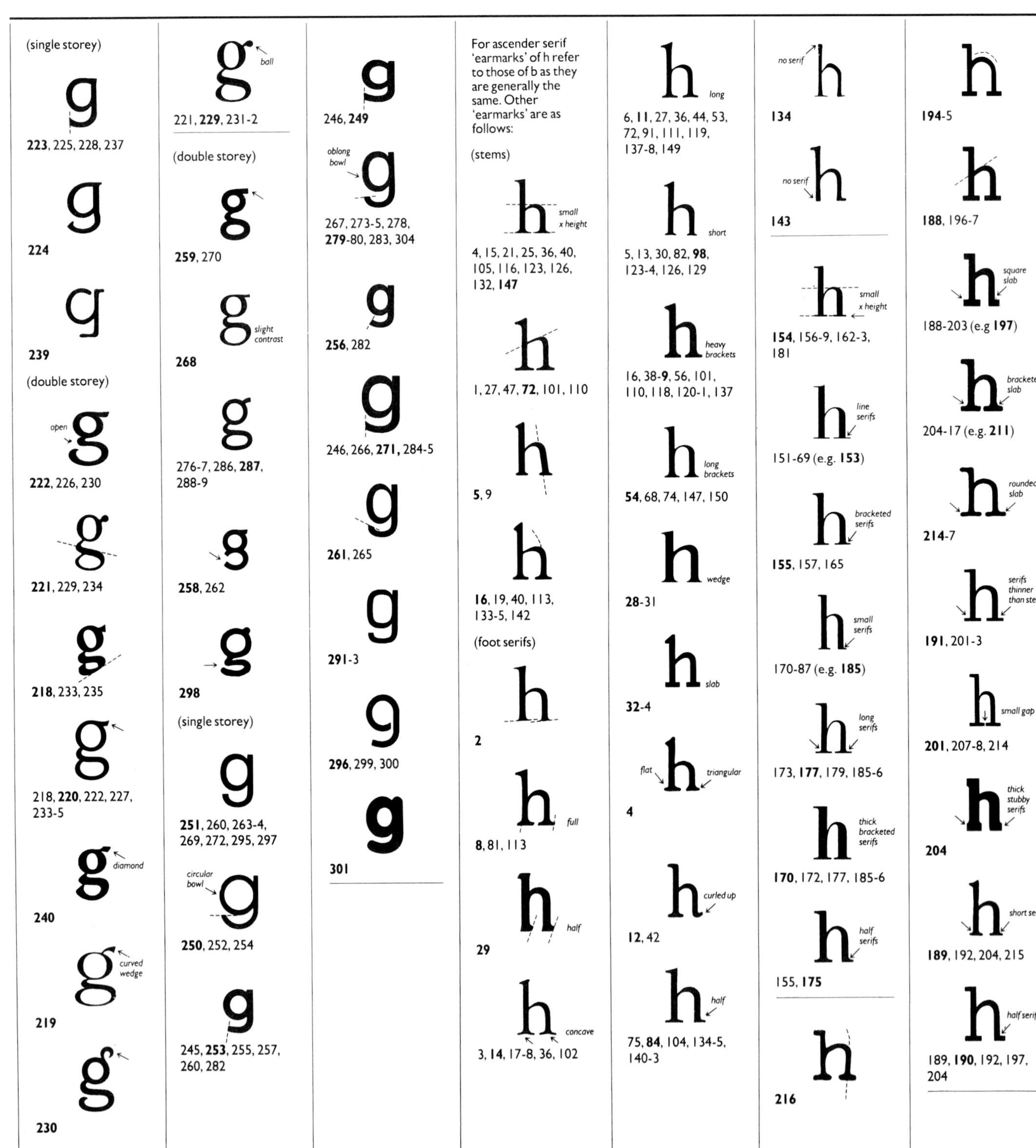
(single storey)
223, 225, 228, 237
224
239
(double storey)
open
222, 226, 230
221, 229, 234
218, 233, 235
218, **220**, 222, 227, 233-5
diamond
240
curved wedge
219
230
ball
221, **229**, 231-2
(double storey)
259, 270
slight contrast
268
276-7, 286, **287**, 288-9
258, 262
298
(single storey)
251, 260, 263-4, 269, 272, 295, 297
circular bowl
250, 252, 254
245, **253**, 255, 257, 260, 282
246, **249**
oblong bowl
267, 273-5, 278, **279**-80, 283, 304
256, 282
246, 266, **271**, 284-5
261, 265
291-3
296, 299, 300
301
For ascender serif 'earmarks' of h refer to those of b as they are generally the same. Other 'earmarks' are as follows:
(stems)
small x height
4, 15, 21, 25, 36, 40, 105, 116, 123, 126, 132, **147**
1, 27, 47, **72**, 101, 110
5, 9
16, 19, 40, 113, 133-5, 142
(foot serifs)
2
full
8, 81, 113
half
29
concave
3, **14**, 17-8, 36, 102
long
6, **11**, 27, 36, 44, 53, 72, 91, 111, 119, 137-8, 149
short
5, 13, 30, 82, **98**, 123-4, 126, 129
heavy brackets
16, 38-**9**, 56, 101, 110, 118, 120-1, 137
long brackets
54, 68, 74, 147, 150
wedge
28-31
slab
32-4
flat
triangular
4
curled up
12, 42
half
75, **84**, 104, 134-5, 140-3
no serif
134
no serif
143
small x height
154, 156-9, 162-3, 181
line serifs
151-69 (e.g. **153**)
bracketed serifs
155, 157, 165
small serifs
170-87 (e.g. **185**)
long serifs
173, **177**, 179, 185-6
thick bracketed serifs
170, 172, 177, 185-6
half serifs
155, **175**
216
194-5
188, 196-7
square slab
188-203 (e.g **197**)
bracketed slab
204-17 (e.g. **211**)
rounded slab
214-7
serifs thinner than stems
191, 201-3
small gap
201, 207-8, 214
thick stubby serifs
204
short serifs
189, 192, 204, 215
half serif
189, **190**, 192, 197, 204

***NB.** Bold figures indicate the specimen illustrated above.*

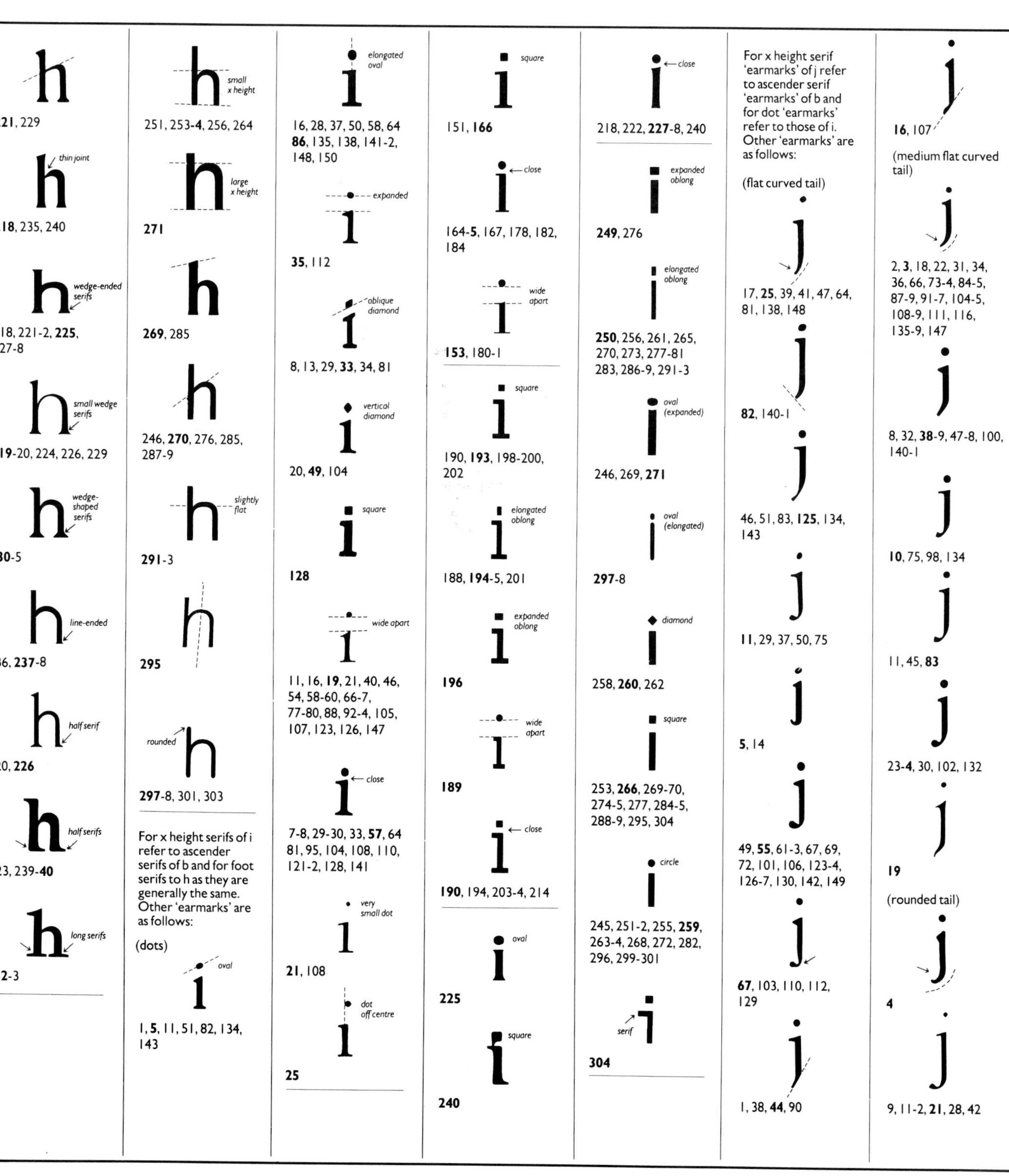
221, 229
thin joint
218, 235, 240
wedge-ended serifs
218, 221-2, 225, 227-8
small wedge serifs
219-20, 224, 226, 229
wedge-shaped serifs
230-5
line-ended
236, 237-8
half serif
220, 226
half serifs
223, 239-40
long serifs
232-3
small x height
251, 253-4, 256, 264
large x height
271
269, 285
246, 270, 276, 285, 287-9
slightly flat
291-3
295
rounded
297-8, 301, 303
For x height serifs of i refer to ascender serifs of b and for foot serifs to h as they are generally the same. Other 'earmarks' are as follows:
(dots)
oval
1, 5, 11, 51, 82, 134, 143
elongated oval
16, 28, 37, 50, 58, 64, 86, 135, 138, 141-2, 148, 150
expanded
35, 112
oblique diamond
8, 13, 29, 33, 34, 81
vertical diamond
20, 49, 104
square
128
wide apart
11, 16, 19, 21, 40, 46, 54, 58-60, 66-7, 77-80, 88, 92-4, 105, 107, 123, 126, 147
close
7-8, 29-30, 33, 57, 64, 81, 95, 104, 108, 110, 121-2, 128, 141
very small dot
21, 108
dot off centre
25
square
151, 166
close
164-5, 167, 178, 182, 184
wide apart
153, 180-1
square
190, 193, 198-200, 202
elongated oblong
188, 194-5, 201
expanded oblong
196
wide apart
189
close
190, 194, 203-4, 214
oval
225
square
240
close
218, 222, 227-8, 240
expanded oblong
249, 276
elongated oblong
250, 256, 261, 265, 270, 273, 277-81, 283, 286-9, 291-3
oval (expanded)
246, 269, 271
oval (elongated)
297-8
diamond
258, 260, 262
square
253, 266, 269-70, 274-5, 277, 284-5, 288-9, 295, 304
circle
245, 251-2, 255, 259, 263-4, 268, 272, 282, 296, 299-301
serif
304
For x height serif 'earmarks' of j refer to ascender serif 'earmarks' of b and for dot 'earmarks' refer to those of i. Other 'earmarks' are as follows:
(flat curved tail)
17, 25, 39, 41, 47, 64, 81, 138, 148
82, 140-1
46, 51, 83, 125, 134, 143
11, 29, 37, 50, 75
5, 14
49, 55, 61-3, 67, 69, 72, 101, 106, 123-4, 126-7, 130, 142, 149
67, 103, 110, 112, 129
1, 38, 44, 90
16, 107
(medium flat curved tail)
2, 3, 18, 22, 31, 34, 36, 66, 73-4, 84-5, 87-9, 91-7, 104-5, 108-9, 111, 116, 135-9, 147
8, 32, 38-9, 47-8, 100, 140-1
10, 75, 98, 134
11, 45, 83
23-4, 30, 102, 132
19
(rounded tail)
4
9, 11-2, 21, 28, 42

'Special Earmarks'

The 'special earmarks' (or distinctive identifying features) are indicated on each letter. The general 'style' of typefaces with the same 'earmark' may vary. The figures refer to specimen numbers.

***NB.** Bold figures indicate the specimen illustrated above.*

'Special Earmarks'

The 'special earmarks' (or distinctive identifying features) are indicated on each letter. The general 'style' of typefaces with the same 'earmark' may vary. The figures refer to specimen numbers.

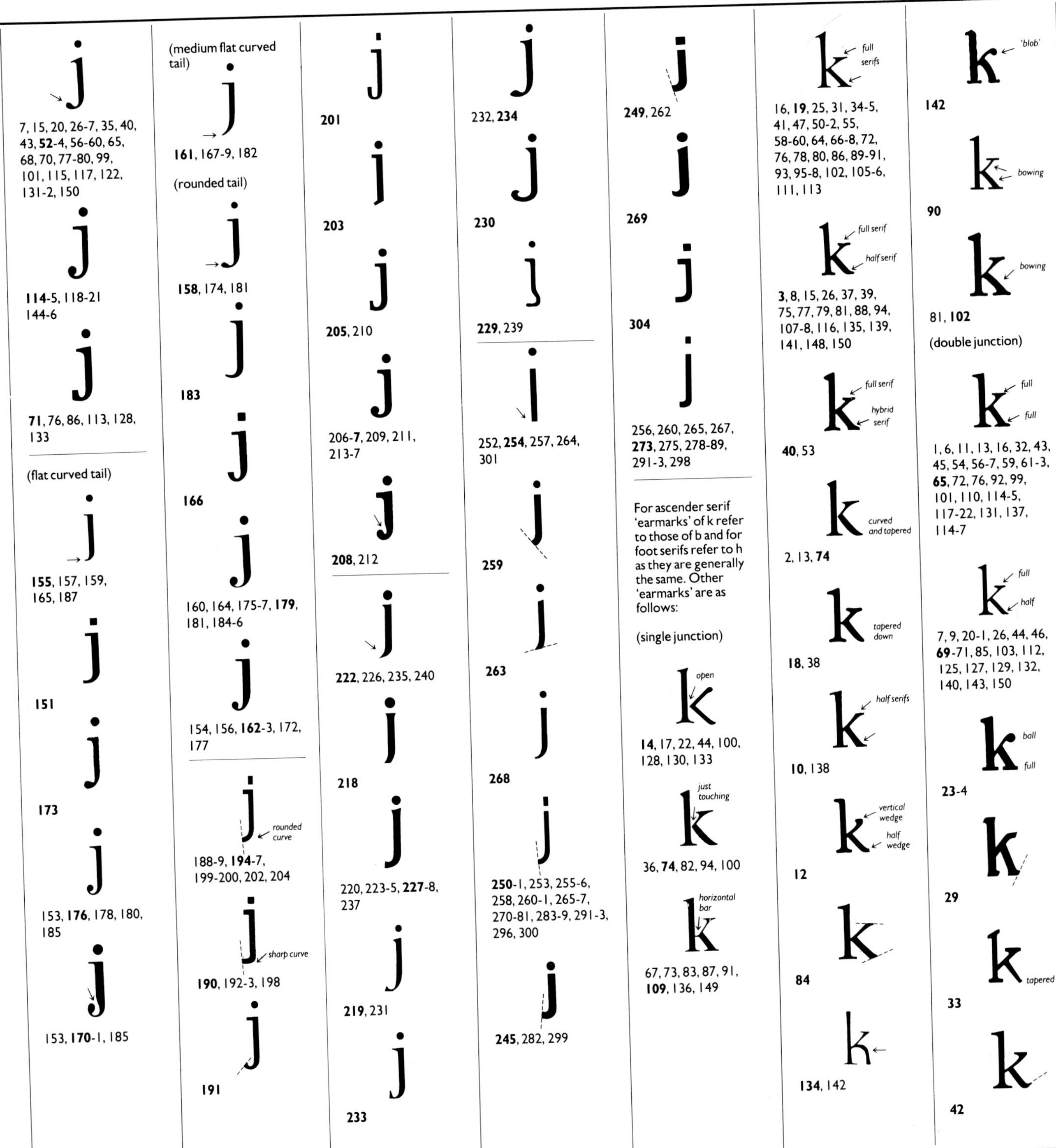
7, 15, 20, 26-7, 35, 40, 43, 52-4, 56-60, 65, 68, 70, 77-80, 99, 101, 115, 117, 122, 131-2, 150
114-5, 118-21 144-6
71, 76, 86, 113, 128, 133
(flat curved tail)
155, 157, 159, 165, 187
151
173
153, 176, 178, 180, 185
153, 170-1, 185
(medium flat curved tail)
161, 167-9, 182
(rounded tail)
158, 174, 181
183
166
160, 164, 175-7, 179, 181, 184-6
154, 156, 162-3, 172, 177
rounded curve
188-9, 194-7, 199-200, 202, 204
sharp curve
190, 192-3, 198
191
201
203
205, 210
206-7, 209, 211, 213-7
208, 212
222, 226, 235, 240
218
220, 223-5, 227-8, 237
219, 231
233
232, 234
230
229, 239
252, 254, 257, 264, 301
259
263
268
250-1, 253, 255-6, 258, 260-1, 265-7, 270-81, 283-9, 291-3, 296, 300
245, 282, 299
249, 262
269
304
256, 260, 265, 267, 273, 275, 278-89, 291-3, 298
For ascender serif 'earmarks' of k refer to those of b and for foot serifs refer to h as they are generally the same. Other 'earmarks' are as follows:
(single junction)
open
14, 17, 22, 44, 100, 128, 130, 133
just touching
36, 74, 82, 94, 100
horizontal bar
67, 73, 83, 87, 91, 109, 136, 149
full serifs
16, 19, 25, 31, 34-5, 41, 47, 50-2, 55, 58-60, 64, 66-8, 72, 76, 78, 80, 86, 89-91, 93, 95-8, 102, 105-6, 111, 113
full serif
half serif
3, 8, 15, 26, 37, 39, 75, 77, 79, 81, 88, 94, 107-8, 116, 135, 139, 141, 148, 150
full serif
hybrid serif
40, 53
curved and tapered
2, 13, 74
tapered down
18, 38
half serifs
10, 138
vertical wedge
half wedge
12
84
134, 142
'blob'
142
bowing
90
bowing
81, 102
(double junction)
full
full
1, 6, 11, 13, 16, 32, 43, 45, 54, 56-7, 59, 61-3, 65, 72, 76, 92, 99, 101, 110, 114-5, 117-22, 131, 137, 114-7
full
half
7, 9, 20-1, 26, 44, 46, 69-71, 85, 103, 112, 125, 127, 129, 132, 140, 143, 150
ball
full
23-4
29
tapered
33
42

***NB.** Bold figures indicate the specimen illustrated above.*

wedge
104

no serif
143

full
full
5

overlap
27

28

30

(single junction)

open
154, 162-**3**, 182

horizontal bar
155-6, 158, **161**, 167-8, 187

155

full
full
152, 154, 159, 165, 181, **183**-4

ball
181

(double junction)

full
full
153, 157, 160, 164, 170-1, 173, 176-80, 185-6

full
half
151, 166, 169, 174-5

172

(single junction)

210

188, 194-6, 199-200, 205, 210

189, 197, 203-4

192

(double junction)

193, 198, 201-2, 206-9, 211-7

190

(single junction)

open
222, 230, **234**, 237

horizontal bar
235

218, **220**, 226, 233, 239-40

219, 223

(double junction)

221, **224**-5, 227-9, 231-2

(single junction)

246, 254, **259**, 263, 271, 283, 285, 295

270

horizontal bar
268, 291-**2**

246, 249, 252-3, **255**, 260, 264, 266-7, 278, 283, 304

251, 262

297-8, **301**

272

296-7

299-300

(double junction)

245, 250, 256-7, 261, 265, 269, 273-7, **279**-82, 284, 286-9, 293

long
short
250, 284

For ascender serif 'earmarks' of l refer to those of b and for foot serifs to h as they are generally the same. Exceptions and other 'earmarks' are as follows:

very slight thinning
2, 8, 10-1, **19**, 36, 81, 104, 113, 130, 133

thinning
98

no serif
134

1, 36

142

14, 17, 33-4

135

143

curled in
157

214-7

long
215-7

218, 227-9

220, 222-**3**, 225, 230, 237

half serif
239-**40**

263, 269, 285

268, 295

tail
282, 304

297-8, **301**

For x height serif 'earmarks' of m refer to ascender serif 'earmarks' of b and for foot serifs to h. Exceptions and other 'earmarks' are as follows:

(stems)

1, 16, 19, 27, 32, 35-6, 46-7, **72**, 82, 101-2, 110, 125, 139

angular pen stroke
10, 75, 108

5, 9

11, **113**, 133

slight bowing
14-7

89

(foot serifs)

2

12, 42

half serif
75, 84, 141

'Special Earmarks'

The 'special earmarks' (or distinctive identifying features) are indicated on each letter. The general 'style' of typefaces with the same 'earmark' may vary. The figures refer to specimen numbers.

***NB.** Bold figures indicate the specimen illustrated above.*

'Special Earmarks'

The 'special earmarks' (or distinctive identifying features) are indicated on each letter. The general 'style' of typefaces with the same 'earmark' may vary. The figures refer to specimen numbers.

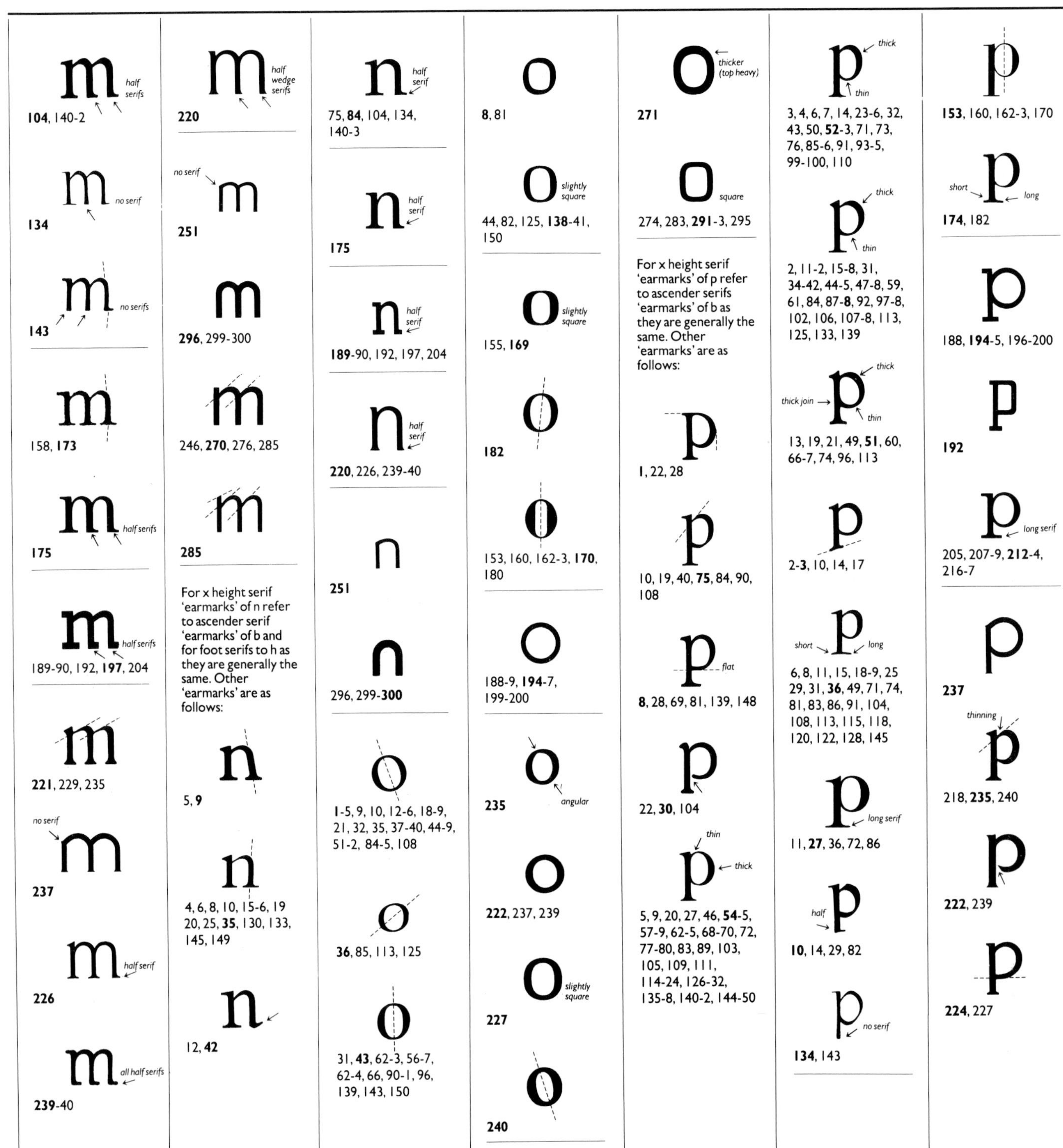
half serifs
104, 140-2
no serif
134
no serifs
143
158, 173
half serifs
175
half serifs
189-90, 192, 197, 204
221, 229, 235
no serif
237
half serif
226
all half serifs
239-40
half wedge serifs
220
no serif
251
296, 299-300
246, 270, 276, 285
285
For x height serif 'earmarks' of n refer to ascender serif 'earmarks' of b and for foot serifs to h as they are generally the same. Other 'earmarks' are as follows:
5, 9
4, 6, 8, 10, 15-6, 19
20, 25, 35, 130, 133,
145, 149
12, 42
half serif
75, 84, 104, 134,
140-3
half serif
175
half serif
189-90, 192, 197, 204
half serif
220, 226, 239-40
251
296, 299-300
1-5, 9, 10, 12-6, 18-9,
21, 32, 35, 37-40, 44-9,
51-2, 84-5, 108
36, 85, 113, 125
31, 43, 62-3, 56-7,
62-4, 66, 90-1, 96,
139, 143, 150
8, 81
slightly square
44, 82, 125, 138-41,
150
slightly square
155, 169
182
153, 160, 162-3, 170,
180
188-9, 194-7,
199-200
angular
235
222, 237, 239
slightly square
227
240
thicker (top heavy)
271
square
274, 283, 291-3, 295
For x height serif 'earmarks' of p refer to ascender serifs 'earmarks' of b as they are generally the same. Other 'earmarks' are as follows:
1, 22, 28
10, 19, 40, 75, 84, 90,
108
flat
8, 28, 69, 81, 139, 148
22, 30, 104
thin
thick
5, 9, 20, 27, 46, 54-5,
57-9, 62-5, 68-70, 72,
77-80, 83, 89, 103,
105, 109, 111,
114-24, 126-32,
135-8, 140-2, 144-50
thick
thin
3, 4, 6, 7, 14, 23-6, 32,
43, 50, 52-3, 71, 73,
76, 85-6, 91, 93-5,
99-100, 110
thick
thin
2, 11-2, 15-8, 31,
34-42, 44-5, 47-8, 59,
61, 84, 87-8, 92, 97-8,
102, 106, 107-8, 113,
125, 133, 139
thick
thick join
thin
13, 19, 21, 49, 51, 60,
66-7, 74, 96, 113
2-3, 10, 14, 17
short
long
6, 8, 11, 15, 18-9, 25
29, 31, 36, 49, 71, 74,
81, 83, 86, 91, 104,
108, 113, 115, 118,
120, 122, 128, 145
long serif
11, 27, 36, 72, 86
half
10, 14, 29, 82
no serif
134, 143
153, 160, 162-3, 170
short
long
174, 182
188, 194-5, 196-200
192
long serif
205, 207-9, 212-4,
216-7
237
thinning
218, 235, 240
222, 239
224, 227

NB. *Bold figures indicate the specimen illustrated above.*

p ← long serif
232

p short → ← long
234

p
231

p circular bowl
251, 253, **255**, 257-8, 262

no serif → p
251, **259**, 295, 297

p
296, 299-**300**

p
269, 296

For bowl and foot serif 'earmarks' of q refer to those of p as they are generally the same. Exceptions and other 'earmarks' are as follows:

q ← no serif
8, 104, 111, 113, **116**, 133-4, 139, 148

q
3, **4**, 12-3, 23-4, 27, 36, 42, 51, 107

q ← flat 'nib'
1, 28

q
125, **150**

q
22, 44, **104**

q ← thick join
34

q ← small 'nib'
6, 15-6, 25, 33, 40, 44, 61, 63, 66, 69, 74, 76, 83, 85, 87, 123-4, 128, 139

q
14, 17, 89, 98, 112, **131**, 136, 141-2, 147, 149

q
57, 132, **140**, 147

q
2, 3, 10, **14**, 17, 29, 81, 117, 143

half serif → q
29, **40**, 82, 123, 126

q ← no serif
134

q
65

q ← no serif
183

q ← 'nib'
182

q ← extended stroke
151, 166-**8**, 187

q
153, 160, **162**-3, 170

q
169

q
191

q
203-4, 214-7

q ← 'nib'
218, 220, 222-3, 227-8, 234, 237

q ← no 'nib'
233

q ← full serif
231

q ← half serif
234, 239-40

q
285

For foot serif 'earmarks' of r refer to those of h as they are generally the same. Other 'earmarks' are as follows:

(angled stem)

r
23-4, 78-80, 122-4

r
30, **77**

r
8, **28**, 40

r
108

(heavy triangular x height serif)

r ← squashed pear
102

r ← pear
6, 17, 22, 43, **53**, 55-6, 59, 61-4, 66-7, 69, 72, 74, 88, 92-3, 95-6, 99, 110

r ← hanging pear
4, 7, 9, **65**, 69, 103, 109

r ← club
9, 15, 26, **38**-41, 47-9, 51, 60, 70, 73, 87, 89, 94, 106-7

r ← flag
16, 20, **25**, 34-5, 37, 50, 83

r
5, **32**

r
13, 33, **45**, 85

r
71

(concave x height serif)

r
27, **68**, 91, 110

(thin triangular x height serif)

r ← pear
18, 27, **31**, 36, 44, 46, 52, 54, 57, 62-4, 72, 90, 97, 101, 105, 126-7, 129-30, 132, 139, 148

r hanging pear
58, 80, 103, 106, 125, 131, 136-7, 145-6, 149-50

r curled in
114-5, 117-21, 142, 144

r
111, 138

r
10-11, 86, 100, 106, 141, 147

r
2, **19**-20, 76, 83, 104

r
3, 12, 21, 42, 128

r
8, 81

r
14, 82, 84-5, 113, 128, 133-5, 140

r
75, 98

r
112, 141

r
116, 143

r ← ball
152-4, **159**-63, 167, 169, 171-2, 178, 180-1, 184, 186-7

r ← hanging pear
156, **168**, 170, 185

r ← ball
164, 175-**77**, 179

r ← club
173-**4**, 183

r ← flag
158

r ← wedge
151, 157, 182

r wedge
155, 166

r ← spiked
165

'Special Earmarks'

The 'special earmarks' (or distinctive identifying features) are indicated on each letter. The general 'style' of typefaces with the same 'earmark' may vary. The figures refer to specimen numbers.

NB. *Bold figures indicate the specimen illustrated above.*

'Special Earmarks'

The 'special earmarks' (or distinctive identifying features) are indicated on each letter. The general style of typefaces with the same 'earmark' may vary. The figures refer to specimen numbers.

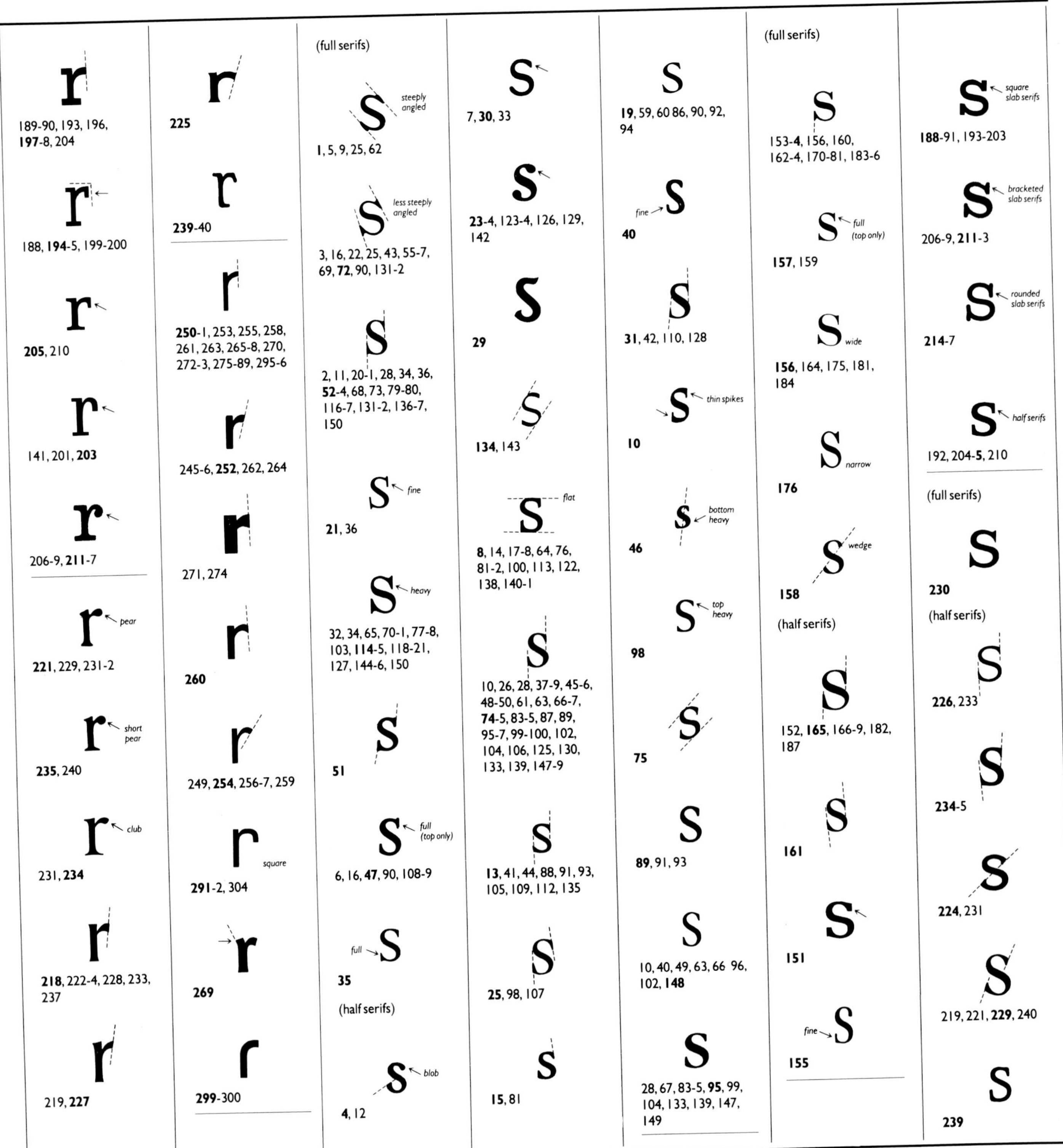
189-90, 193, 196, 197-8, 204
188, 194-5, 199-200
205, 210
141, 201, 203
206-9, 211-7
pear
221, 229, 231-2
short pear
235, 240
club
231, 234
218, 222-4, 228, 233, 237
219, 227
225
239-40
250-1, 253, 255, 258, 261, 263, 265-8, 270, 272-3, 275-89, 295-6
245-6, 252, 262, 264
271, 274
260
249, 254, 256-7, 259
square
291-2, 304
269
299-300
(full serifs)
steeply angled
1, 5, 9, 25, 62
less steeply angled
3, 16, 22, 25, 43, 55-7, 69, 72, 90, 131-2
2, 11, 20-1, 28, 34, 36, 52-4, 68, 73, 79-80, 116-7, 131-2, 136-7, 150
fine
21, 36
heavy
32, 34, 65, 70-1, 77-8, 103, 114-5, 118-21, 127, 144-6, 150
51
full (top only)
6, 16, 47, 90, 108-9
full
35
(half serifs)
blob
4, 12
7, 30, 33
23-4, 123-4, 126, 129, 142
29
134, 143
flat
8, 14, 17-8, 64, 76, 81-2, 100, 113, 122, 138, 140-1
10, 26, 28, 37-9, 45-6, 48-50, 61, 63, 66-7, 74-5, 83-5, 87, 89, 95-7, 99-100, 102, 104, 106, 125, 130, 133, 139, 147-9
13, 41, 44, 88, 91, 93, 105, 109, 112, 135
25, 98, 107
15, 81
19, 59, 60 86, 90, 92, 94
fine
40
31, 42, 110, 128
thin spikes
10
bottom heavy
46
top heavy
98
75
89, 91, 93
10, 40, 49, 63, 66 96, 102, 148
28, 67, 83-5, 95, 99, 104, 133, 139, 147, 149
(full serifs)
153-4, 156, 160, 162-4, 170-81, 183-6
full (top only)
157, 159
wide
156, 164, 175, 181, 184
narrow
176
wedge
158
(half serifs)
152, 165, 166-9, 182, 187
161
151
fine
155
square slab serifs
188-91, 193-203
bracketed slab serifs
206-9, 211-3
rounded slab serifs
214-7
half serifs
192, 204-5, 210
(full serifs)
230
(half serifs)
226, 233
234-5
224, 231
219, 221, 229, 240
239

***NB.** Bold figures indicate the specimen illustrated above.*

218, 220, 223, 228, 237
222
225
227, 236
large opening
251-3, 256, 258, 260, 262, 264, 270, 285-9, 300
245, 254, 257, 261, 265, 276-7, 282
255, 273, 274-5, 281
250, 267, 278-80, 283, 304
291-2
246, 249, 259, 263, 266, 269, 271-2, 284
269, 272
thick top
271
295
268
296-9
299
298, 301
(head)
2-3, 10
1, 29, 49, 98
thickening
25, 134-5
33
triangle
20, 39-41, 47, 52, 59, 63, 67, 71, 73, 79, 86-90, 92, 99, 102, 108, 111
wide
6-7, 14-6, 19, 21, 25-6, 37, 48, 60-1, 65-6, 74, 83, 93, 105, 107, 109, 116, 132
concave
27, 43, 55, 57, 62, 64 69, 72, 100, 103, 106, 110, 114-5, 118-22, 137, 144-6
wide concave
11, 14, 27, 31, 72, 147
1, 3, 32
blob
4, 142
8, 17, 28, 128
36, 123-4, 126-7, 129, 148
18, 22-4, 29, 33, 46, 75, 82, 84, 112-3, 125, 131, 135-6, 138, 141
34
(tail)
flat
30
1, 8, 12, 38, 51, 71, 81, 84, 90, 93, 104, 128, 136, 143, 150
18, 22, 39, 56, 59-60 63, 66, 73-4, 123-4, 127-9, 138, 140, 148
45, 134
curled up
114-5, 118-20, 121, 137, 144-6
(head)
triangle
158, 183
concave
152-3, 159, 164, 167-8, 173, 184
tall and concave
170, 172, 176-9, 181-2
151, 154-5, 157, 161-3, 165, 174, 186
156, 160, 166, 169, 171, 180, 185, 187
(tail)
flat
151, 169
curled up
164-5, 175-80, 182, 185
(head)
concave
205-7, 210, 211-3
tall and concave
201, 208-9
188, 190, 192, 194-6, 199, 203
189, 191, 193, 197-8, 204
202
(tail)
188, 194-5, 199-200
189, 190, 192, 196-7, 204
191, 203
curled up
193, 198, 201-2, 205-8, 209-217
round and curled up
214-7
(head)
triangle
218, 220, 223, 230, 235, 237
slightly concave
219, 231-2, 233
tall concave
221-2, 229
225, 228
224, 226-7, 234, 240
(tail)
239
237
219
t45
222, 235, 240
227
(head)
triangle
259
concave
271, 280
269

'Special Earmarks'

The 'special earmarks' (or distinctive identifying features) are indicated on each letter. The general style of typefaces with the same 'earmark' may vary. The figures refer to specimen numbers.

***NB.** Bold figures indicate the specimen illustrated above.*

'Special Earmarks'

The 'special earmarks' (or distinctive identifying features) are indicated on each letter. The general 'style' of typefaces with the same 'earmark' may vary. The figures refer to specimen numbers.

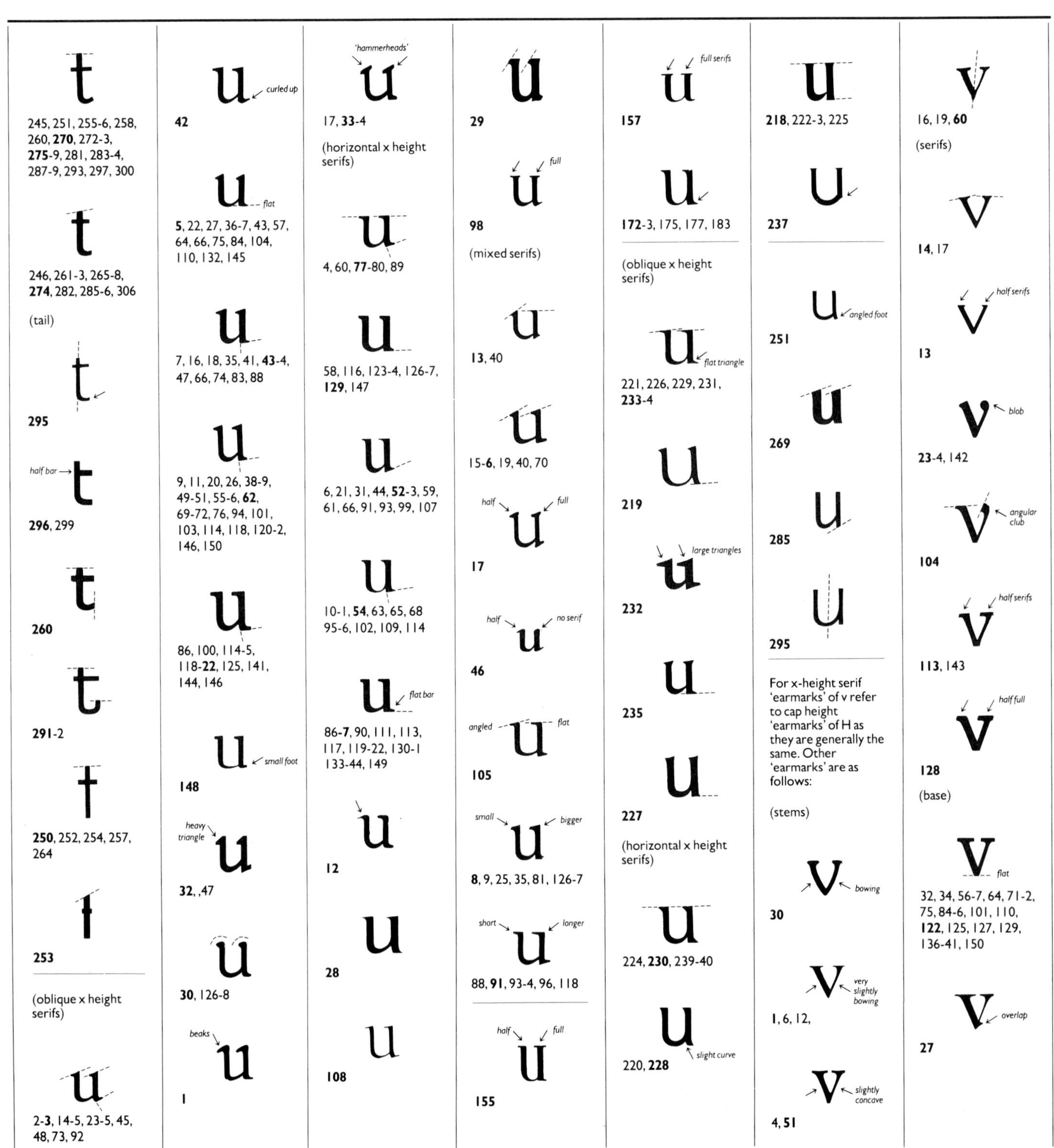
245, 251, 255-6, 258, 260, 270, 272-3, 275-9, 281, 283-4, 287-9, 293, 297, 300
246, 261-3, 265-8, 274, 282, 285-6, 306
(tail)
295
half bar
296, 299
260
291-2
250, 252, 254, 257, 264
253
(oblique x height serifs)
2-3, 14-5, 23-5, 45, 48, 73, 92
curled up
42
flat
5, 22, 27, 36-7, 43, 57, 64, 66, 75, 84, 104, 110, 132, 145
7, 16, 18, 35, 41, 43-4, 47, 66, 74, 83, 88
9, 11, 20, 26, 38-9, 49-51, 55-6, 62, 69-72, 76, 94, 101, 103, 114, 118, 120-2, 146, 150
86, 100, 114-5, 118-22, 125, 141, 144, 146
small foot
148
heavy triangle
32, 47
30, 126-8
beaks
1
'hammerheads'
17, 33-4
(horizontal x height serifs)
4, 60, 77-80, 89
58, 116, 123-4, 126-7, 129, 147
6, 21, 31, 44, 52-3, 59, 61, 66, 91, 93, 99, 107
10-1, 54, 63, 65, 68 95-6, 102, 109, 114
flat bar
86-7, 90, 111, 113, 117, 119-22, 130-1 133-44, 149
12
28
108
29
full
98
(mixed serifs)
13, 40
15-6, 19, 40, 70
half
full
17
half
no serif
46
angled
flat
105
small
bigger
8, 9, 25, 35, 81, 126-7
short
longer
88, 91, 93-4, 96, 118
half
full
155
full serifs
157
172-3, 175, 177, 183
(oblique x height serifs)
flat triangle
221, 226, 229, 231, 233-4
219
large triangles
232
235
227
(horizontal x height serifs)
224, 230, 239-40
slight curve
220, 228
218, 222-3, 225
237
angled foot
251
269
285
295
For x-height serif 'earmarks' of v refer to cap height 'earmarks' of H as they are generally the same. Other 'earmarks' are as follows:
(stems)
bowing
30
very slightly bowing
1, 6, 12,
slightly concave
4, 51
16, 19, 60
(serifs)
14, 17
half serifs
13
blob
23-4, 142
angular club
104
half serifs
113, 143
half full
128
(base)
flat
32, 34, 56-7, 64, 71-2, 75, 84-6, 101, 110, 122, 125, 127, 129, 136-41, 150
overlap
27

***NB.** Bold figures indicate the specimen illustrated above.*

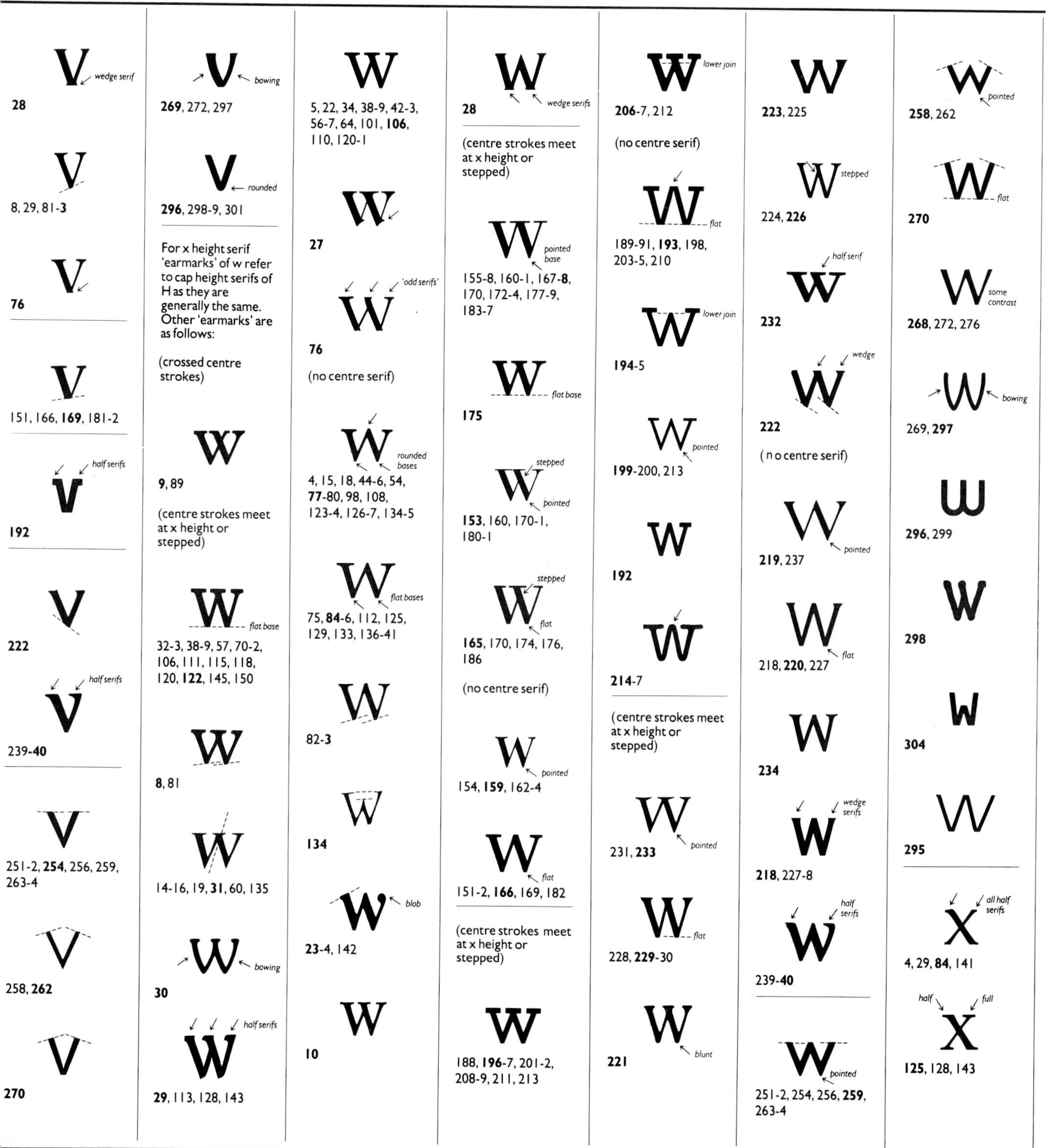
wedge serif
28
8, 29, 81-3
76
151, 166, 169, 181-2
half serifs
192
222
half serifs
239-40
251-2, 254, 256, 259, 263-4
258, 262
270
bowing
269, 272, 297
rounded
296, 298-9, 301
For x height serif 'earmarks' of w refer to cap height serifs of H as they are generally the same. Other 'earmarks' are as follows:
(crossed centre strokes)
9, 89
(centre strokes meet at x height or stepped)
flat base
32-3, 38-9, 57, 70-2, 106, 111, 115, 118, 120, 122, 145, 150
8, 81
14-16, 19, 31, 60, 135
bowing
30
half serifs
29, 113, 128, 143
5, 22, 34, 38-9, 42-3, 56-7, 64, 101, 106, 110, 120-1
27
'odd serifs'
76
(no centre serif)
rounded bases
4, 15, 18, 44-6, 54, 77-80, 98, 108, 123-4, 126-7, 134-5
flat bases
75, 84-6, 112, 125, 129, 133, 136-41
82-3
134
blob
23-4, 142
10
wedge serifs
28
(centre strokes meet at x height or stepped)
pointed base
155-8, 160-1, 167-8, 170, 172-4, 177-9, 183-7
flat base
175
stepped
pointed
153, 160, 170-1, 180-1
stepped
flat
165, 170, 174, 176, 186
(no centre serif)
pointed
154, 159, 162-4
flat
151-2, 166, 169, 182
(centre strokes meet at x height or stepped)
188, 196-7, 201-2, 208-9, 211, 213
lower join
206-7, 212
(no centre serif)
flat
189-91, 193, 198, 203-5, 210
lower join
194-5
pointed
199-200, 213
192
214-7
(centre strokes meet at x height or stepped)
pointed
231, 233
flat
228, 229-30
blunt
221
223, 225
stepped
224, 226
half serif
232
wedge
222
(no centre serif)
pointed
219, 237
flat
218, 220, 227
234
wedge serifs
218, 227-8
half serifs
239-40
pointed
251-2, 254, 256, 259, 263-4
pointed
258, 262
flat
270
some contrast
268, 272, 276
bowing
269, 297
296, 299
298
304
295
all half serifs
4, 29, 84, 141
half
full
125, 128, 143

'Special Earmarks'

The 'special earmarks' (or distinctive identifying features) are indicated on each letter. The general 'style' of typefaces with the same 'earmark' may vary. The figures refer to specimen numbers.

NB. *Bold figures indicate the specimen illustrated above.*

'Special Earmarks'

The 'special earmarks' (or distinctive identifying features) are indicated on each letter. The general 'style' of typefaces with the same 'earmark' may vary. The figures refer to specimen numbers.

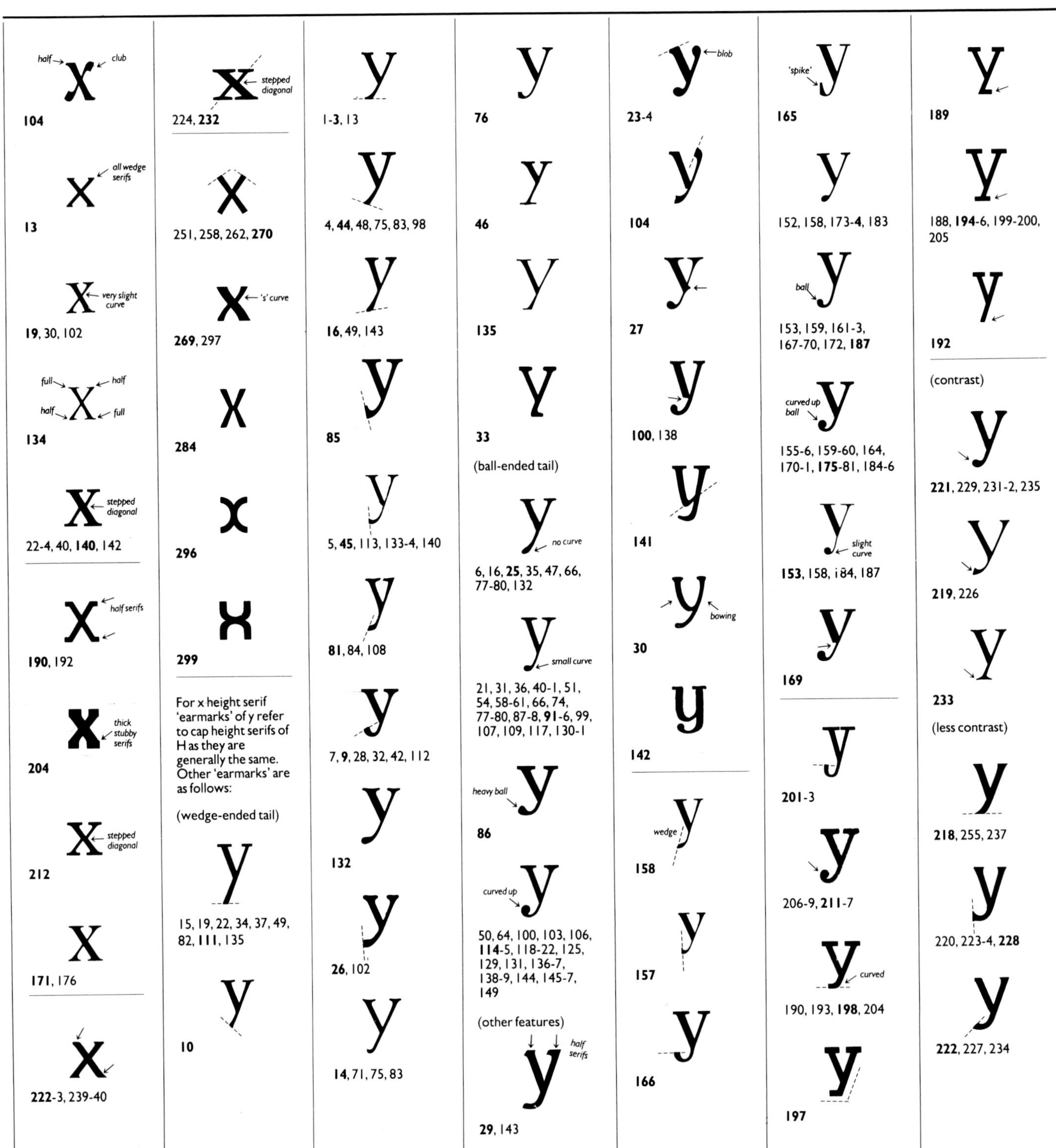
half
club
104
all wedge serifs
13
very slight curve
19, 30, 102
full
half
half
full
134
stepped diagonal
22-4, 40, 140, 142
half serifs
190, 192
thick stubby serifs
204
stepped diagonal
212
171, 176
222-3, 239-40
stepped diagonal
224, 232
251, 258, 262, 270
's' curve
269, 297
284
296
299
For x height serif 'earmarks' of y refer to cap height serifs of H as they are generally the same. Other 'earmarks' are as follows:
(wedge-ended tail)
15, 19, 22, 34, 37, 49, 82, 111, 135
10
1-3, 13
4, 44, 48, 75, 83, 98
16, 49, 143
85
5, 45, 113, 133-4, 140
81, 84, 108
7, 9, 28, 32, 42, 112
132
26, 102
14, 71, 75, 83
76
46
135
33
(ball-ended tail)
no curve
6, 16, 25, 35, 47, 66, 77-80, 132
small curve
21, 31, 36, 40-1, 51, 54, 58-61, 66, 74, 77-80, 87-8, 91-6, 99, 107, 109, 117, 130-1
heavy ball
86
curved up
50, 64, 100, 103, 106, 114-5, 118-22, 125, 129, 131, 136-7, 138-9, 144, 145-7, 149
(other features)
half serifs
29, 143
blob
23-4
104
27
100, 138
141
bowing
30
142
wedge
158
157
166
'spike'
165
152, 158, 173-4, 183
ball
153, 159, 161-3, 167-70, 172, 187
curved up ball
155-6, 159-60, 164, 170-1, 175-81, 184-6
slight curve
153, 158, 184, 187
169
201-3
206-9, 211-7
curved
190, 193, 198, 204
197
189
188, 194-6, 199-200, 205
192
(contrast)
221, 229, 231-2, 235
219, 226
233
(less contrast)
218, 255, 237
220, 223-4, 228
222, 227, 234

***NB.** Bold figures indicate the specimen illustrated above.*

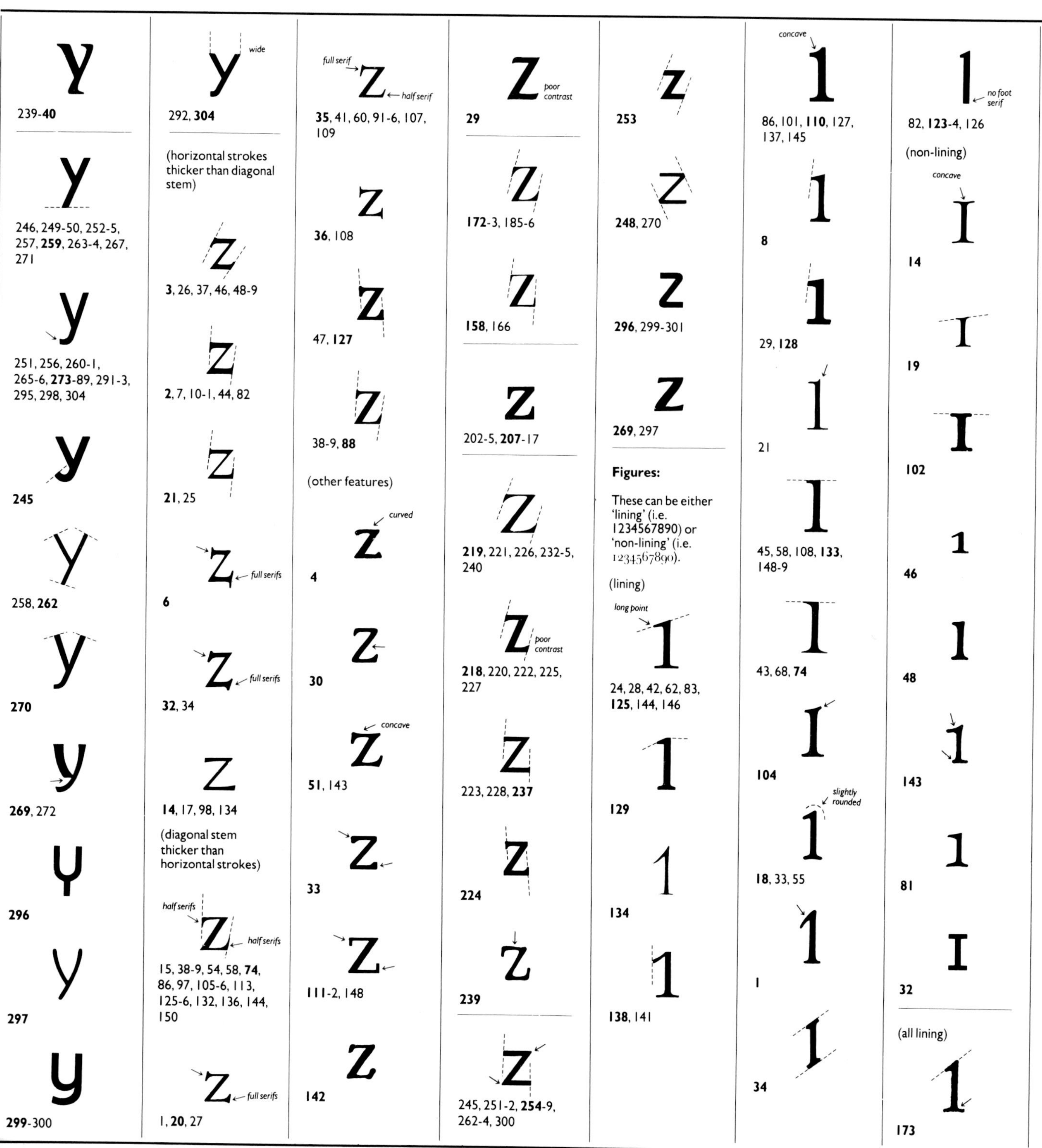
239-40
246, 249-50, 252-5, 257, 259, 263-4, 267, 271
251, 256, 260-1, 265-6, 273-89, 291-3, 295, 298, 304
245
258, 262
270
269, 272
296
297
299-300
wide
292, 304
(horizontal strokes thicker than diagonal stem)
3, 26, 37, 46, 48-9
2, 7, 10-1, 44, 82
21, 25
full serifs
6
full serifs
32, 34
14, 17, 98, 134
(diagonal stem thicker than horizontal strokes)
half serifs
half serifs
15, 38-9, 54, 58, 74, 86, 97, 105-6, 113, 125-6, 132, 136, 144, 150
full serifs
1, 20, 27
full serif
half serif
35, 41, 60, 91-6, 107, 109
36, 108
47, 127
38-9, 88
(other features)
curved
4
30
concave
51, 143
33
111-2, 148
142
poor contrast
29
172-3, 185-6
158, 166
202-5, 207-17
219, 221, 226, 232-5, 240
poor contrast
218, 220, 222, 225, 227
223, 228, 237
224
239
245, 251-2, 254-9, 262-4, 300
253
248, 270
296, 299-301
269, 297
Figures:
These can be either 'lining' (i.e. 1234567890) or 'non-lining' (i.e. 1234567890).
(lining)
long point
24, 28, 42, 62, 83, 125, 144, 146
129
134
138, 141
concave
86, 101, 110, 127, 137, 145
8
29, 128
21
45, 58, 108, 133, 148-9
43, 68, 74
104
slightly rounded
18, 33, 55
1
34
no foot serif
82, 123-4, 126
(non-lining)
concave
14
19
102
46
48
143
81
32
(all lining)
173

'Special Earmarks'

The 'special earmarks' (or distinctive identifying features) are indicated on each letter. The general 'style' of typefaces with the same 'earmark' may vary. The figures refer to specimen numbers.

NB. *Bold figures indicate the specimen illustrated above.*

'Special Earmarks'

The 'special earmarks' (or distinctive identifying features) are indicated on each letter. The general 'style' of typefaces with the same 'earmark' may vary. The figures refer to specimen numbers.

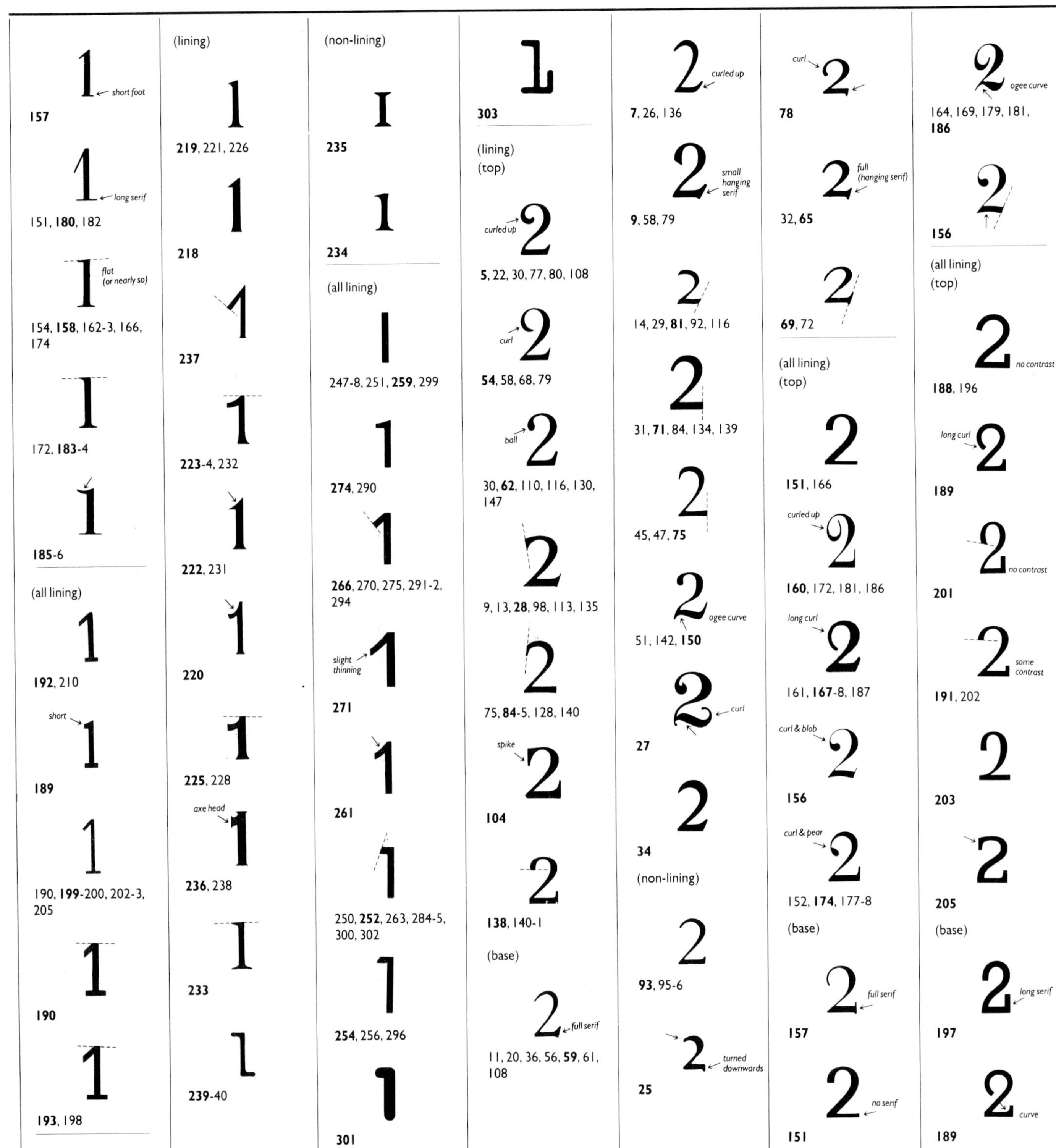
short foot
157
long serif
151, 180, 182
flat (or nearly so)
154, 158, 162-3, 166, 174
172, 183-4
185-6
(all lining)
192, 210
short
189
190, 199-200, 202-3, 205
190
193, 198
(lining)
219, 221, 226
218
237
223-4, 232
222, 231
220
225, 228
axe head
236, 238
233
239-40
(non-lining)
235
234
(all lining)
247-8, 251, 259, 299
274, 290
266, 270, 275, 291-2, 294
slight thinning
271
261
250, 252, 263, 284-5, 300, 302
254, 256, 296
301
303
(lining)
(top)
curled up
5, 22, 30, 77, 80, 108
curl
54, 58, 68, 79
ball
30, 62, 110, 116, 130, 147
9, 13, 28, 98, 113, 135
75, 84-5, 128, 140
spike
104
138, 140-1
(base)
full serif
11, 20, 36, 56, 59, 61, 108
curled up
7, 26, 136
small hanging serif
9, 58, 79
14, 29, 81, 92, 116
31, 71, 84, 134, 139
45, 47, 75
ogee curve
51, 142, 150
curl
27
34
(non-lining)
93, 95-6
turned downwards
25
curl
78
full (hanging serif)
32, 65
69, 72
(all lining)
(top)
151, 166
curled up
160, 172, 181, 186
long curl
161, 167-8, 187
curl & blob
156
curl & pear
152, 174, 177-8
(base)
full serif
157
no serif
151
ogee curve
164, 169, 179, 181, 186
156
(all lining)
(top)
no contrast
188, 196
long curl
189
no contrast
201
some contrast
191, 202
203
205
(base)
long serif
197
curve
189

***NB.** Bold figures indicate the specimen illustrated above.*

203

191, **213**

201-2, **205**

206

203

blob

ogee curve

214

(lining)
(top)

218, 236-8

222, 240

239

230-1

226

(base)

228, 236, 238

230-1, **233**, 239

238

227, 237

(non-lining)

full serif

232

half serif

234-5

(all lining)
(top)

249

246, **259**-60, 266, 271, 304

curl

265

longer curl

258, **261**-2, 296, 298

295, **297**

(base)

271

290

298

(lining)
(top)

curved

1

54, 58, 68, 77-80

16, 125, 139

82, 113, 123-4, 126

pear

86

138

13, 45

pointed wedge serif

75, 84, 98, 140

angular

6

36

flat

spiked serifs

104

50, 128, 147

22

5

134

111, **135**, 141

112

9, 28

(bottom tail endings where different from top – curved top typefaces only)

12, **42**, 44, 108

17, 71

58, **68**

27

6, 20, 35, 38-9, 41, **52**-3, 55-6, 59, 61, 63, 70, 73, 87-8, 92, 94, 101, 105, 109, 125, 139

79-80

86

76

98

148

(non-lining)

65

14

78

32

8, **81**

(all lining)
(top)

182

159, 173, **181**

172, 186

173

158

152, **174**

165

'Special Earmarks'

The 'special earmarks' (or distinctive identifying features) are indicated on each letter. The general 'style' of typefaces with the same 'earmark' may vary. The figures refer to specimen numbers.

NB. *Bold figures indicate the specimen illustrated above.*

'Special Earmarks'
The 'special earmarks' (or distinctive identifying features) are indicated on each letter. The general 'style' of typefaces with the same 'earmark' may vary. The figures refer to specimen numbers.

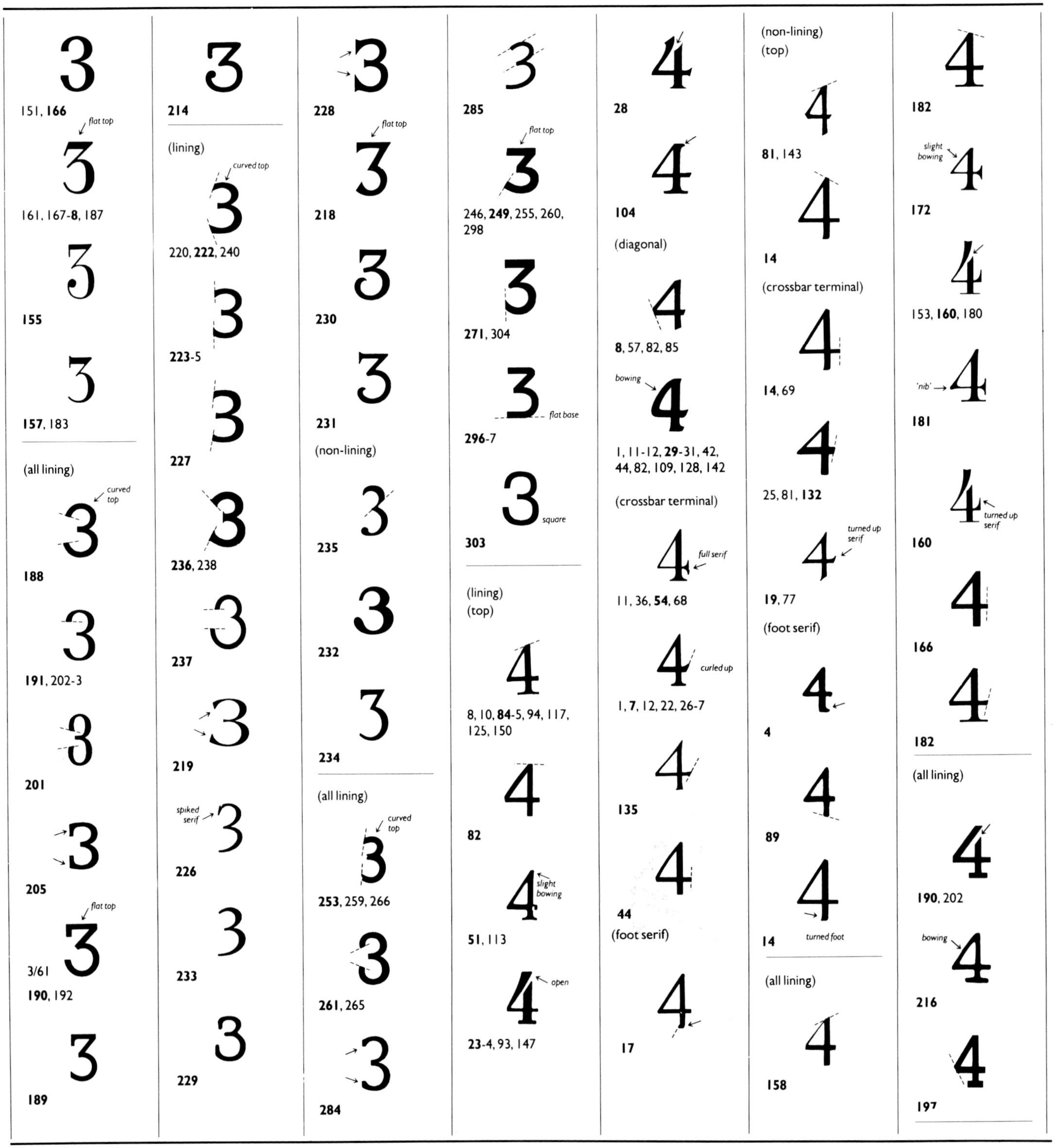

151, **166**

flat top
161, 167-**8**, 187

155

157, 183

(all lining)

curved top
188

191, 202-3

201

205

flat top
3/61
190, 192

189

214

(lining)

curved top
220, **222**, 240

223-5

227

236, 238

237

219

spiked serif
226

233

229

228

flat top
218

230

231

(non-lining)

235

232

234

(all lining)

curved top
253, 259, 266

261, 265

284

285

flat top
246, **249**, 255, 260, 298

271, 304

flat base
296-7

square
303

(lining)
(top)

8, 10, **84**-5, 94, 117, 125, 150

82

slight bowing
51, 113

open
23-4, 93, 147

28

104

(diagonal)

8, 57, 82, 85

bowing
1, 11-12, **29**-31, 42, 44, 82, 109, 128, 142

(crossbar terminal)

full serif
11, 36, **54**, 68

curled up
1, **7**, 12, 22, 26-7

135

44

(foot serif)

17

(non-lining)
(top)

81, 143

14

(crossbar terminal)

14, 69

25, 81, **132**

turned up serif
19, 77

(foot serif)

4

89

turned foot
14

(all lining)

158

182

slight bowing
172

153, **160**, 180

'nib'
181

turned up serif
160

166

182

(all lining)

190, 202

bowing
216

197

NB. *Bold figures indicate the specimen illustrated above.*

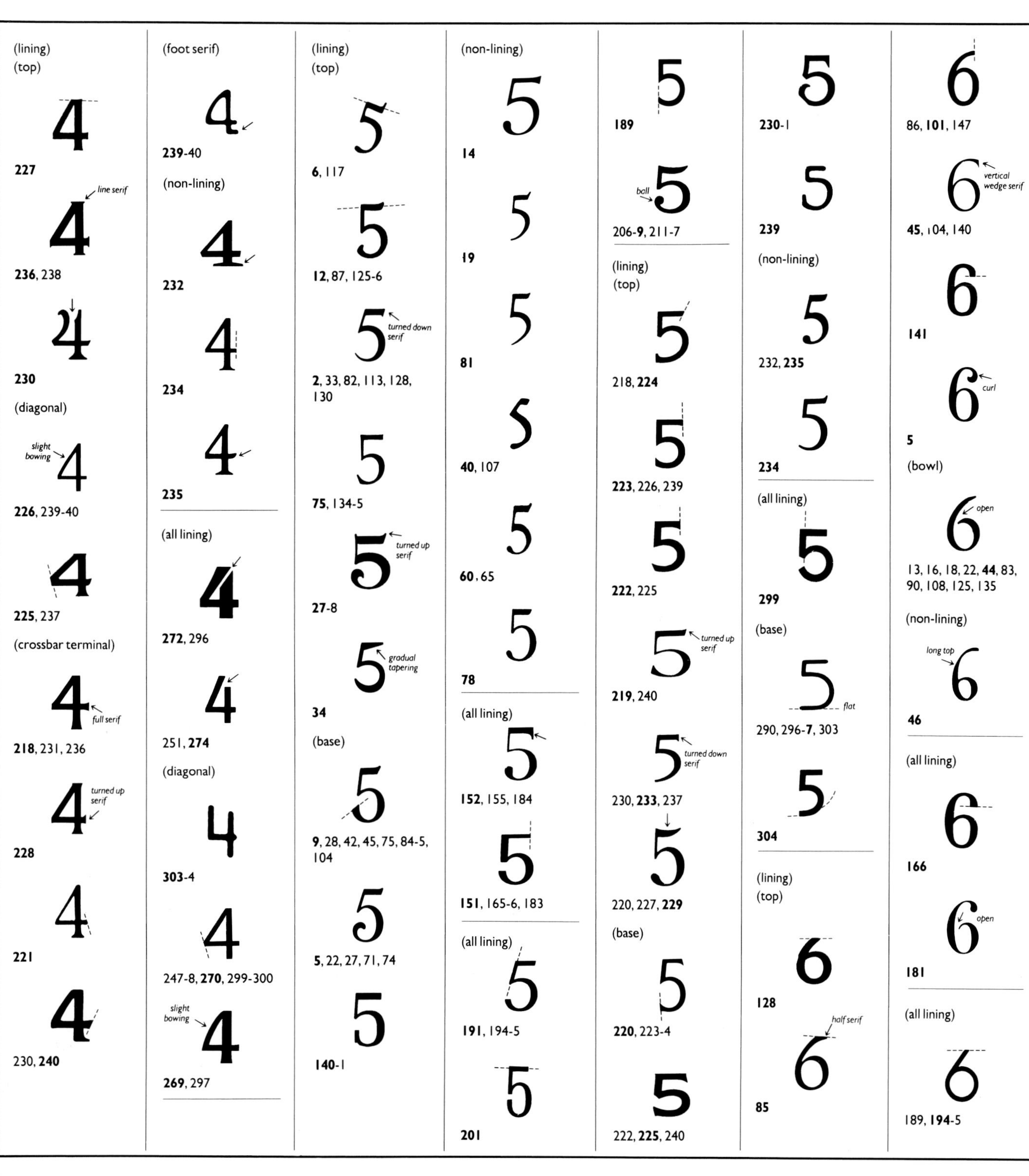
(lining)
(top)
227
line serif
236, 238
230
(diagonal)
slight bowing
226, 239-40
225, 237
(crossbar terminal)
full serif
218, 231, 236
turned up serif
228
221
230, 240
(foot serif)
239-40
(non-lining)
232
234
235
(all lining)
272, 296
251, 274
(diagonal)
303-4
247-8, 270, 299-300
slight bowing
269, 297
(lining)
(top)
6, 117
12, 87, 125-6
turned down serif
2, 33, 82, 113, 128, 130
75, 134-5
turned up serif
27-8
gradual tapering
34
(base)
9, 28, 42, 45, 75, 84-5, 104
5, 22, 27, 71, 74
140-1
(non-lining)
14
19
81
40, 107
60, 65
78
(all lining)
152, 155, 184
151, 165-6, 183
(all lining)
191, 194-5
201
189
ball
206-9, 211-7
(lining)
(top)
218, 224
223, 226, 239
222, 225
turned up serif
219, 240
turned down serif
230, 233, 237
220, 227, 229
(base)
220, 223-4
222, 225, 240
230-1
239
(non-lining)
232, 235
234
(all lining)
299
(base)
flat
290, 296-7, 303
304
(lining)
(top)
128
half serif
85
86, 101, 147
vertical wedge serif
45, 104, 140
141
curl
5
(bowl)
open
13, 16, 18, 22, 44, 83, 90, 108, 125, 135
(non-lining)
long top
46
(all lining)
166
open
181
(all lining)
189, 194-5

'Special Earmarks'

The 'special earmarks' (or distinctive identifying features) are indicated on each letter. The general 'style' of typefaces with the same 'earmark' may vary. The figures refer to specimen numbers.

NB. *Bold figures indicate the specimen illustrated above.*

'Special Earmarks'

The 'special earmarks' (or distinctive identifying features) are indicated on each letter. The general 'style' of typefaces with the same 'earmark' may vary. The figures refer to specimen numbers.

205
ball
206-9, 211-4, 216-7
(lining)
vertical serif
224-5
219, 227
hook serif
231
228
236, 238
221, 229
240
230
open
222, 239
(non-lining)
232
215
(all lining)
251-2, 254, 258-9, 262-4
265
303
295-6
(lining)
(top)
turned up serif
44
wedge serif
17, 134
71, 92, 139
short top
7
92
(back)
bowing
15, 21, 51, 82
tapering
31, 33, 44
142
(foot)
long serif
36
82, 85, 128
bent
108
'nib'
12-13, 76
(non-lining)
wedge serif
14
turned down serif
143
81, 97
4
(all lining)
bowing
156
ball
153
full serif
157, 165, 181
(all lining)
191, 203
(lining)
240
thickening
228
bend
220
231
239-40
(all lining)
vertical half serif
273, 281, 290, 298, 303
298
303
(lining)
open
open
22
open
104
bottom heavy
29, 34, 47, 125, 128, 142, 150
slightly square
140
(non-lining)
14
65, 78
stepped crossover
8, 72
(all lining)
151
flattened
169
(all lining)
bottom heavy
194-5
(lining)
bottom heavy
237
open
239
(non-lining)
stepped crossover
232
stepped crossover
266, 284
bottom heavy
265, 296, 298-300
303
(lining)
16, 18, 22, 90, 104, 108, 125, 135
104, 140
5
9, 28
pear
54, 62, 77, 79, 110, 117, 125, 130, 138, 150

NB. *Bold figures indicate the specimen illustrated above.*

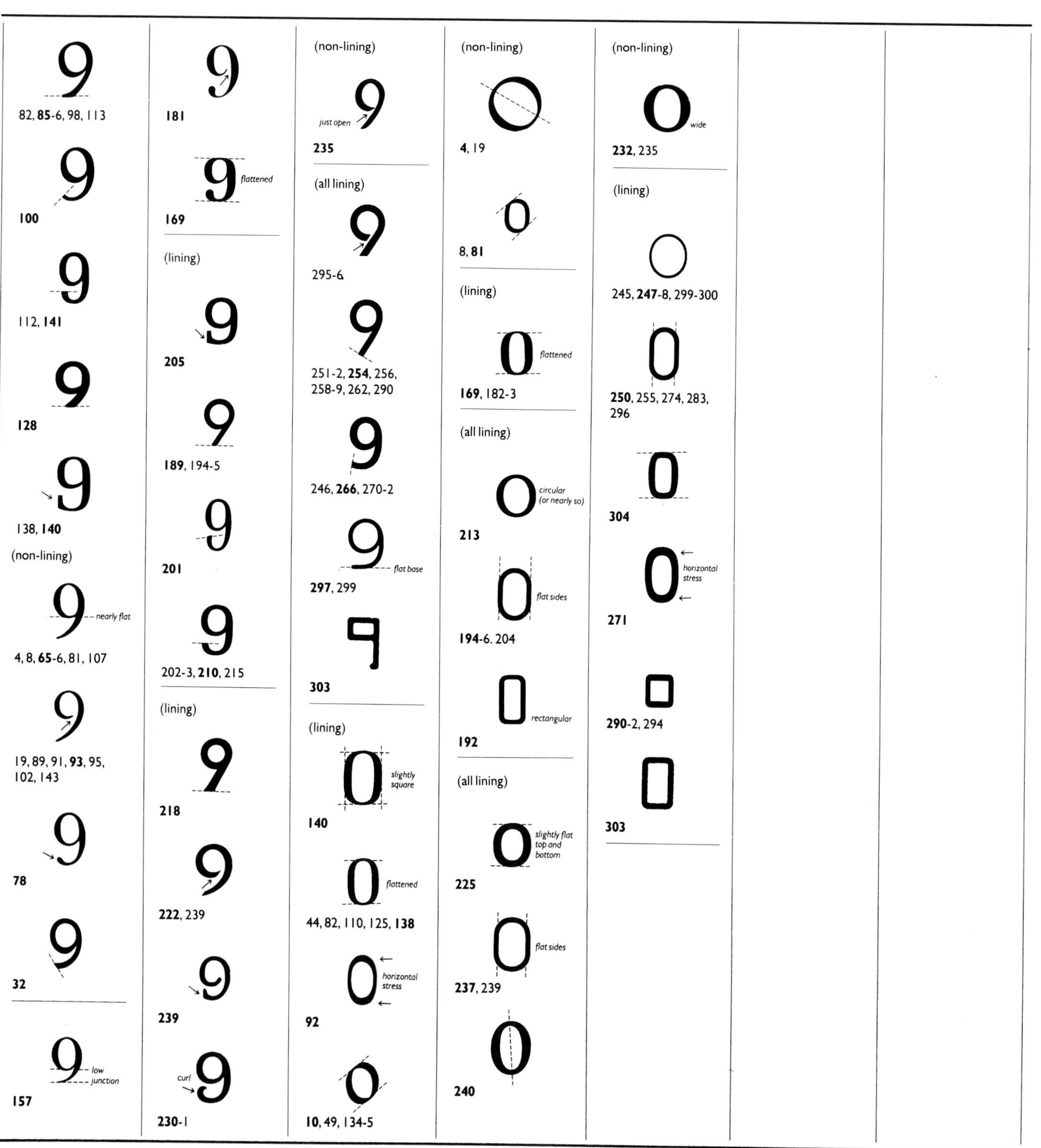
82, **85**-6, 98, 113
100
112, **141**
128
138, **140**
(non-lining)
nearly flat
4, 8, **65**-6, 81, 107
19, 89, 91, **93**, 95, 102, 143
78
32
low junction
157
181
flattened
169
(lining)
205
189, 194-5
201
202-3, **210**, 215
(lining)
218
222, 239
239
curl
230-1
(non-lining)
just open
235
(all lining)
295-**6**
251-2, **254**, 256, 258-9, 262, 290
246, **266**, 270-2
flat base
297, 299
303
(lining)
slightly square
140
flattened
44, 82, 110, 125, **138**
horizontal stress
92
10, 49, 134-5
(non-lining)
4, 19
8, **81**
(lining)
flattened
169, 182-3
(all lining)
circular (or nearly so)
213
flat sides
194-6. 204
rectangular
192
(all lining)
slightly flat top and bottom
225
flat sides
237, 239
240
(non-lining)
wide
232, 235
(lining)
245, **247**-8, 299-300
250, 255, 274, 283, 296
304
horizontal stress
271
290-2, 294
303

'Special Earmarks'

The 'special earmarks' (or distinctive identifying features) are indicated on each letter. The general 'style' of typefaces with the same 'earmark' may vary. The figures refer to specimen numbers.

NB. *Bold figures indicate the specimen illustrated above.*

pt.2:

(non-continuous text)

Deco
rative]
ypefaces

DECORATIVE TYPEFACE CATEGORIES

THIS PART OF the book contains a cross-section of decorative typefaces, i.e. those not normally used for continuous text setting. Instead, they are used for headings and titling or in limited quantities and situations for display purposes. The characteristic features of each of the eight typeface categories are described below and are illustrated on the opposite page.

As with *Text* typefaces **the classification system and terminology is entirely new and does not follow established type classifications.** Categories are based on specific design features.

Each category is further divided into smaller groups according to more specific design features which are explained at the beginning of each section. Typeface specimens are then arranged alphabetically within each group and have an individual specimen number which is cross-referenced to the index.

NB. There is inevitably a small overlap between the *Text* and *Decorative* parts of the book. For instance, some *Decorative* typefaces in special circumstances may be used for continuous text setting and vice-versa.

Categories are as follows:

1. Flowing Scripts *Nos. 305-322*

This category includes script typefaces which, when typeset, give a 'joined up' script effect so that words appear to be 'flowing' as in handwriting. The category is divided into smaller groups of quill pen, felt or graphic pen and brush script effects. A further division is made into sloping, upright, rounded and angular forms.

2. Non-Flowing Scripts (including Blackletter & Uncial)

Nos. 323-381

As the term describes, this category includes script typefaces in which the letters remain unjoined when typeset and are, therefore, 'non-flowing'. As in the 'flowing' category there are groups for quill pen, felt or graphic pen and brush. This category includes blackletter and uncial typefaces together with a small group of roman italic typefaces based on pen scripts.

3. Unmodified (Formal Text Shape)

Nos. 382-428

This category contains typefaces that generally adhere to the formal and traditional letter shapes normally associated with continuous text typefaces but which are usually used for decorative applications. However, it excludes those typefaces which, though conforming to this criteria, are either very bold or very thin. These will be found in the next category Fat & Thin Face. The category is arranged in groups according to whether the design is roman, slab, wedge or sans serif in origin and within each of these divisions there are separate groups for outline, inline, shaded, or with background versions.

4. Fat Face & Thin Face (Unmodified & Modified)

Nos Fat 429-515, Thin 516-536

This category is divided into two parts and contains a selection of typefaces which represent the extremes in weight – very bold (Fat Face) and very light (Thin Face). As with the Unmodified Section, arrangement is by roman, slab, wedge and sans serif groups. The substantial roman serif group is further sub-divided depending on whether the typefaces have thin, medium or thick serifs. The sans serif group is also divided into typefaces of wide, medium or narrow design or of a special rounded shape. *NB. A small number of typefaces with Fat Face characteristics are to be found in the Modified Serif and Sans Serif categories as they were felt better placed there.*

5. Ornamental *Nos. 537-563*

Grouped here are typefaces of a particularly elaborate (often 'floriated') and highly decorated nature. In addition, those with 'swash style' characteristics or flourishes have been included. Consistent with the previous two sections, typefaces are arranged into roman, slab, wedge and sans serif groups. There is also a small group of script-based typefaces.

6. Modified Serif *Nos. 564-603*

The term 'modified' means non-formal or non-traditional letter shapes. Modification is by distortion, added or other subtracted elements (such as, for example, stencil letters) or by axis (sloping backwards). Arrangement is by roman, slab, wedge and sans serif groups. *NB. This category includes some typefaces with Fat Face characteristics that were felt better placed here.*

7. Modified Sans Serif *Nos. 604-665*

This section covers all 'modified' typefaces without serifs. Due to the varied and unusual nature of this typeface category new explanatory group headings have been created such as: vertical and horizontal thick and thin stress, electronic, cut, stencil or stencil effect, and striped or inline. *NB. This category includes some typefaces with Fat Face characteristics which were felt better placed here.*

8. Modified Outrageous *Nos. 666-700*

This final category includes both 'modified' serif and sans serif typefaces that are of a particularly unusual or 'way out' nature. They are highly stylised and often humorous and intended for special, very limited use only. Typeface groups include: heavy, inline or striped, dot-formed, shaded and 3D, with backgrounds and pictorial.

NB. A very small number of typeface specimens in this part of the book do not include an ampersand.

The Typefinding Process

1. To identify a typeface, first decide into which one of main categories shown opposite the typeface specimen you wish to identify belongs.

2. Using the thumb index on the edge of the page turn to the appropriate category introduction page.

3. From the listings there select the specific group within the category to which the specimen relates.

4. Read off the specimen numbers given for this group and find them in the following listings of typeface specimens.

5. Decide which of the typefaces in the group it equates to by 'scanning' the alphabetical listings until you find a typeface to which your specimen matches.

Type categories	*General characteristics*				
1. Flowing Scripts. *Nos 305-322* e.g. **310** Palace Script, **316** ITC Zapf Chancery, **319** Kaufmann and **322** Mistral.	*Groups include: quill pen sloping and rounded* 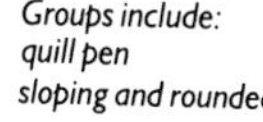	*quill pen upright and rounded* Scr	*felt or graphic pen sloping* Scr	*felt or graphic pen upright* Scr	*brush* Scr
2. Non-Flowing Scripts. (including Blackletter & Uncial) *Nos 323-381* e.g. **323** Bernhard Tango, **333** Bologna, **372** Old English Text and **380** Blado Italic.	*Groups include: quill pen* Scr	*felt or graphic pen* Scr	*brush* Scr	*blackletter* BL	*uncial* un
3. Unmodified. *Nos 382-428* e.g. **385** Engravers Roman, **392** Castellar, **412** Latin Antique No 9 and **422** Helvetica Outline.	*roman serif* ROM	*slab serif* SL	*wedge serif* WE	*sans serif* SA	
4. Fat Face & Thin Face. *Nos 429-536* **(Modified & Unmodified)** e.g. **434** Falstaff, **467** Cooper Black, **514** Harry Fat and **536** Harry Thin.	*roman serif* F	*slab serif* FT	*wedge serif* FT	*sans serif* FT	
5. Ornamental. *Nos 537-563* e.g. **540** Fry's Ornamented, **548** Lettres Ornées **554** Davida and **561** Ballé Initials.	*roman serif* R	*slab serif* 	*wedge serif* 	*sans serif* 	*script* 
. Modified Serif. *Nos 564-603* .g. **566** Belwe, **575** Stencil Bold,**579** Profil nd **585** Charleston.	*roman serif* ROM	*slab serif* SL	*wedge serif* WE	*wedge serif (sloping backwards)* WE	
. Modified Sans Serif. *Nos 604-665* g. **608** Peignot, **619** Frankfurter Medium, **26** Countdown and **646** Neon.	*Groups include: thick and thin stress (vertical)* TH	*rounded* RO	*electronic* EL	*cut* CU	*shaded or 3D* 3D
Modified Outrageous. *Nos 666-700* g. **668** Litzenburg, **679** Shatter, **682** Pinball d **688** Calypso.	*Groups include: heavy distorted* HE	*inline or striped* ST	*dot-formed* 	*shaded or 3D* 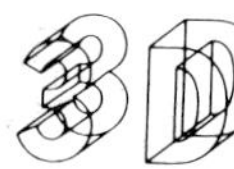	*pictorial* PIC

1. FLOWING SCRIPTS

Specimen nos		Basic characteristics	Secondary characteristics	
305-315	Flow	*quill pen*	*sloping and rounded*	e.g. **310** Palace Script
316	Flow	,,	*sloping and angular*	e.g. **316** ITC Zapf Chancery
317-318	Flow	,,	*upright*	e.g. **318** Linoscript
319	Flow	*felt pen or graphic pen*	*sloping*	e.g. **319** Kaufmann
320	Flow	,,	*upright*	e.g. **320** Jiffy
321-322	Flow	*brush*		e.g. **322** Mistral

NB. *Typefaces in each group are arranged in alphabetical order.*

OWING
RIPTS
Scr

quill pen sloping and rounded

305 Ariston Light Script

ABCDEFGHIJKLMNOPQRSTUVWXYZ&

306 Bank Script

ABCDEFGHIJKLMNOPQRSTUVWXYZ

307 Commercial Script

ABCDEFGHIJKLMNOPQRSTUVWXYZ&

308 Diskus

ABCDEFGHIJKLMNOPQRSTUVWXYZ&

309 Künstler Schreibschrift

ABCDEFGHIJKLMNOPQRSTUVWXYZ&

310 Palace Script

ABCDEFGHIJKLMNOPQRSTUVWXYZ&

311 Park Avenue

ABCDEFGHIJKLMNOPQRSTUVWXYZ&

312 Shelley Allegro Script

ABCDEFGHIJKLMNOPQRSTUVWXYZ&

313 Shelley Andante Script

ABCDEFGHIJKLMNOPQRSTUVWXYZ&

314 Snell Roundhand

ABCDEFGHIJKLMNOPQRSTUVWXYZ&

FLOWIN
SCRIP

Ariston Light Script **305**

abcdefghijklmnopqrstuvwxyz1234567890

Bank Script **306**

abcdefghijklmnopqrstuvwxyz1234567890

Commercial Script **307**

abcdefghijklmnopqrstuvwxyz 1234567890

Diskus **308**

abcdefghijklmnopqrstuvwxyz1234567890

Künstler Schreibschrift **309**

abcdefghijklmnopqrstuvwxyz1234567890

Palace Script **310**

abcdefghijklmnopqrstuvwxyz 1234567890

Park Avenue **311**

abcdefghijklmnopqrstuvwxyz1234567890

Shelley Allegro Script **312**

abcdefghijklmnopqrstuvwxyz1234567890

Shelley Andante Script **313**

abcdefghijklmnopqrstuvwxyz1234567890

Snell Roundhand **314**

abcdefghijklmnopqrstuvwxyz1234567890

315 Yale Script

ABCDEFGHIJKLMNOPQRSTUVWXYZ

quill pen sloping and angular

316 ITC Zapf Chancery

ABCDEFGHIJKLMNOPQRSTUVWXYZ&

felt or graphic pen upright

317 Gando Ronde Script

ABCDEFGHIJKLMNOPQRSTUVWXYZ&

quill pen upright rounded

318 Linoscript

ABCDEFGHIJKLMNOPQRSTUVWXYZ &

felt or graphic pen sloping

319 Kaufmann

ABCDEFGHIJKLMNOPQRSTUVWXYZ&

320 Jiffy

ABCDEFGHIJKLMNOPQRSTUVWXYZ&

brush

321 Brush Script

ABCDEFGHIJKLMNOPQRSTUVWXYZ&

322 Mistral

ABCDEFGHIJKLMNOPQRSTUVWXYZ&

Yale Script **315**

abcdefghijklmnopqrstuvwxyz1234567890

ITC Zapf Chancery **316**

abcdefghijklmnopqrstuvwxyz1234567890

Gando Ronde Script **317**

abcdefghijklmnopqrstuvwxyz1234567890

Linoscript **318**

abcdefghijklmnopqrstuvwxyz1234567890

Kaufmann **319**

abcdefghijklmnopqrstuvwxyz1234567890

Jiffy **320**

abcdefghijklmnopqrstuvwxyz1234567890

Brush Script **321**

abcdefghijklmnopqrstuvwxyz1234567890

Mistral **322**

abcdefghijklmnopqrstuvwxyz1234567890

FLOWIN
SCRIPT
Scr

NON-FLOWING
SCRIPTS
(INCLUDING
BLACKLETTER & UNCIAL)
Scr

2. NON-FLOWING SCRIPTS
(INCLUDING BLACKLETTER & UNCIAL)

Specimen nos	Basic characteristics	Secondary characteristics	
323-326	*quill pen*	*sloping and rounded*	e.g. **323** Bernhard Tango
327-331	"	*sloping and angular*	e.g. **330** Noris Script
332	"	*upright and rounded*	e.g. **332** Murray Hill Bold
333-336	"	*upright and angular*	e.g. **333** Bologna
337-338	"	*'oriental'*	e.g. **337** Auriol
339-343	"	*decorative sloping*	e.g. **343** Vivaldi
344-345	"	*decorative upright*	e.g. **344** Delphin No I
346-352	*felt or graphic pen*	*sloping*	e.g. **350** Sallwey Script
353-356	"	*upright*	e.g. **353** Artic
357-362	*brush*		e.g. **359** Flash

NB. *Typefaces in each group are arranged in alphabetical order.*

continued on next page

continued from previous page

Specimen nos				
363-374	Nofl	*blackletter*	*text*	e.g. **372** Old English Text
375-376	Nofl	"	*decorative*	e.g. **376** St. Clair
377-378	nofl	*uncial*		e.g. **378** Libra
379-381	*Nofl*	*roman italic (based on pen scripts)*		e.g. **380** Blado Italic

NB. *Typefaces in each group are arranged in alphabetical order.*

NON-FLOWIN
SCRIPT
(INCLUDIN
BLACKLETTER & UNCIAL
Scr

quill pen sloping and rounded

323 Bernhard Tango

ABCDEFGHIJKLMNOPQRSTUVWXYZ&

324 Dorchester Script

ABCDEFGHIJKLMNOPQRSTUVWXYZ&

325 Nuptial Script

ABCDEFGHIJKLMNOPQRSTUVWXYZ&

326 Stradivarius

ABCDEFGHIJKLMNOPQRSTUVWXYZ&

quill pen sloping and angular

327 Cascade

ABCDEFGHIJKLMNOPQRSTUVWXYZ&

328 Klang

ABCDEFGHIJKLMNOPQRSTUVWXYZ&

329 Medici Script

ABCDEFGHIJKLMNOPQRSTUVWXYZ&

330 Noris Script

ABCDEFGHIJKLMNOPQRSTUVWXYZ&

331 Temple Script

ABCDEFGHIJKLMNOPQRSTUVWXYZ&

quill pen upright and rounded

332 Murray Hill Bold

ABCDEFGHIJKLMNOPQRSTUVWXYZ&

Bernhard Tango **323**

abcdefghijklmnopqrstuvwxyz 1234567890

Dorchester Script **324**

abcdefghijklmnopqrstuvwxyz1234567890

Nuptial Script **325**

abcdefghijklmnopqrstuvwxyz1234567890

Stradivarius **326**

abcdefghijklmnopqrstuvwxyz1234567890

Cascade **327**

abcdefghijklmnopqrstuvwxyz 1234567890

Klang **328**

abcdefghijklmnopqrstuvwxyz1234567890

Medici Script **329**

abcdefghijklmnopqrstuvwxyz1234567890

Noris Script **330**

abcdefghijklmnopqrstuvwxyz1234567890

Temple Script **331**

abcdefghijklmnopqrstuvwxyz1234567890

Murray Hill Bold **332**

bcdefghijklmnopqrstuvwxyz 1234567890

NON-FLOWING SCRIPTS (INCLUDING BLACKLETTER & UNCIAL)
Scr

NON-FLOWING SCRIPTS (INCLUDING BLACKLETTER & UNCIAL)

Scr

Bologna
Codex
Lydian
Ondine
Auriol
Boutique
Crayonette
Kalligraphia
Le Griffe
Treasury Open

quill pen
upright and angular

333 Bologna

ABCDEFGHIJKLMNOPQRSTUVWXYZ&

334 Codex

ABCDEFGHIJKLMNOPQRSTUVWXYZ&

335 Lydian

ABCDEFGHIJKLMNOPQRSTUVWXYZ&

336 Ondine

ABCDEFGHIJKLMNOPQRSTUVWXYZ

quill pen
'oriental'

337 Auriol

ABCDEFGHIJKLMNOPQRSTUVWXYZ&

338 Boutique

ABCDEFGHIJKLMNOPQRSTUVWXYZ&

quill pen
decorative sloping

339 Crayonette

ABCDEFGHIJKLMNOPQRSTUVWXYZ&

340 Kalligraphia

ABCDEFGHIJKLMNOPQRSTUVWXYZ&

341 Le Griffe

ABCDEFGHIJKLMNOPQRSTUVWXYZ&

342 Treasury Open

ABCDEFGHIJKLMNOPQRSTUVWXYZ&

Bologna **333**

abcdefghijklmnopqrstuvwxyz1234567890

Codex **334**

abcdefghijklmnopqrstuvwxyz 1234567890

Lydian **335**

abcdefghijklmnopqrstuvwxyz 1234567890

Ondine **336**

abcdefghijklmnopqrstuvwxyz 1234567890

Auriol **337**

abcdefghijklmnopqrstuvwxyz1234567890

Boutique **338**

abcdefghijklmnopqrstuvwxyz 1234567890

Crayonette **339**

abcdefghijklmnopqrstuvwxyz 1234567890

Kalligraphia **340**

abcdefghijklmnopqrstuvwxyz1234567890

Le Griffe **341**

abcdefghijklmnopqrstuvwxyz 1234567890

Treasury Open **342**

abcdefghijklmnopqrstuvwxyz1234567890

343 Vivaldi

ABCDEFGHIJKLMNOPQRSTUVWXYZ&

quill pen
decorative
upright

344 Delphin No I

ABCDEFGHIJKLMNOPQRSTUVWXYZ&

345 Matura

ABCDEFGHIJKLMNOPQRSTUVWXYZ&

felt or
graphic pen
sloping

346 Balloon Extra Bold

ABCDEFGHIJKLMNOPQRSTUVWXYZ&

347 Caprice

ABCDEFGHIJKLMNOPQRSTUVWXYZ&

348 Gillies Extra Bold

ABCDEFGHIJKLMNOPQRSTUVWXYZ&

349 Lateinische Ausgangsschrift

ABCDEFGHIJKLMNOPQRSTUVWXYZ

350 Sallwey Script

ABCDEFGHIJJKLMNOPQRSTUVWXYZ&

351 Venture

ABCDEFGHIJKLMNOPQRSTUVWXYZ&

352 Vertex

ABCDEFGHIJKLMNOPQRSTUVWXYZ&

N-FLOWING
RIPTS
CLUDING
CKLETTER & UNCIAL)

Scr

valdi
elphin No I
atura
alloon Extra Bold
aprice
illies Extra Bold
ateinische
usgangsschrift
allwey Script
enture
ertex

Vivaldi **343**

abcdefghijklmnopqrstuvwxyz1234567890

Delphin No I **344**

abcdefghijklmnopqrstuvwxyz1234567890

Matura **345**

abcdefghijklmnopqrstuvwxyz1234567890

Balloon Extra Bold **346**

1234567890 *no lower case*

Caprice **347**

abcdefghijklmnopqrstuvwxyz1234567890

Gillies Extra Bold **348**

abcdefghijklmnopqrstuvwxyz1234567890

Lateinische Ausgangsschrift **349**

abcdefghijklmnopqrstuvwxyz1234567890

Sallwey Script **350**

abcdefghijklmnopqrstuvwxyz1234567890

Venture **351**

abcdefghijklmnopqrstuvwxyz1234567890

Vertex **352**

abcdefghijklmnopqrstuvwxyz1234567890

NON-FLOWING SCRIPTS (INCLUDING BLACKLETTER & UNCIAL)
Scr

NON-FLOWING SCRIPTS (INCLUDING BLACKLETTER & UNCIAL)

Scr

felt or graphic pen upright

353 Artic

ABCDEFGHIJKLMNOPQRSTUVWXYZ&

354 Dom Casual

ABCDEFGHIJKLMNOPQRSTUVWXYZ&

355 Present

ABCDEFGHIJKLMNOPQRSTUVWXYZ&

356 Studio

ABCDEFGHIJKLMNOPQRSTUVWXYZ&

brush

357 Ashley Script

ABCDEFGHIJKLMNOPQRSTUVWXYZ&

358 Bison

ABCDEFGHIJKLMNOPQRSTUVWXYZ&

359 Flash

ABCDEFGHIJKLMNOPQRSTUVWXYZ&

360 Forte

ABCDEFGHIJKLMNOPQRSTUVWXYZ&

361 Pepita

ABCDEFGHIJKLMNOPQRSTUVWXYZ&

362 Reporter No 2

ABCDEFGHIJKLMNOPQRSTUVWXYZ&

Artic **353**

abcdefghijklmnopqrstuvwxyz1234567890

Dom Casual **354**

abcdefghijklmnopqrstuvwxyz1234567890

Present **355**

abcdefghijklmnopqrstuvwxyz1234567890

Studio **356**

abcdefghijklmnopqrstuvwxyz1234567890

Ashley Script **357**

abcdefghijklmnopqrstuvwxyz1234567890

Bison **358**

abcdefghijklmnopqrstuvwxyz1234567890

Flash **359**

abcdefghijklmnopqrstuvwxyz1234567890

Forte **360**

abcdefghijklmnopqrstuvwxyz1234567890

Pepita **361**

abcdefghijklmnopqrstuvwxyz1234567890

Reporter No 2 **362**

abcdefghijklmnopqrstuvwxyz1234567890

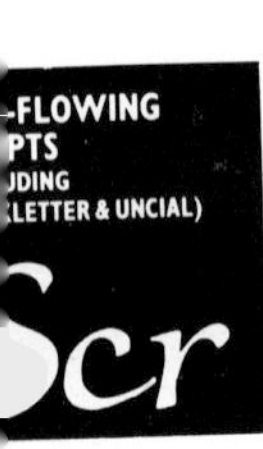
-FLOWING
PTS
JDING
LETTER & UNCIAL)
Scr

blackletter text

363 Caligra

ABCDEFGHIJKLMNOPQRSTUVWXYZ

364 Cloister Black

ABCDEFGHIJKLMNOPQRSTUVVWWXYZ&

365 Fette Fraktur

ABCDEFGHIJKLMNOPQRSTUVWXYZ&

366 Fraktur Bold

ABCDEFGHIJKLMNOPQRSTUVWXYZ&

367 Gothique

ABCDEFGHIJKLMNOPQRSTUVWXYZ&

368 Goudy Text

ABCDEFGHIJKLMNOPQRSTUVWXYZ&

369 ITC Honda

ABCDEFGHIJKLMNOPQRSTUVWXYZ&

370 Linotext

ABCDEFGHIJKLMNOPQRSTUVWXYZ&

371 Luthersche Fraktur

ABCDEFGHIJKLMNOPQRSTUVWXYZ&

372 Old English Text

ABCDEFGHIJKLMNOPQRSTUVWXYZ&

Caligra **363**

abcdefghijklmnopqrstuvwxyz1234567890

Cloister Black **364**

abcdefghijklmnopqrstuvwxyz1234567890

Fette Fraktur **365**

abcdefghijklmnopqrstuvwxyz1234567890

Fraktur Bold **366**

abcdefghijklmnopqrstuvwxyz1234567890

Gothique **367**

abcdefghijklmnopqrstuvwxyz1234567890

Goudy Text **368**

abcdefghijklmnopqrstuvwxyz1234567890

ITC Honda **369**

abcdefghijklmnopqrstuvwxyz1234567890

Linotext **370**

abcdefghijklmnopqrstuvwxyz1234567890

Luthersche Fraktur **371**

abcdefghijklmnopqrstuvwxyz1234567890

Old English Text **372**

abcdefghijklmnopqrstuvwxyz1234567890

NON-FLOWI
SCRIP
(INCLUDI
BLACKLETTER & UNCI
Scr

373 Venetian Text Condensed

ABCDEFGHIJKLMNOPQRSTUVWXYZ&

374 Wilhelm Klingspor Gotisch

ABCDEFGHIJKLMNOPQRSTUVWXYZ&

blackletter decorative

375 Pamela

ABCDEFGHIJKLMNOPQRSTUVWXYZ&

376 St. Clair

ABCDEFGHIJKLMNOPQRSTUVWXYZ&

uncial

377 American Uncial

abcdefghijklmnopqrstuvwxyz&

378 Libra

abcdefghijklmnopqrstuvwxyz

roman italic (based on pen scripts)

379 Arrighi Italic (Centaur Italic)

ABCDEFGHIJKLMNOPQRSTUVWXYZ&

380 Blado Italic

ABCDEFGHIJKLMNOPQRSTUVWXYZ&

381 Cancelleresca Bastarda

ABCDEFGHIJKLMNOPQRSTUVWXYZ

Venetian Text Condensed **373**

abcdefghijklmnopqrstuvwxyz 1234567890

Wilhelm Klingspor Gotisch **374**

abcdefghijklmnopqrstuvwxyz1234567890

Pamela **375**

abcdefghijklmnopqrstuvwxyz *no figures*

St. Clair **376**

abcdefghijklmnopqrstuvwxyz1234567890

American Uncial **377**

1234567890 *no lower case*

Libra **378**

1234567890 *no lower case*

Arrighi Italic (Centaur Italic) **379**

abcdefghijklmnopqrstuvwxyz1234567890

Blado Italic **380**

abcdefghijklmnopqrstuvwxyz 1234567890

Cancelleresca Bastarda **381**

abcdefghijklmnopqrstuvwxyz1234567890

NON-FLOWIN
SCRIPT
(INCLUDIN
BLACKLETTER & UNCIA
Scr

3. UNMODIFIED
(FORMAL TEXT SHAPE)

Specimen nos		Basic characteristics	Secondary characteristics	
382-390	R	roman serif		e.g. **385** Engravers Roman
391-399	R	"	inline and outline	e.g. **392** Castellar
400-402	R	"	shaded	e.g. **402** Thorne Shaded
403	SL	slab serif		e.g. **403** Hellenic Wide
404-405	SL	"	inline and outline	e.g. **405** Egyptian Outline
406-408	SL	"	shaded	e.g. **407** Gold Rush
409-415	W	wedge serif		e.g. **412** Latin Antique No 9
416-419	W	"	inline	e.g. **417** Chisel
420-421	SA	sans serif		e.g. **420** Fleet
422	SA	"	outline	e.g. **422** Helvetica Outline

NB. *Typefaces in each group are arranged in alphabetical order.*

continued on next page

UNMODIFI
(FORMAL TEXT SHA
UN

continued from previous page

423-426		*(sans serif)*	*inline and outline shaded*	e.g. **425** Gill Sans Shadow 408
427-428		"	*with backgrounds*	e.g. **427** Gill Cameo

NB. *Typefaces in each group are arranged in alphabetical order.*

UNMODIFIED
(FORMAL TEXT SHAPE)
UN

UNMODIFIED
(FORMAL TEXT SHAPE)

UN

Bauer Classic Roman
Caslon Antique
Elizabeth Roman
Engravers Roman
Engravers Roman Bold
Felix Titling
Fleet Titling
Horizon
Victoria Titling
Caslon Open Face

roman serif

382 Bauer Classic Roman

ABCDEFGHIJKLMNOPQRSTUVWXYZ&

383 Caslon Antique

ABCDEFGHIJKLMNOPQRSTUVWXYZ&

384 Elizabeth Roman

ABCDEFGHIJKLMNOPQRSTUVWXYZ&

385 Engravers Roman

ABCDEFGHIJKLMNOPQRSTUVWXYZ&

386 Engravers Roman Bold

ABCDEFGHIJKLMNOPQRSTUVWXYZ&

387 Felix Titling

ABCDEFGHIJKLMNOPQRSTUVWXYZ

388 Fleet Titling

ABCDEFGHIJKLMNOPQRSTUVWXYZ&

389 Horizon

ABCDEFGHIJKLMNOPQRSTUVWXYZ&

390 Victoria Titling

ABCDEFGHIJKLMNOPQRSTUVWXYZ&

roman serif
inline and outline

391 Caslon Open Face

ABCDEFGHIJKLMNOPQRSTUVWXYZ&

Bauer Classic Roman **382**

abcdefghijklmnopqrstuvwxyz1234567890

Caslon Antique **383**

abcdefghijklmnopqrstuvwxyz1234567890

Elizabeth Roman **384**

abcdefghijklmnopqrstuvwxyz 1234567890

small capitals (no lower case)

Engravers Roman **385**

ABCDEFGHIJKLMNOPQRSTUVWXYZ1234567890

small capitals (no lower case)

Engravers Roman Bold **386**

ABCDEFGHIJKLMNOPQRSTUVWXYZ1234567890

Felix Titling **387**

1234567890 *no lower case*

Fleet Titling **388**

1234567890 *no lower case*

Horizon **389**

abcdefghijklmnopqrstuvwxyz1234567890

Victoria Titling **390**

1234567890 *no lower case*

Caslon Open Face **391**

abcdefghijklmnopqrstuvwxyz1234567890

UNMODIFIED
(FORMAL TEXT SHAPE)
UN

Bauer Classic Roman
Caslon Antique
Elizabeth Roman
Engravers Roman
Engravers Roman Bold
Felix Titling
Fleet Titling
Horizon
Victoria Titling
Caslon Open Face

UNMODIFIED
(FORMAL TEXT SHAPE)

UN

Castellar
Cloister Open Face
Goudy Handtooled
Hadriano Stonecut
Old Style Bold Outline
Times English Black Outline
Windsor Bold Outline
Windsor Elongated
Bank Note
Cheque

392 Castellar

ABCDEFGHIJKLMNOPQRSTUVWXYZ&

393 Cloister Open Face

ABCDEFGHIJKLMNOPQRSTUVWXYZ&

394 Goudy Handtooled

ABCDEFGHIJKLMNOPQRSTUVWXYZ

395 Hadriano Stonecut

ABCDEFGHIJKLMNOPQRSTUVWXYZ&

396 Old Style Bold Outline

ABCDEFGHIJKLMNOPQRSTUVWXYZ&

397 Times English Black Outline

ABCDEFGHIJKLMNOPQRSTUVWXYZ&

398 Windsor Bold Outline

ABCDEFGHIJKLMNOPQRSTUVWXYZ&

399 Windsor Elongated

ABCDEFGHIJKLMNOPQRSTUVWXYZ&

roman serif shaded

400 Bank Note

ABCDEFGHIJKLMNOPQRSTUVWXYZ&

401 Cheque

ABCDEFGHIJKLMNOPQRSTUVWXYZ&

Castellar **392**

1234567890 *no lower case*

Cloister Open Face **393**

abcdefghijklmnopqrstuvwxyz1234567890

Goudy Handtooled **394**

abcdefghijklmnopqrstuvwxyz1234567890

Hadriano Stonecut **395**

1234567890 *no lower case*

Old Style Bold Outline **396**

abcdefghijklmnopqrstuvwxyz1234567890

Times English Black Outline **397**

abcdefghijklmnopqrstuvwxyz1234567890

Windsor Bold Outline **398**

abcdefghijklmnopqrstuvwxyz1234567890

Windsor Elongated **399**

abcdefghijklmnopqrstuvwxyz 1234567890

Bank Note **400**

1234567890 *no lower case*

Cheque **401**

1234567890 *no lower case*

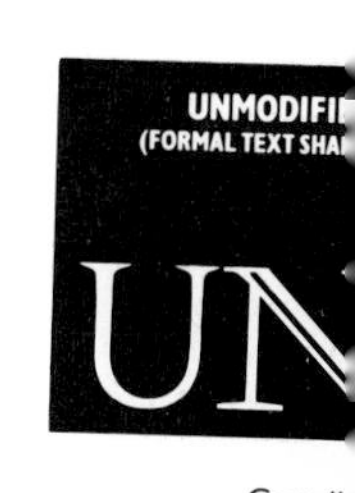
UNMODIFI
(FORMAL TEXT SHA
UN

MODIFIED
MAL TEXT SHAPE)
JN

orne Shaded
llenic Wide
C American
pewriter
old Outline
yptian Outline
yptienne Filette
old Rush
ockwell Shadow
ugustea Nova
olumna
na

402 Thorne Shaded

ABCDEFGHIJKLMNOPQRSTUVWXYZ

slab serif
inline and outline

403 Hellenic Wide

ABCDEFGHIJKLMNOPQRSTUVWXYZ&

slab serif

404 ITC American Typewriter Bold Outline

ABCDEFGHIJKLMNOPQRSTUVWXYZ&

405 Egyptian Outline

ABCDEFGHIJKLMNOPQRSTUVWXYZ&

slab serif
shaded or 3D

406 Egyptienne Filette

ABCDEFGHIJKLMNOPQRSTUVWXYZ

407 Gold Rush

ABCDEFGHIJKLMNOPQRSTUVWXYZ&

408 Rockwell Shadow

ABCDEFGHIJKLMNOPQRSTUVWXYZ&

wedge serif

409 Augustea Nova

ABCDEFGHIJKLMNOPQRSTUVWXYZ&

410 Columna

ABCDEFGHIJKLMNOPQRSTUVWXYZ&

411 Jana

ABCDEFGHIJKLMNOPQRSTUVWXYZ&

Thorne Shaded **402**

1234567890 *no lower case*

Hellenic Wide **403**

abcdefghijklmnopqrstuvwxyz 1234567890

ITC American Typewriter Bold Outline **404**

abcdefghijklmnopqrstuvwxyz 1234567890

Egyptian Outline **405**

1234567890 *no lower case*

Egyptienne Filette **406**

no lower case or figures

Gold Rush **407**

1234567890 *no lower case*

Rockwell Shadow **408**

1234567890 *no lower case*

Augustea Nova **409**

abcdefghijklmnopqrstuvwxyz1234567890

Columna **410**

1234567890 *no lower case*

Jana **411**

abcdefghijklmnopqrstuvwxyz 1234567890

412 Latin Antique No 9

ABCDEFGHIJKLMNOPQRSTUVWXYZ&

413 Latin Condensed No 2

ABCDEFGHIJKLMNOPQRSTUVWXYZ&

414 Latin Wide

ABCDEFGHIJKLMNOPQRSTUVWXYZ&

UNMODIFIED
(FORMAL TEXT SHAPE)

UN

Latin Antique No 9
Latin Condensed No 2
Latin Wide
Runic Condensed
Augustea Inline
Chisel
Contura
Crystal
Fleet
Hanseatic Bold

415 Runic Condensed

ABCDEFGHIJKLMNOPQRSTUVWXYZ&

wedge serif

inline and outline

416 Augustea Inline

ABCDEFGHIJKLMNOPQRSTUVWXYZ&

417 Chisel

ABCDEFGHIJKLMNOPQRSTUVWXYZ&

418 Contura

ABCDEFGHIJKLMNOPQRSTUVWXYZ&

419 Crystal

ABCDEFGHIJKLMNOPQRSTUVWXYZ&

sans serif

420 Fleet

ABCDEFGHIJKLMNOPQRSTUVWXYZ&

421 Hanseatic Bold

ABCDEFGHIJKLMNOPQRSTUVWXYZ&

Latin Antique No 9 **412**

abcdefghijklmnopqrstuvwxyz1234567890

Latin Condensed No 2 **413**

abcdefghijklmnopqrstuvwxyz1234567890

Latin Wide **414**

abcdefghijklmnopqrstuvwxyz 1234567890

Runic Condensed **415**

abcdefghijklmnopqrstuvwxyz1234567890

Augustea Inline **416**

1234567890 *no lower case*

Chisel **417**

abcdefghijklmnopqrstuvwxyz1234567890

Contura **418**

abcdefghijklmnopqrstuvwxyz1234567890

Crystal **419**

1234567890 *no lower case*

Fleet **420**

abcdefghijklmnopqrstuvwxyz1234567890

Hanseatic Bold **421**

abcdefghijklmnopqrstuvwxyz1234567890

UNMODIFIED
(FORMAL TEXT SHAPE)
UN

Latin Antique No 9
Latin Condensed No 2
Latin Wide
Runic Condensed
Augustea Inline
Chisel
Contura
Crystal
Fleet
Hanseatic Bold

sans serif outline

422 Helvetica Outline

ABCDEFGHIJKLMNOPQRSTUVWXYZ&

sans serif inline and outline shaded

423 Festival Titling

ABCDEFGHIJKLMNOPQRSTUVWXYZ&

424 Gill Sans Shadow Line 290

ABCDEFGHIJKLMNOPQRSTUVWXYZ&

425 Gill Sans Shadow 408

ABCDEFGHIJKLMNOPQRSTUVWXYZ&

426 Sans Serif Shaded

ABCDEFGHIJKLMNOPQRSTUVWXYZ&

sans serif with backgrounds

427 Gill Cameo

ABCDEFGHIJKLMNOPQRSTUVWXYZ&

428 Gill Cameo Ruled

ABCDEFGHIJKLMNOPQRSTUVWXYZ&

NMODIFIED
ORMAL TEXT SHAPE)

UN

Ielvetica Outline
estival Titling
Gill Sans Shadow
ine 290
Gill Sans Shadow 408
Sans Serif Shaded
Gill Cameo
Gill Cameo Ruled

Helvetica Outline **422**

abcdefghijklmnopqrstuvwxyz1234567890

Festival Titling **423**

1234567890 *no lower case*

Gill Sans Shadow Line 290 **424**

abcdefghijklmnopqrstuvwxyz1234567890

Gill Sans Shadow 408 **425**

1234567890 *no lower case*

Sans Serif Shaded **426**

1234567890 *no lower case*

Gill Cameo **427**

1234567890 *no lower case*

Gill Cameo Ruled **428**

1234567890 *no lower case*

4. FAT & THIN FACE
(UNMODIFIED & MODIFIED)

FAT FACE

Specimen nos		*Basic characteristics*	*Secondary characteristics*	
429-443	R	*roman serif*	*thin serifs*	e.g. **434** Falstaff
444-449	R	”	*medium weight serifs*	e.g. **445** Caslon Black
450-452	R	”	*heavy serifs*	e.g. **451** Kompakt
453-458	SL	*slab serif*		e.g. **453** Figaro
459-466	W	*wedge serif*	*thin/medium serifs*	e.g. **459** Americana True
467-469	W	”	*heavy serifs*	e.g. **467** Cooper Black
470-471	W	”	*heavy serifs and outline*	e.g. **471** ITC Souvenir Bold Outline
472-481	SA	*sans serif*	*wide*	e.g. **472** Annonce Grotesque
482	SA	”	*wide outline*	e.g. **482** Gill Kayo Outline
483-498	SA	”	*medium width*	e.g. **493** Helvetica Heavy

NB. *Typefaces in each group are arranged in alphabetical order.*

continued on next page

FAT FACE
& THIN FACE
(UNMODIFIED & MODIFIED)
FT

continued from previous page

499-506	SA	(sans serif)	narrow	e.g. **501** Compacta Bold
507-509	SA	,,	narrow outline	e.g. **508** Impact Outline
510-514	SA	,,	rounded shape	e.g. **514** Harry Fat
515	SA	,,	rounded shape outline	e.g. **515** ITC Bauhaus Heavy Outline

THIN FACE

516-519	LS	slab serif		e.g. **519** ITC Stymie Hairline
520-521	W	wedge serif		e.g. **520** ITC Newtext Light
522-533	SA	sans serif		e.g. **530** Helvetica Ultra Light
534-536	SA	,,	rounded shape	e.g. **535** Churchward 70 Hairline

NB. *Typefaces in each group are arranged in alphabetical order.*

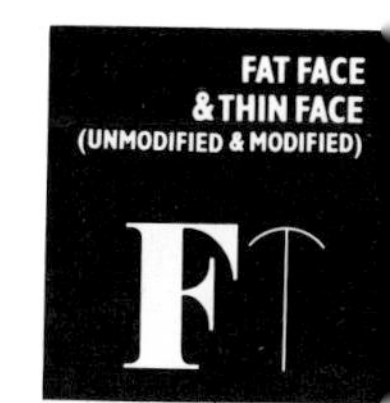
FAT FACE
& THIN FACE
(UNMODIFIED & MODIFIED)
FT

AT FACE
THIN FACE
(UNMODIFIED & MODIFIED)

Annlie Extra Bold
Brace Condensed
Carousel
ITC Didi
Elongated Roman
Falstaff
ITC Firenze
Normande
Orator
Perpetua Black

roman serif with thin serifs

429 Annlie Extra Bold

ABCDEFGHIJKLMNOPQRSTUVWXYZ&

430 Brace Condensed

ABCDEFGHIJKLMNOPQRSTUVWXYZ&

431 Carousel

ABCDEFGHIJKLMNOPQRSTUVWXYZ&

432 ITC Didi

ABCDEFGHIJKLMMNOPQRSTUVWWXYZ&

433 Elongated Roman

ABCDEFGHIJKLMNOPQRSTUVWXYZ&

434 Falstaff

ABCDEFGHIJKLMNOPQRSTUVWXYZ&

435 ITC Firenze

ABCDEFGHIJKLMNOPQRSTUVWXYZ&

436 Normande

ABCDEFGHIJKLMNOPQRSTUVWXYZ&

437 Orator

ABCDEFGHIJKLMNOPQRSTUVWXYZ&

438 Perpetua Black

ABCDEFGHIJKLMNOPQRSTUVWXYZ&

Annlie Extra Bold **429**

abcdefghijklmnopqrstuvwxyz1234567890

Brace Condensed **430**

abcdefghijklmnopqrstuvwxyz 1234567890

Carousel **431**

abcdefghijklmnopqrstuvwxyz1234567890

ITC Didi **432**

abcdefghijklmnopqrstuvwxyz1234567890

Elongated Roman **433**

1234567890 *no lower case*

Falstaff **434**

abcdefghijklmnopqrstuvwxyz1234567890

ITC Firenze **435**

abcdefghijklmnopqrstuvwxyz1234567890

Normande **436**

abcdefghijklmnopqrstuvwxyz1234567890

Orator **437**

abcdefghijklmnopqrstuvwxyz1234567890

Perpetua Black **438**

abcdefghijklmnopqrstuvwxyz1234567890

FAT FACE & THIN FACE (UNMODIFIED & MODIFIED)

Annlie Extra Bold
Brace Condensed
Carousel
ITC Didi
Elongated Roman
Falstaff
ITC Firenze
Normande
Orator
Perpetua Black

439 Pistilli Roman

ABCDEFGHIJKLMNOPQRSTUVWXYZ&

440 Poster Bodoni

ABCDEFGHIJKLMNOPQRSTUVWXYZ&

441 Thorowgood

ABCDEFGHIJKLMNOPQRSTUVWXYZ&

442 ITC Tiffany Heavy

ABCDEFGHIJKLMNOPQRSTUVWXYZ&

443 ITC Zapf Book Heavy

ABCDEFGHIJKLMNOPQRSTUVWXYZ&

roman serif with medium thickness serifs

444 Aetna

ABCDEFGHIJKLMNOPQRSTUVWXYZ&

445 Caslon Black

ABCDEFGHIJKLMNOPQRSTUVWXYZ&

446 ITC Century Ultra

ABCDEFGHIJKLMNOPQRSTUVWXYZ&

447 ITC Galliard Ultra

ABCDEFGHIJKLMNOPQRSTUVWXYZ&

448 ITC Garamond Ultra

ABCDEFGHIJKLMNOPQRSTUVWXYZ&

FAT FACE
& THIN FACE
(UNMODIFIED & MODIFIED)
F

Pistilli Roman
Poster Bodoni
Thorowgood
ITC Tiffany Heavy
ITC Zapf Book Heavy
Aetna
Caslon Black
ITC Century Ultra
ITC Galliard Ultra
ITC Garamond Ultra

Pistilli Roman **439**

abcdefghijklmnopqrstuvwxyz1234567890

Poster Bodoni **440**

abcdefghijklmnopqrstuvwxyz1234567890

Thorowgood **441**

abcdefghijklmnopqrstuvwxyz1234567890

ITC Tiffany Heavy **442**

abcdefghijklmnopqrstuvwxyz1234567890

ITC Zapf Book Heavy **443**

abcdefghijklmnopqrstuvwxyz1234567890

Aetna **444**

1234567890 *no lower case*

Caslon Black **445**

abcdefghijklmnopqrstuvwxyz1234567890

ITC Century Ultra **446**

abcdefghijklmnopqrstuvwxyz1234567890

ITC Galliard Ultra **447**

abcdefghijklmnopqrstuvwxyz1234567890

ITC Garamond Ultra **448**

abcdefghijklmnopqrstuvwxyz1234567890

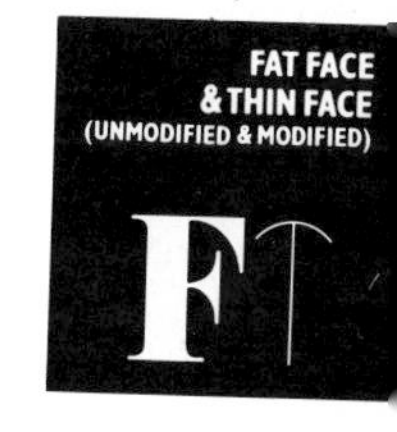

Pistilli Roman
Poster Bodoni
Thorowgood
ITC Tiffany Heavy
ITC Zapf Book Heavy
Aetna
Caslon Black
ITC Century Ultra
ITC Galliard Ultra
ITC Garamond Ultra

449 ITC Grouch

ABCDEFGHIJKLMNOPQRSTUVWXYZ&

roman serifs with heavy serifs

450 ITC Cheltenham Ultra

ABCDEFGHIJKLMNOPQRSTUVWXYZ&

451 Kompakt

ABCDEFGHIJKLMNOPQRSTUVWXYZ&

452 Whitin Black

ABCDEFGHIJKLMNOPQRSTUVWXYZ&

slab serif

453 Figaro

ABCDEFGHIJKLMNOPQRSTUVWXYZ&

454 Hidalgo

ABCDEFGHIJKLMNOPQRSTUVWXYZ&

455 Karnak Black

ABCDEFGHIJKLMNOPQRSTUVWXYZ&

456 Memphis Extra Bold

ABCDEFGHIJKLMNOPQRSTUVWXYZ&

457 Playbill

ABCDEFGHIJKLMNOPQRSTUVWXYZ&

458 Rockwell Extra Bold

ABCDEFGHIJKLMNOPQRSTUVWXYZ&

AT FACE
THIN FACE
UNMODIFIED & MODIFIED)
F

TC Grouch
TC Cheltenham Ultra
Kompakt
Whitin Black
Figaro
Hidalgo
Karnak Black
Memphis Extra Bold
Playbill
Rockwell Extra Bold

ITC Grouch **449**

abcdefghijklmnopqrstuvwxyz1234567890

ITC Cheltenham Ultra **450**

abcdefghijklmnopqrstuvwxyz1234567890

Kompakt **451**

abcdefghijklmnopqrstuvwxyz1234567890

Whitin Black **452**

abcdefghijklmnopqrstuvwxyz1234567890

Figaro **453**

abcdefghijklmnopqrstuvwxyz1234567890

Hidalgo **454**

1234567890 *no lower case*

Karnak Black **455**

abcdefghijklmnopqrstuvwxyz1234567890

Memphis Extra Bold **456**

abcdefghijklmnopqrstuvwxyz1234567890

Playbill **457**

abcdefghijklmnopqrstuvwxyz1234567890

Rockwell Extra Bold **458**

abcdefghijklmnopqrstuvwxyz1234567890

FAT FACE
& THIN FACE
(UNMODIFIED & MODIFIED)
F

ITC Grouch
ITC Cheltenham Ultra
Kompakt
Whitin Black
Figaro
Hidalgo
Karnak Black
Memphis Extra Bold
Playbill
Rockwell Extra Bold

wedge serif
with thin or medium serifs

459 Americana True

ABCDEFGHIJKLMNOPQRSTUVWXYZ&

460 Hawthorn

ABCDEFGHIJKLMNOPQRSTUVWXYZ&

461 Hess Neobold

ABCDEFGHIJKLMNOPQRSTUVWXYZ&

462 Las Vegas

ABCDEFGHIJKLMNOPQRSTUVWXYZ&

FAT FACE
& THIN FACE
(UNMODIFIED & MODIFIED)

Americana True
Hawthorn
Hess Neobold
Las Vegas
Macbeth
ITC Novarese Ultra
ITC Serif Gothic Heavy
Trooper Black
Cooper Black
Pabst

463 Macbeth

ABCDEFGHIJKLMNOPQRSTUVWXYZ&

464 ITC Novarese Ultra

ABCDEFGHIJKLMNOPQRSTUVWXYZ&

465 ITC Serif Gothic Heavy

ABCDEFGHIJKLMNOPQRSTUVWXYZ&

466 Trooper Black

ABCDEFGHIJKLMNOPQRSTUVWXYZ&

wedge serif
with heavy serifs

467 Cooper Black

ABCDEFGHIJKLMNOPQRSTUVWXYZ&

468 Pabst

ABCDEFGHIJKLMNOPQRSTUVWXYZ&

Americana True **459**

abcdefghijklmnopqrstuvwxyz1234567890

Hawthorn **460**

abcdefghijklmnopqrstuvwxyz1234567890

Hess Neobold **461**

1234567890 *no lower case*

Las Vegas **462**

abcdefghijklmnopqrstuvwxyz1234567890

Macbeth **463**

abcdefghijklmnopqrstuvwxyz1234567890

ITC Novarese Ultra **464**

abcdefghijklmnopqrstuvwxyz1234567890

ITC Serif Gothic Heavy **465**

abcdefghijklmnopqrstuvwxyz1234567890

Trooper Black **466**

abcdefghijklmnopqrstuvwxyz1234567890

Cooper Black **467**

abcdefghijklmnopqrstuvwxyz1234567890

Pabst **468**

abcdefghijklmnopqrstuvwxyz1234567890

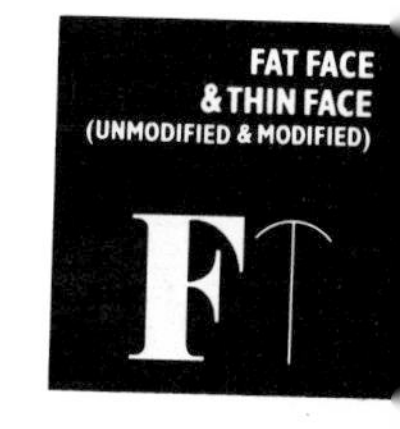

Americana True
Hawthorn
Hess Neobold
Las Vegas
Macbeth
ITC Novarese Ultra
ITC Serif Gothic Heavy
Trooper Black
Cooper Black
Pabst

469 ITC Souvenir Bold

ABCDEFGHIJKLMNOPQRSTUVWXYZ&

wedge serif with heavy serifs and outline

470 Cooper Black Outline

ABCDEFGHIJKLMNOPQRSTUVWXYZ&

471 ITC Souvenir Bold Outline

ABCDEFGHIJKLMNOPQRSTUVWXYZ&

sans serif wide

472 Annonce Grotesque

ABCDEFGHIJKLMNOPQRSTUVWXYZ&

473 Antique Olive Nord

ABCDEFGHIJKLMNOPQRSTUVWXYZ&

474 ITC Bolt Bold

ABCDEFGHIJKLMNOPQRSTUVWXYZ&

475 Fehrle Display

ABCDEFGHIJKLMNOPQRSTUVWXYZ&

476 Gill Kayo

ABCDEFGHIJKLMNOPQRSTUVWXYZ&

477 Helvetica Bold Extended

ABCDEFGHIJKLMNOPQRSTUVWXYZ&

478 Information Black Extended

ABCDEFGHIJKLMNOPQRSTUVWXYZ&

AT FACE
THIN FACE
UNMODIFIED & MODIFIED)

TC Souvenir Bold
Cooper Black Outline
TC Souvenir Bold Outline
Annonce Grotesque
Antique Olive Nord
ITC Bolt Bold
Fehrle Display
Gill Kayo
Helvetica Bold Extended
Information Black Extended

ITC Souvenir Bold 469

abcdefghijklmnopqrstuvwxyz1234567890

Cooper Black Outline 470

abcdefghijklmnopqrstuvwxyz1234567890

ITC Souvenir Bold Outline 471

abcdefghijklmnopqrstuvwxyz1234567890

Annonce Grotesque 472

abcdefghijklmnopqrstuvwxyz1234567890

Antique Olive Nord 473

abcdefghijklmnopqrstuvwxyz1234567890

ITC Bolt Bold 474

abcdefghijklmnopqrstuvwxyz 1234567890

Fehrle Display 475

abcdefghijklmnopqrstuvwxyz1234567890

Gill Kayo 476

abcdefghijklmnopqrstuvwxyz1234567890

Helvetica Bold Extended 477

abcdefghijklmnopqrstuvwxyz1234567890

Information Black Extended 478

abcdefghijklmnopqrstuvwxyz1234567890

FAT FACE
& THIN FACE
(UNMODIFIED & MODIFIED)

ITC Souvenir Bold
Cooper Black Outline
ITC Souvenir Bold Outline
Annonce Grotesque
Antique Olive Nord
ITC Bolt Bold
Fehrle Display
Gill Kayo
Helvetica Bold Extended
Information Black Extended

479 Koloss

ABCDEFGHIJKLMNOPQRSTUVWXYZ&

480 Spartan Extra Black

ABCDEFGHIJKLMNOPQRSTUVWXYZ&

481 Univers 83

ABCDEFGHIJKLMNOPQRSTUVWXYZ&

sans serif wide outline

482 Gill Kayo Outline

ABCDEFGHIJKLMNOPQRSTUVWXYZ&

sans serif medium width

483 Antique Olive Compact

ABCDEFGHIJKLMNOPQRSTUVWXYZ&

484 Broadway

ABCDEFGHIJKLMNOPQRSTUVWXYZ&

485 Broadway Engraved

ABCDEFGHIJKLMNOPQRSTUVWXYZ&

486 Bullion Solid

ABCDEFGHIJKLMNOPQRSTUVWXYZ&

487 Dynamo

ABCDEFGHIJKLMNOPQRSTUVWXYZ&

488 Folio Extra Bold

ABCDEFGHIJKLMNOPQRSTUVWXYZ&

Koloss
Spartan Extra Black
Univers 83
Gill Kayo Outline
Antique Olive Compact
Broadway
Broadway Engraved
Bullion Solid
Dynamo
Folio Extra Bold

Koloss **479**

abcdefghijklmnopqrstuvwxyz1234567890

Spartan Extra Black **480**

abcdefghijklmnopqrstuvwxyz1234567890

Univers 83 **481**

abcdefghijklmnopqrstuvwxyz1234567890

Gill Kayo Outline **482**

abcdefghijklmnopqrstuvwxyz1234567890

Antique Olive Compact **483**

abcdefghijklmnopqrstuvwxyz1234567890

Broadway **484**

abcdefghijklmnopqrstuvwxyz1234567890

Broadway Engraved **485**

abcdefghijklmnopqrstuvwxyz1234567890

Bullion Solid **486**

1234567890 *no lower case*

Dynamo **487**

abcdefghijklmnopqrstuvwxyz1234567890

Folio Extra Bold **488**

abcdefghijklmnopqrstuvwxyz1234567890

FAT FACE
& THIN FACE
(UNMODIFIED & MODIFIED)
F

Koloss
Spartan Extra Black
Univers 83
Gill Kayo Outline
Antique Olive Compact
Broadway
Broadway Engraved
Bullion Solid
Dynamo
Folio Extra Bold

489 Frutiger 75 Black

ABCDEFGHIJKLMNOPQRSTUVWXYZ&

490 Gothic No 16

ABCDEFGHIJKLMNOPQRSTUVWXYZ&

491 ITC Grizzly

ABCDEFGHIJKLMNOPQRSTUVWXYZ&

492 Haas Unica Black

ABCDEFGHIJKLMNOPQRSTUVWXYZ&

493 Helvetica Heavy

ABCDEFGHIJKLMNOPQRSTUVWXYZ&

494 Helvetica No 2 Bold

ABCDEFGHIJKLMNOPQRSTUVWXYZ&

495 Neil Bold

ABCDEFGHIJKLMNOPQRSTUVWXYZ&

496 Plak Heavy

ABCDEFGHIJKLMNOPQRSTUVWXYZ&

497 Syntax Ultra Black

ABCDEFGHIJKLMNOPQRSTUVWXYZ&

498 Univers 75

ABCDEFGHIJKLMNOPQRSTUVWXYZ&

AT FACE
THIN FACE
NMODIFIED & MODIFIED)
F

rutiger 75 Black
Gothic No 16
TC Grizzly
Haas Unica Black
Helvetica Heavy
Helvetica No 2 Bold
Neil Bold
Plak Heavy
Syntax Ultra Black
Univers 75

Frutiger 75 Black **489**

abcdefghijklmnopqrstuvwxyz1234567890

Gothic No 16 **490**

abcdefghijklmnopqrstuvwxyz1234567890

ITC Grizzly **491**

abcdefghijklmnopqrstuvwxyz1234567890

Haas Unica Black **492**

abcdefghijklmnopqrstuvwxyz1234567890

Helvetica Heavy **493**

abcdefghijklmnopqrstuvwxyz1234567890

Helvetica No 2 Bold **494**

abcdefghijklmnopqrstuvwxyz1234567890

Neil Bold **495**

abcdefghijklmnopqrstuvwxyz1234567890

Plak Heavy **496**

abcdefghijklmnopqrstuvwxyz1234567890

Syntax Ultra Black **497**

abcdefghijklmnopqrstuvwxyz1234567890

Univers 75 **498**

abcdefghijklmnopqrstuvwxyz1234567890

Frutiger 75 Black
Gothic No 16
ITC Grizzly
Haas Unica Black
Helvetica Heavy
Helvetica No 2 Bold
Neil Bold
Plak Heavy
Syntax Ultra Black
Univers 75

sans serif narrow

499 Anzeigen Grotesque

ABCDEFGHIJKLMNOPQRSTUVWXYZ&

500 Block Black Condensed

ABCDEFGHIJKLMNOPQRSTUVWXYZ&

501 Compacta Bold

ABCDEFGHIJKLMNOPQRSTUVWXYZ&

502 Futura Display

ABCDEFGHIJKLMNOPQRSTUVWXYZ&

503 Headline Bold

ABCDEFGHIJKLMNOPQRSTUVWXYZ&

504 Impact

ABCDEFGHIJKLMNOPQRSTUVWXYZ&

505 ITC Machine

ABCDEFGHIJKLMNOPQRSTUVWXYZ&

506 Placard Extra Bold Condensed

ABCDEFGHIJKLMNOPQRSTUVWXYZ&

sans serif narrow outline or inline

507 Compacta Bold Outline

ABCDEFGHIJKLMNOPQRSTUVWXYZ&

508 Impact Outline

ABCDEFGHIJJKLMNOPQRSTUVWXYZ&

FT

Anzeigen Grotesque
Block Black Condensed
Compacta Bold
Futura Display
Headline Bold
Impact
ITC Machine
Placard Extra Bold Condensed
Compacta Bold Outline
Impact Outline

Anzeigen Grotesque **499**

abcdefghijklmnopqrstuvwxyz1234567890

Block Black Condensed **500**

abcdefghijklmnopqrstuvwxyz1234567890

Compacta Bold **501**

abcdefghijklmnopqrstuvwxyz1234567890

Futura Display **502**

abcdefghijklmnopqrstuvwxyz1234567890

Headline Bold **503**

abcdefghijklmnopqrstuvwxyz1234567890

Impact **504**

abcdefghijklmnopqrstuvwxyz1234567890

ITC Machine **505**

1234567890 *no lower case*

Placard Extra Bold Condensed **506**

abcdefghijklmnopqrstuvwxyz1234567890

Compacta Bold Outline **507**

1234567890 *no lower case*

Impact Outline **508**

abcdefghijklmnopqrstuvwxyz1234567890

Anzeigen Grotesque
Block Black Condensed
Compacta Bold
Futura Display
Headline Bold
Impact
ITC Machine
Placard Extra Bold Condensed
Compacta Bold Outline
Impact Outline

509 Superstar

ABCDEFGHIJKLMNOPQRSTUVWXYZ&

sans serif rounded shape

510 ITC Bauhaus Heavy

ABCDEFGHIJKLMNOPQRSTUVWXYZ&

511 Blippo Black

ABCDEFGHIJKLMNOPQRSTUVWXYZ&

512 Cable Heavy (Klingspor)

ABCDEFGHIJKLMNOPQRSTUVWXYZ&

513 Churchward 70 Ultra Black

ABCDEFGHIJKLMNOPQRSTUVWXYZ&

514 Harry Fat

ABCDEFGHIJKLMNOPQRSTUVWXYZ&

sans serif rounded shape outline

515 ITC Bauhaus Heavy Outline

ABCDEFGHIJKLMNOPQRSTUVWXYZ&

slab serif

516 ITC American Typewriter Light

ABCDEFGHIJKLMNOPQRSTUVWXYZ&

517 Glypha 35 Thin

ABCDEFGHIJKLMNOPQRSTUVWXYZ&

518 Serifa 35 Thin

ABCDEFGHIJKLMNOPQRSTUVWXYZ&

uperstar
TC Bauhaus Heavy
lippo Black
able Heavy (Klingspor)
hurchward 70 Jltra Black
Harry Fat
TC Bauhaus Heavy Outline
ITC American Typewriter Light
Glypha 35 Thin
Serifa 35 Thin

Superstar **509**

1234567890 *no lower case*

ITC Bauhaus Heavy **510**

abcdefghijklmnopqrstuvwxyz1234567890

Blippo Black **511**

abcdefghijklmnopqrstuvwxyz1234567890

Cable Heavy (Klingspor) **512**

abcdefghijklmnopqrstuvwxyz1234567890

Churchward 70 Ultra Black **513**

abcdefghijklmnopqrstuvwxyz1234567890

Harry Fat **514**

abcdefghijklmnopqrstuvwxyz1234567890

ITC Bauhaus Heavy Outline **515**

abcdefghijklmnopqrstuvwxyz1234567890

ITC American Typewriter Light **516**

abcdefghijklmnopqrstuvwxyz1234567890

Glypha 35 Thin **517**

abcdefghijklmnopqrstuvwxyz1234567890

Serifa 35 Thin **518**

abcdefghijklmnopqrstuvwxyz1234567890

Superstar
ITC Bauhaus Heavy
Blippo Black
Cable Light (Klingspor)
Churchward 70 Ultra Black
Harry Fat
ITC Bauhaus Heavy Outline
ITC American Typewriter Light
Glypha 35 Thin
Serifa 35 Thin

T FACE
THIN FACE
NMODIFIED & MODIFIED)
FT

C Stymie Hairline
C Newtext Light
irgin Roman
C Avant Garde Gothic
xtra Light
able Light (Klingspor)
mpire
C Eras Light
utura Light
ill Sans Light
rotesque 126

519 ITC Stymie Hairline

ABCDEFGHIJKLMNOPQRSTUVWXYZ&

wedge serif

520 ITC Newtext Light

ABCDEFGHIJKLMNOPQRSTUVWXYZ&

521 Virgin Roman

ABCDEFGHIJKLMNOPQRSTUVWXYZ&

sans serif

522 ITC Avant Garde Gothic Extra Light

ABCDEFGHIJKLMNOPQRSTUVWXYZ&

523 Cable Light (Klingspor)

ABCDEFGHIJKLMNOPQRSTUVWXYZ&

524 Empire

525 ITC Eras Light

ABCDEFGHIJKLMNOPQRSTUVWXYZ&

526 Futura Light

ABCDEFGHIJKLMNOPQRSTUVWXYZ&

527 Gill Sans Light

ABCDEFGHIJKLMNOPQRSTUVWXYZ&

528 Grotesque 126

ABCDEFGHIJKLMNOPQRSTUVWXYZ&

ITC Stymie Hairline **519**

abcdefghijklmnopqrstuvwxyz 1234567890

ITC Newtext Light **520**

abcdefghijklmnopqrstuvwxyz1234567890

Virgin Roman **521**

abcdefghijklmnopqrstuvwxyz1234567890

ITC Avant Garde Gothic Extra Light **522**

abcdefghijklmnopqrstuvwxyz 1234567890

Cable Light (Klingspor) **523**

abcdefghijklmnopqrstuvwxyz1234567890

Empire **524**

1234567890 *no lower case*

ITC Eras Light **525**

abcdefghijklmnopqrstuvwxyz1234567890

Futura Light **526**

abcdefghijklmnopqrstuvwxyz1234567890

Gill Sans Light **527**

abcdefghijklmnopqrstuvwxyz1234567890

Grotesque 126 **528**

abcdefghijklmnopqrstuvwxyz1234567890

FAT FACE
& THIN FACE
(UNMODIFIED & MODIFIED)
FT

ITC Stymie Hairline
ITC Newtext Light
Virgin Roman
ITC Avant Garde Gothic Extra Light
Cable Light (Klingspor)
Empire
ITC Eras Light
Futura Light
Gill Sans Light
Grotesque 126

529 Helvetica Thin

ABCDEFGHIJKLMNOPQRSTUVWXYZ&

530 Helvetica Ultra Light

ABCDEFGHIJKLMNOPQRSTUVWXYZ&

531 L & C Hairline

ABCDEFGHIJKLMNOPQRSTUVWXYZ&

532 Penny Bee

ABCDEFGHIJKLMNOPQRSTUVWXYZ&

533 Stark Debonair

ABCDEFGHIJKLMNOPQRSTUVWXYZ&

sans serif rounded shape

534 ITC Busorama Light

ABCDEFGHIJKLMNOPQRSTUVWXYZ&

535 Churchward 70 Hairline

ABCDEFGHIJKLMNOPQRSTUVWXYZ&

536 Harry Thin

ABCDEFGHIJKLMNOPQRSTUVWXYZ&

Helvetica Thin
Helvetica Ultra Light
L & C Hairline
Penny Bee
Stark Debonair
ITC Busorama Light
Churchward 70 Hairline
Harry Thin

Helvetica Thin **529**

abcdefghijklmnopqrstuvwxyz1234567890

Helvetica Ultra Light **530**

abcdefghijklmnopqrstuvwxyz1234567890

L & C Hairline **531**

abcdefghijklmnopqrstuvwxyz1234567890

Penny Bee **532**

1234567890 *no lower case*

Stark Debonair **533**

abcdefghijklmnopqrstuvwxyz1234567890

ITC Busorama Light **534**

1234567890 *no lower case*

Churchward 70 Hairline **535**

abcdefghijklmnopqrstuvwxyz1234567890

Harry Thin **536**

abcdefghijklmnopqrstuvwxyz1234567890

FAT FACE
& THIN FACE
(UNMODIFIED & MODIFIED)
FT

Helvetica Thin
Helvetica Ultra Light
L & C Hairline
Penny Bee
Stark Debonair
ITC Busorama Light
Churchward 70 Hairline
Harry Thin

5. ORNAMENTAL

Specimen nos		Basic characteristics	Secondary characteristics	
537-546		*roman serif*		e.g. **540** Fry's Ornamented
547		,,	*sloping*	e.g. **547** Goudy Fancy
548-551		*slab serif*		e.g. **548** Lettres Ornées
552-559		*wedge serif*		e.g. **554** Davida
560		*sans serif*		e.g. **560** Abramesque
561-563		*script*		e.g. **561** Ballé Initials

NB. *Typefaces in each group are arranged in alphabetical order.*

roman serif

537 Flirt

ABCDEFGHIJKLMNOPQRSTUVWXYZ&

538 Floriated Capitals

ABCDEFGHIJKLMNOPQRSTUVWXYZ

539 Fontanesi

ABCDEFGHIJKLMNOPQRSTUVWXYZ&

540 Fry's Ornamented

ABCDEFGHIJKLMNOPQRSTUVWXYZ&

541 Gallia

ABCDEFGHIJKLMNOPQRSTUVWXYZ&

542 Lexington

ABCDEFGHIJKLMNOPQRSTUVWXYZ&

543 Modernistic

ABCDEFGHIJKLMNOPQRSTUVWXYZ&

544 Mole Foliate

ABCDEFGHIJKLMNOPQRSTUVWXYZ&

545 Nymphic

ABCDEFGHIJKLMNOPQRSTUVWXYZ&

546 Sapphire

ABCDEFGHIJKLMNOPQRSTUVWXYZ&

Flirt **537**

abcdefghijklmnopqrstuvwxyz1234567890

Floriated Capitals **538**

no lower case or figures

Fontanesi **539**

1234567890 *no lower case*

Fry's Ornamented **540**

no lower case or figures

Gallia **541**

1234567890 *no lower case*

Lexington **542**

1234567890 *no lower case*

Modernistic **543**

1234567890 *no lower case*

Mole Foliate **544**

1234567890 *no lower case*

Nymphic **545**

abcdefghijklmnopqrstuvwxyz 1234567890

Sapphire **546**

1234567890 *no lower case*

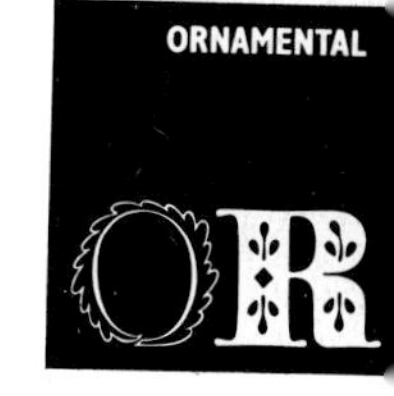

roman serif

sloping

547 Goudy Fancy

ABCDEFGHIJKLMNOPQRSTUVWXYZ&

slab serif

548 Lettres Ornées

ABCDEFGHIJKLMNOPQRSTUVWXYZ

549 Quentin

ABCDEFGHIJKLMNOPQRSTUVWXYZ&

550 Romantiques No 5

ABCDEFGHIJKLMNOPQRSTUVWXYZ&

551 Trocadero

ABCDEFGHIJKLMNOPQRSTUVWXYZ&

ORNAMENTAL
OR

Goudy Fancy
Lettres Ornées
Quentin
Romantiques No 5
Trocadero
Aesthetic Ornamented
Arnold Böcklin
Davida
Karnac
Kismet

wedge serif

552 Aesthetic Ornamented

ABCDEFGHIJKLMNOPQRSTUVWXYZ&

553 Arnold Böcklin

ABCDEFGHIJKLMNOPQRSTUVWXYZ&

554 Davida

ABCDEFGHIJKLMNOPQRSTUVWXYZ&

555 Karnac

ABCDEFGHIJKLMNOPQRSTUVWXYZ&

556 Kismet

ABCDEFGHIJKLMNOPQRSTUVWXYZ&

Goudy Fancy **547**

abcdefghijklmnopqrstuvwxyz1234567890

Lettres Ornées **548**

no lower case or figures

Quentin **549**

1234567890 *no lower case*

Romantiques No 5 **550**

123456789 *no lower case*

Trocadero **551**

1234567890 *no lower case*

Aesthetic Ornamented **552**

ABCDEFGHIJKLMNOPQRSTUVWXYZ1234567890 *small capitals (no lower case)*

Arnold Böcklin **553**

abcdefghijklmnopqrstuvwxyz1234567890

Davida **554**

1234567890 *no lower case*

Karnac **555**

abcdefghijklmnopqrstuvwxyz1234567890

Kismet **556**

abcdefghijklmnopqrstuvwxyz1234567890

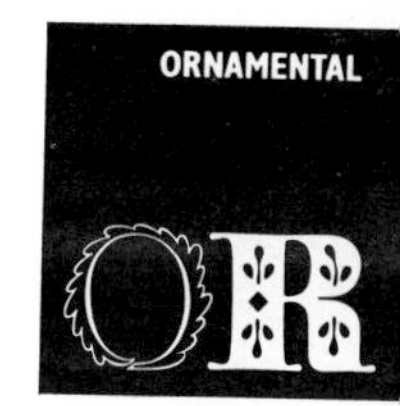

557 Recherche

ABCDEFGHIJKLMNOPQRSTUVWXYZ&

558 Ringlet

ABCDEFGHIJKLMNOPQRSTUVWXYZ

559 Victorian

ABCDEFGHIJKLMNOPQRSTUVWXYZ&

sans serif

560 Abramesque

ABCDEFGHIJKLMNOPQRSTUVWXYZ&

script

561 Ballé Initials

ABCDEFGHIJKLMNOPQRSTUVWXYZ

562 Lilith

ABCDEFGHIJKLMNOPQRSTUVWXYZ&

563 Raffia Initials

ABCDEFGHIJKLMNOPQRSTUVWXYZ

Recherche **557**

abcdefghijklmnopqrstuvwxyz1234567890

Ringlet **558**

abcdefghijklmnopqrstuvwxyz1234567890

Victorian **559**

abcdefghijklmnopqrstuvwxyz1234567890

Abramesque **560**

no lower case or figures

Ballé Initials **561**

no lower case or figures

Lilith **562**

abcdefghijklmnopqrstuvwxyz1234567890

Raffia Initials **563**

1234567890 *no lower case*

6. MODIFIED SERIF

Specimen nos		Basic characteristics	Secondary characteristics	
564-574	R	*roman serif*		e.g. **566** Belwe
575-576	R	,,	*stencil or stencil effect*	e.g. **575** Stencil Bold
577-579	SL	*slab serif*		e.g. **579** Profil
580-601	W	*wedge serif*		e.g. **585** Charleston
602-603	W	,,	*sloping backwards*	e.g. **602** Alfereta

NB. *Typefaces in each group are arranged in alphabetical order.*

MODIFIED SERIF
MS

roman serif

564 Abbott Old Style

ABCDEFGHIJKLMNOPQRSTUVWXYZ&

565 Antikva Margaret

ABCDEFGHIJKLMNOPQRSTUVWXYZ&

566 Belwe

ABCDEFGHIJKLMNOPQRSTUVWXYZ&

567 Bernhard Antique

ABCDEFGHIJKLMNOPQRSTUVWXYZ&

568 Greco Bold

ABCDEFGHIJKLMNOPQRSTUVWXYZ&

569 Koch Antiqua

ABCDEFGHIJKLMNOPQRSTUVWXYZ&

570 Milton

ABCDEFGHIJKLMNOPQRSTUVWXYZ&

571 Packhard

ABCDEFGHIJKLMNOPQRSTUVWXYZ&

572 Richmond

ABCDEFGHIJKLMNOPQRSTUUVWXYZ&

573 Skyjald

ABCDEFGHIJKLMNOPQRSTUVWXYZ&

MODIFIED SERIF
MS

Abbott Old Style
Antikva Margaret
Belwe
Bernhard Antique
Greco Bold
Koch Antiqua
Milton
Packhard
Richmond
Skyjald

Abbott Old Style **564**

abcdefghijklmnopqrstuvwxyz1234567890

Antikva Margaret **565**

abcdefghijklmnopqrstuvwxyz1234567890

Belwe **566**

abcdefghijklmnopqrstuvwxyz 1234567890

Bernhard Antique **567**

abcdefghijklmnopqrstuvwxyz1234567890

Greco Bold **568**

abcdefghijklmnopqrstuvwxyz1234567890

Koch Antiqua **569**

abcdefghijklmnopqrstuvwxyz1234567890

Milton **570**

abcdefghijklmnopqrstuvwxyz1234567890

Packhard **571**

abcdefghijklmnopqrstuvwxyz1234567890

Richmond **572**

abcdefghijklmnopqrstuvwxyz1234567890

Skyjald **573**

abcdefghijklmnopqrstuvwxyz1234567890

MS

574 University Roman

ABCDEFGHIJKLMNOPQRSTUVWXYZ&

roman serif

stencil or stencil effect

575 Stencil Bold

ABCDEFGHIJKLMNOPQRSTUVWXYZ&

576 Teachest

ABCDEFGHIJKLMNOPQRSTUVWXYZ&

slab serif

577 Antiqua Pointed

ABCDEFGHIJKLMNOPQRSTUVWXYZ

578 Nubian

ABCDEFGHIJKLMNOPQRSTUVWXYZ&

579 Profil

ABCDEFGHIJKLMNOPQRSTUVWXYZ&

wedge serif

580 Algerian

ABCDEFGHIJKLMNOPQRSTUVWXYZ&

581 Blackfriars Roman

ABCDEFGHIJKLMNOPQRSTUVWXYZ&

582 Brutus

ABCDEFGHIJKLMNOPQRSTUVWXYZ&

583 Bullfinch

ABCDEFGHIJKLMNOPQRSTUVWXYZ&

University Roman **574**

abcdefghijklmnopqrstuvwxyz1234567890

Stencil Bold **575**

abcdefghijklmnopqrstuvwxyz1234567890

Teachest **576**

1234567890 *no lower case*

Antiqua Pointed **577**

1234567890 *no lower case*

Nubian **578**

abcdefghijklmnopqrstuvwxyz1234567890

Profil **579**

1234567890 *no lower case*

Algerian **580**

1234567890 *no lower case*

Blackfriars Roman **581**

abcdefghijklmnopqrstuvwxyz1234567890

Brutus **582**

abcdefghijklmnopqrstuvwxyz1234567890

Bullfinch **583**

abcdefghijklmnopqrstuvwxyz1234567890

584 Chantrey

ABCDEFGHIJKLMNOPQRSTUVWXYZ&

585 Charleston

ABCDEFGHIJKLMNOPQRSTUVWXYZ&

586 Columbus

ABCDEFGHIJKLMNOPQRSTUVWXYZ&

587 Croydon

ABCDEFGHIJKLMNOPQRSTUVWXYZ&

588 Desdemona

ABCDEFGHIJKLMNOPQRSTUVWXYZ&

589 Eckmann

ABCDEFGHIJKLMNOPQRSTUVWXYZ&

590 Edda

ABCDEFGHIJKLMNOPQRSTUVWXYZ&

591 Fantail

ABCDEFGHIJKLMNOPQRSTUVWXYZ&

592 Hermosa

ABCDEFGHIJKLMNOPQRSTUVWXYZ

593 Hobo

ABCDEFGHIJKLMNOPQRSTUVWXYZ&

MS

Chantrey **584**

abcdefghijklmnopqrstuvwxyz1234567890

Charleston **585**

abcdefghijklmnopqrstuvwxyz1234567890

Columbus **586**

abcdefghijklmnopqrstuvwxyz1234567890

Croydon **587**

1234567890 *no lower case*

Desdemona **588**

1234567890 *no lower case*

Eckmann **589**

abcdefghijklmnopqrstuvwxyz1234567890

Edda **590**

1234567890 *no lower case*

Fantail **591**

abcdefghijklmnopqrstuvwxyz1234567890

Hermosa **592**

abcdefghijklmnopqrstuvwxyz1234567890

Hobo **593**

abcdefghijklmnopqrstuvwxyz1234567890

MS

594 Hogarth

ABCDEFGHIJKLMNOPQRSTUVWXYZ&

595 Lafayette

ABCDEFGHIJKLMNOPQRSTUVWXYZ&

596 Mikado Black

ABCDEFGHIJKLMNOPQRSTUVWXYZ&

597 Neptune

ABCDEFGHIJKLMNOPQRSTUVWXYZ&

598 Pretorian

ABCDEFGHIJKLMNOPQRSTUVWXYZ&

599 Tango

ABCDEFGHIJKLMNOPQRSTUVWXYZ&

600 Thalia

ABCDEFGHIJKLMNOPQRSTUVWXYZ&

601 Tip Top

ABCDEFGHIJKLMNOPQRSTUVWXYZ&

wedge serif sloping backwards

602 Alfereta

ABCDEFGHIJKLMNOPQRSTUVWXYZ&

603 Blanchard

ABCDEFGHIJKLMNOPQRSTUVWXYZ&

Hogarth **594**

abcdefghijklmnopqrstuvwxyz1234567890

Lafayette **595**

abcdefghijklmnopqrstuvwxyz1234567890

Mikado Black **596**

abcdefghijklmnopqrstuvwxyz1234567890

Neptune **597**

abcdefghijklmnopqrstuvwxyz1234567890

Pretorian **598**

abcdefghijklmnopqrstuvwxyz1234567890

Tango **599**

abcdefghijklmnopqrstuvwxyz1234567890

Thalia **600**

abcdefghijklmnopqrstuvwxyz1234567890

Tip Top **601**

abcdefghijklmnopqrstuvwxyz1234567890

Alfereta **602**

abcdefghijklmnopqrstuvwxyz1234567890

Blanchard **603**

abcdefghijklmnopqrstuvwxyz1234567890

7. MODIFIED SANS SERIF

Specimen nos	Basic characteristics	
604-609	*thick and thin stress (vertical)*	e.g. **608** Peignot
610	*thick and thin stress (horizontal)*	e.g. **610** Sintex I
611-612	*heavy bow-shaped*	e.g. **611** Becket
613-614	*square-shaped*	e.g. **613** Tamil
615	*sloping*	e.g. **615** Condensa
616-623	*rounded shape*	e.g. **619** Frankfurter Medium
624	*rounded shape outline*	e.g. **624** Helvetica Rounded Outline
625-629	*electronic*	e.g. **626** Countdown
630-633	*cut*	e.g. **632** Neuland
634-642	*stencil or stencil effect*	e.g. **636** Futura Black

NB. *Typefaces in each group are arranged in alphabetical order.*

continued on next page

continued from previous page

643-654	 INL	*inline or striped*	e.g. **646** Neon
655-662	 SH	*shaded or 3D*	e.g. **659** Superstar Shadow
663-665	 SH	*shaded or 3D* *inline or patterned*	e.g. **663** Baby Arbuckle

NB. *Typefaces in each group are arranged in alphabetical order.*

MODIFIED
SANS SERIF
MSS

thick and thin stress (vertical)

604 Britannic

ABCDEFGHIJKLMNOPQRSTUVWXYZ&

605 Florentine

ABCDEFGHIJKLMNOPQRSTUVWXYZ&

606 Inga

ABCDEFGHIJKLMNOPQRSTUVWXYZ&

607 Parisian

ABCDEEFGHIJKLMNOPQRSTUVWXYZ&

608 Peignot

ABCDEFGHIJKLMNOPQRSTUVWXYZ&

609 Radiant

ABCDEFGHIJKLMNOPQRSTUVWXYZ&

thick and thin stress (horizontal)

610 Sintex I

ABCDEFGHIJKLMNOPQRSTUVWXYZ&

heavy bow-shaped

611 Becket

ABCDEFGHIJKLMNOPQRSTUVWXYZ&

612 Revue

ABCDEFGHIiJKLMNOPQRSTUVWXYZ&

square-shaped

613 Tamil

ABCDEFGHIJKLMNOPQRSTUVWXYZ&

tannic
orentine
ga
risian
ignot
diant
ntex I
ecket
evue
amil

Britannic 604

abcdefghijklmnopqrstuvwxyz1234567890

Florentine 605

abcdefghijklmnopqrstuvwxyz1234567890

Inga 606

abcdefghijklmnopqrstuvwxyz1234567890

Parisian 607

abcdefghijklmnopqrstuvwxyz1234567890

Peignot 608

AbcdEfGHijklMNOPQRSTUVWxyz1234567890

Radiant 609

abcdefghijklmnopqrstuvwxyz1234567890

Sintex I 610

abcdefghijklmnopqrstuvwxyz1234567890

Becket 611

abcdefghijklmnopqrstuvwxyz1234567890

Revue 612

abcdefghijklmnopqrstuvwxyz1234567890

Tamil 613

abcdefghijklmnopqrstuvwxyz1234567890

614 Topic

ABCDEFGHIJKLMNOPQRSTUVWXYZ&

sloping

615 Condensa

ABCDEFGHIJKLMNOPQRSTUVWXYZ&

rounded shape

616 Capone

ABCDEFGHIJKLMNOPQRSTUVWXYZ&

617 Dempsey Medium

ABCDEFGHIJKLMNOPQRSTUVWXYZ&

618 Formula I

ABCDEFGHIJKLMNOPQRSTUVWXYZ&

619 Frankfurter Medium

ABCDEFGHIJKLMNOPQRSTUVWXYZ&

620 Helvetica Rounded

ABCDEFGHIJKLMNOPQRSTUVWXYZ&

621 Horatio Medium

ABCDEFGHIJKLMNOPQRSTUVWXYZ&

622 Octopuss

ABCDEFGHIJKLMNOPQRSTUVWXYZ&

623 Pump

ABCDEFGHIJKLMNOPQRSTUVWXYZ&

ODIFIED
ANS SERIF
MSS

Topic **614**

abcdefghijklmnopqrstuvwxyz 1234567890

Condensa **615**

abcdefghijklmnopqrstuvwxyz 1234567890

Capone **616**

abcdefghijklmnopqrstuvwxyz 1234567890

Dempsey Medium **617**

abcdefghijklmnopqrstuvwxyz 1234567890

Formula 1 **618**

abcdefghijklmnopqrstuvwxyz 1234567890

Frankfurter Medium **619**

abcdefghijklmnopqrstuvwxyz 1234567890

Helvetica Rounded **620**

abcdefghijklmnopqrstuvwxyz 1234567890

Horatio Medium **621**

abcdefghijklmnopqrstuvwxyz 1234567890

Octopuss **622**

abcdefghijklmnopqrstuvwxyz 1234567890

Pump **623**

abcdefghijklmnopqrstuvwxyz 1234567890

MODIFIED
SANS SERIF
MSS

rounded shape outline

624 Helvetica Rounded Outline

ABCDEFGHIJKLMNOPQRSTUVWXYZ&

electronic

625 Amelia

ABCDEFGHIJKLMNOPQRSTUVWXYZ&

626 Countdown

ABCDEFGHIJKLMNOPQRSTUVWXYZ&

627 Data 70

ABCDEFGHIJKLMNOPQRSTUVWXYZ&

628 Digital

ABCDEFGHIJKLMNOPQRSTUVWXYZ

629 Russell Square

ABCDEFGHIJKLMNOPQRSTUVWXYZ&

cut

630 Ad Lib

ABCDEFGHIJKLMNOPQRSTUVWXYZ&

631 Kino

ABCDEFGHIJKLMNOPQRSTUVWXYZ

632 Neuland

ABCDEFGHIJKLMNOPQRSTUVWXYZ&

633 Othello

ABCDEFGHIJKLMNOPQRSTUVWXYZ&

Helvetica Rounded Outline **624**

abcdefghijklmnopqrstuvwxyz1234567890

Amelia **625**

abcdefghijklmnopqrstuvwxyz1234567890

Countdown **626**

abcdefghijklmnopqrstuvwxyz1234567890

Data 70 **627**

abcdefghijklmnopqrstuvwxyz1234567890

Digital **628**

1234567890 *no lower case*

Russell Square **629**

abcdefghijklmnopqrstuvwxyz1234567890

Ad Lib **630**

abcdefghijklmnopqrstuvwxyz1234567890

Kino **631**

abcdefghijklmnopqrstuvwxyz1234567890

Neuland **632**

1234567890 *no lower case*

Othello **633**

1234567890 *no lower case*

stencil or stencil effect

634 Braggadocio

ABCDEFGHIJKLMNOPQRSTUVWXYZ&

635 Folio Stencil

ABCDEFGHIJKLMNOPQRSTUVWXYZ&

636 Futura Black

ABCDEFGHIJKLMNOPQRSTUVWXYZ&

637 Glaser Stencil Bold

ABCDEFGHIJKLMNOPQRSTUVWXYZ&

638 Glyphic

ABCDEFGHIJKLMNOPQRSTUVWXYZ

639 Motter Tektura

ABCDEFGHIJKLMNOPQRSTUVWXYZ&

640 Stop

ABCDEFGHIJKLMNOPQRSTUVWXYZ&

641 Tabasco

ABCDEFGHIJKLMNOPQRSTUVWXYZ&

642 Traffic

no capital letters

inline or striped

643 Fatima

ABCDEFGHIJKLMNOPQRSTUVWXYZ&

Braggadocio **634**

abcdefghijklmnopqrstuvwxyz1234567890

Folio Stencil **635**

1234567890 *no lower case*

Futura Black **636**

abcdefghijklmnopqrstuvwxyz1234567890

Glaser Stencil Bold **637**

1234567890 *no lower case*

Glyphic **638**

1234567890 *no lower case*

Motter Tektura **639**

abcdefghijklmnopqrstuvwxyz1234567890

Stop **640**

1234567890 *no lower case*

Tabasco **641**

abcdefghijklmnopqrstuvwxyz 1234567890

Traffic **642**

abcdefghijklmnopqrstuvwxyz1234567890

Fatima **643**

1234567890 *no lower case*

644 French Flash

ABCDEFGHIJKLMNOPQRSTUVWXYZ

645 Michel

ABCDEFGHIJKLMNOPQRSTUVWXYZ&

646 Neon

ABCDEFGHIJKLMNOPQRSTUVWXYZ&

647 Optex

ABCDEFGHIJKLMNOPQRSTUVWXYZ&

648 Oxford

no capital letters

649 Piccadilly

ABCDEFGHIJKLMNOPQRSTUVWXYZ&

650 Pluto

ABCDEFGHIJKLMNOPQRSTUVWXYZ&

651 Prisma

ABCDEFGHIJKLMNOPQRSTUVWXYZ&

652 Pump Triline

ABCDEFGHIJKLMNOPQRSTUVWXYZ&

653 ITC Uptight Neon

ABCDEFGHIJKLMNOPQRSTUVWXYZ&

French Flash **644**

1234567890 *no lower case*

Michel **645**

abcdefghijklmnopqrstuvwxyz 1234567890

Neon **646**

1234567890 *no lower case*

Optex **647**

abcdefghijklmnopqrstuvwxyz 1234567890

Oxford **648**

abcdefghijklmnopqrstuvwxyz 1234567890

Piccadilly **649**

1234567890 *no lower case*

Pluto **650**

abcdefghijklmnopqrstuvwxyz 1234567890

Prisma **651**

1234567890 *no lower case*

Pump Triline **652**

abcdefghijklmnopqrstuvwxyz 1234567890

ITC Uptight Neon **653**

abcdefghijklmnopqrstuvwxyz 1234567890

654 Zeppelin

ABCDEFGHIJKLMNOPQRSTUVWXYZ&

shaded or 3D

655 Bullion Shadow

ABCDEFGHIJKLMNOPQRSTUVWXYZ&

656 Old Bowery

ABCDEFGHIJKLMNOPQRSTUVWXYZ&

657 Pioneer Shadow

ABCDEFGHIJKLMNOPQRSTUVWXYZ&

658 Premier Shaded

ABCDEFGHIJKLMNOPQRSTUVWXYZ&

659 Superstar Shadow

ABCDEFGHIJKLMNOPQRSTUVWXYZ&

660 Tintoretto

ABCDEFGHIJKLMNOPQRSTUVWXYZ&

661 Umbra

ABCDEFGHIJKLMNOPQRSTUVWXYZ&

662 Uncle Bill

ABCDEFGHIJKLMNOPQRSTUVWXYZ&

shaded or 3D
inline or patterned

663 Baby Arbuckle

ABCDEFGIHJKLMNOPQRSTUVXWYZ&

Zeppelin **654**

abcdefghijklmnopqrstuvwxyz1234567890

Bullion Shadow **655**

1234567890 *no lower case*

Old Bowery **656**

no lower case or figures

Pioneer Shadow **657**

1234567890 *no lower case*

Premier Shaded **658**

1234567890 *no lower case*

Superstar Shadow **659**

1234567890 *no lower case*

Tintoretto **660**

abcdefghijklmnopqrstuvwxyz 1234567890

Umbra **661**

1234567890 *no lower case*

Uncle Bill **662**

1234567890 *no lower case*

Baby Arbuckle **663**

1234567890 *no lower case*

664 Jim Crow

ABCDEFGHIJKLMNOPQRSTUWVXYZ

665 Quicksilver

ABCDEFGHIJKLMNOPQRSTUVWXYZ &

MODIFIED
SANS SERIF
MSS

Jim Crow **664**

1234567890 *no lower case*

Quicksilver **665**

1234567890 *no lower case*

MODIFIED
SANS SERIF
MSS

8. MODIFIED OUTRAGEOUS

Specimen nos	*Basic characteristics*	
666-671	*heavy/distorted*	e.g. **668** Litzenburg
672-678	*inline or striped*	e.g. **672** ITC Aki Lines
679	*broken-surfaced and distorted*	e.g. **679** Shatter
680-684	*dot-formed*	e.g. **682** Pinball
685-694	*shaded or 3D*	e.g. **688** Calypso
695-698	*with backgrounds*	e.g. **697** Process
699-700	*pictorial*	e.g. **700** Zip

NB. *Typefaces in each group are arranged in alphabetical order.*

MODIFIED
OUTRAGEOUS
MO

heavy/ distorted

666 Bottleneck

ABCDEFGHIJKLMNOPQRSTUVWXYZ&

667 Florist

ABCDEFGHIJKLMNOPQRSTUVWXYZ&

668 Litzenburg

ABCDEFGHIJKLMNOPQRSTUVWXYZ&

669 Pierrot

ABCDEFGHIJKLMNOPQRSTUVWXYZ&

670 Starvation

ABCDEFGHIJKLMNOPQRSTUVWXYZ&

671 Talbot

ABCDEFGHIJKLMNOPQRSTUVWXYZ&

inline or striped

672 ITC Aki Lines

ABCDEFGHIJKLMNOPQRSTUVWXYZ&

673 Groove

674 Horseman Sidesaddle

ABCDEFGHIJKLMNOPQRSTUVWXYZ&

675 Matra

ABCDEFGHIJKLMNOPQRSTUVWXYZ

Bottleneck
Florist
Litzenburg
Pierrot
Starvation
Talbot
ITC Aki Lines
Groove
Horseman Sidesaddle
Matra

MODIFIED OUTRAGEOUS

Bottleneck **666**

abcdefghijklmnopqrstuvwxyz 1234567890

Florist **667**

1234567890 *no lower case*

Litzenburg **668**

1234567890 *no lower case*

Pierrot **669**

abcdefghijklmnopqrstuvwxyz1234567890

Starvation **670**

1234567890 *no lower case*

Talbot **671**

1234567890 *no lower case*

ITC Aki Lines **672**

12334556789O *no lower case*

Groove **673**

1234567890 *no lower case*

Horseman Sidesaddle **674**

1234567890 *no lower case*

Matra **675**

1234567890 *no lower case*

Bottleneck
Florist
Litzenburg
Pierrot
Starvation
Talbot
ITC Aki Lines
Groove
Horseman Sidesaddle
Matra

676 Old Glory

ABCDEFGHIJKLMNOPQRSTUVWXYZ&

677 Sinaloa

ABCDEFGHIJKLMNOPQRSTUVWXYZ &

678 Stripes

ABCDEFGHIJKLMNOPQRSTUVWXYZ&

broken surfaced and distorted

679 Shatter

ABCDEFGHIJKLMNOPQRSTUVWXYZ &

dot-formed

680 Astra

ABCDEFGHIJKLMNOPQRSTUVWXYZ &

681 Chequered

ABCDEFGHIJKLMNOPQRSTUVWXYZ&

682 Pinball

ABCDEFGHIJKLMNOPQRSTUVWXYZ &

683 Spangle

ABCDEFGHIJKLMNOPQRSTUVWXYZ

684 Spotty Face

ABCDEFGHIJKLMNOPQRSTUVWXYZ&

shaded or 3D

685 Block up

ABCDEFGHIJKLMNOPQRSTUVWXYZ &

Old Glory **676**

1234567890 *no lower case*

Sinaloa **677**

1234567890 *no lower case*

Stripes **678**

1234567890 *no lower case*

Shatter **679**

abcdefghijklmnopqrstuvwxyz 1234567890

Astra **680**

1234567890 *no lower case*

Chequered **681**

1234567890 *no lower case*

Pinball **682**

abcdefghijklmnopqrstuvwxyz1234567890

Spangle **683**

1234567890 *no lower case*

Spotty Face **684**

1234567890 *no lower case*

Block up **685**

1234567890 *no lower case*

686 Bombere

ABCDEFGHIJKLMNOPQRSTUVWXYZ&

687 Buster

ABCDEFGHIJKLMNOPQRSTUVWXYZ&

688 Calypso

ABCDEFGHIJKLMNOPQRSTUVWXYZ

689 Italiennes Ombrees

ABCDEFGHIJKLMNOPQRSTUVWXYZ&

690 Perspective Italic

ABCDEFGHIJKLMNOPQRSTUVWXYZ

691 Speed Caps

ABCDEFGHIJKLMNOPQRSTUVWXYZ&

692 Stack

ABCDEFGHIJKLMNOPQRSTUVWXYZ&

693 Sunshine

no capitals

694 Talbot's Rocky Mountain

ABCDEFGHIJKLMNOPQRSTUVWXYZ&

with backgrounds

695 Good Vibrations

ABCDEFGHIJKLMNOPQRSTUVWXYZ&

Bombere **686**

1234567890 *no lower case*

Buster **687**

1234567890 *no lower case*

Calypso **688**

no lower case or figures

Italiennes Ombrees **689**

1234567890 *no lower case*

Perspective Italic **690**

no lower case or figures

Speed Caps **691**

1234567890 *no lower case*

Stack **692**

1234567890 *no lower case*

Sunshine **693**

abcdefghijklmnopqrstuvwxyz1234567890

Talbot's Rocky Mountain **694**

1234567890 *no lower case*

Good Vibrations **695**

1234567890 *no lower case*

MO

696 Phase Two

697 Process

ABCDEFGHIJKLMNOPQRSTUVWXYZ&

698 Tonal

ABCDEFGHIJKLMNOPQRSTUVWXYZ&

pictorial

699 Via Face Don Black

ABCDEFGHIJKLMNOPQRSTUVWXYZ

700 Zip

ABCDEFGHIJKLMNOPQRSTUVWXYZ&

MODIFIED
OUTRAGEOUS
MO

Phase Two **696**

abcdefghijklmnopqrstuvwxyz1234567890

Process **697**

1234567890 *no lower case*

Tonal **698**

1234567890 *no lower case*

Via Face Don Black **699**

no lower case or figures

Zip **700**

1234567890 *no lower case*

APPENDIX / COMPARATIVE CHART OF 'TYPEFINDER' CLASSIFICATION TO BRITISH STANDARDS CLASSIFICATION (BS 2961: 1967)

'TYPEFINDER' CLASSIFICATION SYSTEM

TEXT TYPEFACE CATEGORIES

1. Sloping e-Bar (Venetian Serif). *Nos 1-34*
Includes all roman, slab and wedge serif faces with a sloping bar on the lower case e, a traditional feature of 'Venetian' typefaces. The mixture of serif-style typefaces in this category means that other characteristics are mixed – for example, typefaces may have either vertical or angled stress and oblique or straight serifs.

e.g. Kennerley, Centaur, ITC Souvenir.

2. Angled Stress/Oblique Serifs (Old Style Serif). *Nos 35-53*
Includes 'Old Style' or 'Old Face' typefaces providing they have the above characteristics and do not possess a sloping bar on the lower case e.

e.g. Bembo, Plantin, Times New Roman.

3. Vertical Stress/Oblique Serifs (Transitional Serif). *Nos 54-110*
Includes 'Transitional' typefaces providing they have these characteristics and do not have a sloping bar on the lower case e. 'Transitional' typefaces with horizontal serifs or abrupt contrast will be found in either Categories 4 or 5.

e.g. Caslon Old Face, Baskerville 169 (Monotype), Garamond (Stempel).

4. Vertical Stress/Straight Serifs (New Transitional Serif). *Nos 111-150*
Contains 'Transitional' typefaces which have straight (horizontal) serifs or nearly so, as well as 'Twentieth Century Roman' typefaces with the same characteristics.

e. g. Joanna, Century Schoolbook, Cheltenham

5. Abrupt Contrast/Straight Serifs (Modern Serif). *Nos 151-187*
Contains 'Modern', 'Transitional' and 'Twentieth Century Romans' with good contrast and straight (horizontal) serifs.

e.g. Bauer Bodoni, Caledonia, Scotch Roman.

6. Slab Serif. *Nos 188-217*
Typefaces of a generally heavy appearance, either with square or bracketed slab serifs. Also includes rounded slab typefaces (typewriter designs).

e.g. Rockwell, Clarendon, ITC American Typewriter

7. Wedge Serif (Hybrid Serif). *Nos 218-240*
Includes some 'Glyphic' typefaces used for continuous text setting plus typefaces with wedge-ended, or wedge-shaped serifs. The category also includes 'hybrid' typefaces which are neither clearly serif nor sans serif in origin.

e.g. Albertus, Meridien, Copperplate Gothic

BRITISH STANDARDS CLASSIFICATION OF TYPEFACES (BS 2961: 1967)

Category		Description	Examples
No.	Name		
I	Humanist	Typefaces in which the cross stroke of the lower case e is oblique; the axis of the curves is inclined to the left; there is no great contrast between thin and thick strokes; the serifs are bracketed; the serifs of the ascenders in the lower case are oblique. NOTE. This was formerly known as 'Venetian', having been derived from the 15th century minuscule written with a varying stroke thickness by means of an obliquely-held broad pen.	Verona, Centaur, Kennerley
II	Garalde	Typefaces in which the axis of the curves is inclined to the left; there is generally a greater contrast in the relative thickness of the strokes than in Humanist designs; the serifs are bracketed; the bar of the lower case e is horizontal; the serifs of the ascenders in the lower case are oblique. NOTE. These are types in the Aldine and Garamond tradition and were formerly called 'Old Face' and 'Old Style'.	Bembo, Garamond, Caslon, Vendôme
III	Transitional	Typefaces in which the axis of the curves is vertical or inclined slightly to the left; the serifs are bracketed, and those of the ascenders in the lower case are oblique. NOTE. This typeface is influenced by the letter-forms of the copperplate engraver. It may be regarded as a transition from Garalde to Didone, and incorporates some characteristics of each.	Fournier, Baskerville, Bell, Caledonia, Columbia
IV	Didone	Typefaces having an abrupt contrast between thin and thick strokes; the axis of the curves is vertical; the serifs of the ascenders of the lower case are horizontal; there are often no brackets to the serifs. NOTE. These are typefaces as developed by Didot and Bodoni. Formerly called 'Modern'.	Bodoni, Corvinus, Modern Extended
V	Slab-serif	Typefaces with heavy, square-ended serifs, with or without brackets.	Rockwell, Clarendon, Playbill

'Typefinder' Classification System devised by Christopher Perfect & Eiichi Kono.

BRITISH STANDARDS CLASSIFICATION OF TYPEFACES (BS 2961: 1967)

Category		Description	Examples
No.	**Name**		
VI	Lineale	Typefaces without serifs. NOTE. Formerly called 'Sans-serif'.	
	a Grotesque	Lineale typefaces with 19th century origins. There is some contrast in thickness of strokes. They have squareness of curve, and curling close-set jaws. The R usually has a curled leg and the G is spurred. The ends of the curved strokes are usually horizontal.	SB Grot. No. 6, Cond. Sans No. 7, Monotype Headline Bold
	b Neo-grotesque	Lineale typefaces derived from the grotesque. They have less stroke contrast and are more regular in design. The jaws are more open than in the true grotesque and the g is often open-tailed. The ends of the curved strokes are usually oblique.	Edel/Wotan, Univers, Helvetica
	c Geometric	Lineale typefaces constructed on simple geometric shapes, circle or rectangle. Usually monoline, and often with single-storey a.	Futura, Erbar, Eurostyle
	d Humanist	Lineale typefaces based on the proportions of inscriptional Roman capitals and Humanist or Garalde lower-case, rather than on early grotesques. They have some stroke contrast, with two-storey a and g.	Optima, Gill Sans, Pascal
VII	Glyphic	Typefaces which are chiselled rather than calligraphic in form.	Latin, Albertus, Augustea
VIII	Script	Typefaces that imitate cursive writing.	Palace Script, Legend, Mistral
IX	Graphic	Typefaces whose characters suggest that they have been drawn rather than written.	Libra, Cartoon, Old English (Monotype)

'TYPEFINDER' CLASSIFICATION SYSTEM

TEXT TYPEFACE CATEGORIES *continued*

8. Sans Serif. *Nos 245-304*

Includes 'Lineale' designs used for continuous text setting arranged according to the width of the capital G and whether or not it has a spur. There are additional groups for square, sloping, rounded and electronic designs.

e.g. Futura, Gill Sans, Unvers.

DECORATIVE (NON-CONTINUOUS TEXT) TYPEFACE CATEGORIES

3. Unmodified (Formal Text Shape). *Nos 382-428*

'Glyphic' typefaces not usually used for continuous text setting will be found here. The category contains serif or sans serif typefaces of a traditional letter shape normally used for titling or headings but not for continuous text setting.

e.g. Engravers Roman, Castellar, Latin Antique No. 9

1. Flowing Scripts *Nos 305-322* and
2. Non-Flowing Scripts *Nos 323-381*

'Script' and 'Graphic' typefaces are to be found in one of these two categories according to whether their letters are joined when typeset and therefore appear 'flowing' like handwriting. The Non-Flowing category includes blackletter and uncial typefaces as well as roman italic typefaces based on pen scripts.

e.g. **1.** Palace Script, Kaufmann, Mistral.
e.g. **2.** Bernhard Tango, Old English Text, Libra.

4. Fat & Thin Face (Modified & Unmodified). *Nos. 429-536*

Includes serif or sans serif typefaces of the extremes in weight – very bold or very light.

e.g. Falstaff, Cooper Black, Harry Thin.

5. Ornamental. *Nos 537-563*

Serif, sans serif or script typefaces of a very elaborately patterned or 'floriated' design.

e.g. Fry's Ornamented, Lettres Ornées, Ballé Initials.

6. Modified Serif. *Nos 564-603*

Serif typefaces of a 'non-formal/traditional' shape.

e.g. Belwe, Profil, Charleston.

7. Modified Sans Serif. *Nos 604-665*

Sans serif typefaces of a 'non-formal/traditional' shape.

e.g. Peignot, Frankfurter Medium, Countdown.

8. Modified Outrageous. *Nos 666-700*

Serif and sans serif typefaces of a highly unusual or 'way out' nature.

e.g. Shatter, Pinball, Calypso.

BIOGRAPHICAL NOTES ON LEADING TYPE DESIGNERS
by Sarah Rookledge

The information that makes up this section has been compiled from sources too numerous to list here. Major ones include D.B. Updike; *Printing Types, Their History, Forms, and Use*, Sebastian Carter; *Twentieth Century Type Designers*, and Geoffrey Dowding; *An Introduction to the History of Printing Types*.

Ludovico degli Arrighi da Vincenzia, d.c1527
Blado italic, 380

Ludovico degli Arrighi, who lived in Rome, was a professional calligrapher, and later a printer of fine editions, who also designed type. In 1524 he started a small press with Lautitius Perusinus, a printer but also an engraver and as such probably the cutter of the types. They printed fine editions of short contemporary works using type based on Arrighi's formal cursive script. The type was later acquired by Antonio Blado who gives his name to its contemporary version.

Richard Austin and John Bell, 1746-1831
Bell, 172
Scotch Roman, 185/186

In 1788, inspired by Fournier's types, John Bell, a newspaper publisher and pioneer of cheap editions of the classics, started The British Letter Foundry and issued his first type specimen, cut by Richard Austin. A skilful cutter, Austin produced a very sharp letter which Stanley Morison called the first English modern face. Actually the type retains some old style characteristics and should more properly be called a late transitional. Austin went on to cut true moderns, though in 1819 when he had started a foundry of his own he outlined the dangers of such designs being taken to extremes.

The British Letter Foundry closed in 1798. Between this date and Austin's setting up The Imperial Letter Foundry in Worship Street, London he cut types for the Wilson Foundry in Glasgow and for William Miller in Edinburgh. The Miller & Richards types known as the Scotch Romans are probably his work. Austin also worked as a cutter of typographical ornaments.

John Baskerville, 1706-1775
Baskerville, 77-80

John Baskerville's contribution to printing is enormous. He adapted the old face roman to produce highly influential new types; he recognised the important role of typography in book design; he modified inks and the printing press to give blacker, sharper letters on the page and may also be responsible for the introduction of wove paper (though he sold it for writing not printing). Baskerville's work influenced Continental printers like Didot and Bodoni but in his native England it was frequently derided.

Like Caslon, John Baskerville was born in Worcestershire but in 1725 he moved to Birmingham where he worked as a writing master and did some stone engraving. He cut inscriptions on gravestones. Later, when he was to design his own types, he could use the knowledge of lettering he acquired in this period. He taught writing for ten years, then decided to take advantage of the fashion for japanned ornaments (japanning is a method of decorating which gives a glossy finish). The business prospered and made Baskerville a prominent figure in Birmingham society.

In 1750, he set up a printing press but the pace of work and the exacting standards he set himself were such that it was to take him seven years before that press produced its first book. Existing types, inks and presses did not meet his standards. Despite lacking any printing background he determined to create his own. By 1752 he had cut fourteen letters. By 1753 he had enough type to produce an advertisement for his first book, a fine edition of Virgil. The book itself appeared in 1757, as did another specimen sheet, this time showing four sizes of roman.

Baskerville's type was much criticised in England and compared unfavourably to Caslon's. People said it was difficult to read, even that it would damage the sight, but it also had its advocates, notably Benjamin Franklin. The Bible which Baskerville printed (on special dispensation from the Cambridge University Press) brought him great acclaim on the Continent. The appearance of Baskerville's books, unlike those of most of his contemporaries, did not depend on illustrations. He achieved his effects through good types cleanly printed, and a judicious use of leading and letter spacing. Other printers, most notably Bodoni, followed his lead in this.

Baskerville died in 1735 and his wife Sarah sold his remaining stock to Beaumarchais for an edition of the works of Voltaire. His punches eventually came into the hands of Deberny & Peignot who made new matrices from them for their version of Baskerville. In 1953 they presented the punches to the Cambridge University Press.

John Bell, see Richard Austin

Morris Fuller Benton, 1872-1948
Century Schoolbook, 119
Franklin Gothic, 276
News Gothic, 287

Morris Fuller Benton was the son of Linn Boyd Benton, inventor of the pantographic punchcutting machine and cutter of Century for Theodore De Vinne's magazine *The Century*. Like his father, Morris Benton worked for American Typefounders (ATF); he joined Linn Boyd Benton as his assistant in ATF's type design department. This was the first department of its kind in a foundry and had been set up by his father at the instigation of ATF's director Robert Nelson. Benton has been credited with inventing the concept of the type family, and although this is not the case he did do his best work expanding faces into families and adapting existing type styles. Between 1900 and 1928 he designed eighteen variations on Century, including the popular Century Schoolbook (1924). Other Benton types include: Franklin Gothic (1903) and News Gothic (1980).

Giovanni Battista Bodoni, 1740-1813
Bodoni, 154/162/163

Bodoni is one of the first cutters of a modern face; that is, a typeface which has hairline serifs at right angles to the uprights, vertical stress and abrupt contrast between thick and thin strokes. He took French types, such as Fournier's and those of the Didot's as his models. Bodoni was, in his day, the best known printer in Europe.

Bodoni was born in Saluzzo in Piedmont in the north of Italy in 1740, the son of a printer. He was apprenticed to be a compositor at the press of Properganda Fide in Rome but left after the suicide of the Director. At 28 he was made Director of the press of the Duke of Parma, the last of the Ducal private presses.

His early types are based on those of Pierre Simon Fournier, whose work he admired, but he experimented with these letter forms to create his own. The roman letter he cut in 1798 is what we generally mean by a Bodoni. The contrast of light and shade in his types can produce a sparkling effect on the page. The books which he printed reveal a taste for large sizes of type, generous use of white space and few ornaments. In addition to his romans Bodoni also produced a great many script types.

Bodoni set out his principles of typography (although stated in vague and general terms) in his *Manual Tipographico*. This book was completed by his wife and she published it in 1818, five years after his death.

Bodoni's faces appear today in two main recuttings: American Typefounders' and Bauer. The ATF version was cut by M. F. Benton and copied with minor variations by The Monotype Corporation, Haas, Linotype, Intertype, and Ludlow. The more delicate Bauer version is used by Bauer alone.

Margaret Calvert, see Jock Kinneir

Ron Carpenter, b.1950
Calisto, 53A
Cantoria, 240A

Ron Carpenter joined Monotype in 1968 where he trained as a type draftsman. His first experience of typeface design was working on the italic for Nimrod with Robin Nicholas. Since becoming Senior Type Designer in 1984 he has been responsible for designing Cantoria and Calisto and new weights for Times New Roman.

Matthew Carter, b.1937
Auriga, 151
Bell Centenial, 284
Galliard, 74
Olympian, 71
Video, 283

Matthew Carter is the son of printing historian Harry Carter who was archivist to the Oxford University Press. He was taught by Jan Van Krimpen's assistant and worked for Crossfield Electronics and Mergenthaler Linotype, designing Bell Centenial for the latter in 1978. Also in 1978, he designed Galliard with Mike Parker and in 1981 they set up Bitstream to supply new type designs in digital form. Bitstream Charter is the first new design they have issued.

William Caslon, 1692-1766
Caslon, 59-61/99/383/391/445

Worcestershire-born William Caslon began his career engraving and chasing gun barrels (occasionally also cutting brass letters for bookbinders) until a printer called William Bowyer who had seen some of his letters encouraged him to try punchcutting. Bowyer was so confident Caslon would succeed at it he, and two other printers, lent him £500 to start his own foundry which opened in about 1716.

Caslon was the first British typefounder of any reknown. Previously British printers were dependent mainly on imported types, chiefly Dutch and French. In 1722 he produced his second type, a roman based on Dutch models. With the publication of his first specimen sheet in 1734 he became immediately successful. Unlike those of John Baskerville Caslon's designs were not innovative; similar types were in use a hundred years earlier; but it was his skills as an engraver that distinguished him. His roman quickly established itself as a popular book face.

In 1766 the Oxford University Press bought Caslon type to supplement the Fell types. He published further sheets and, later, books of his types. His work found particular favour in America and Caslon type was used by Mary Katherine Goddard of Baltimore for the printing of the Declaration of Independence.

The Caslon foundry continued under the directorship of successive William Caslons until the death of the last male Caslon in 1873. The company remained in existence, for much of the time in the same Chiswell Street premises in London, until 1936. Its stock was bought up by Stephenson Blake and Company.

Thomas J. Cobden Sanderson, 1840-1922, and Emery Walker, 1851-1933

Thomas Cobden Sanderson, an important member of the Arts and Crafts movement in the late nineteenth and early twentieth centuries founded The Doves Press in 1901, with the typographer Emery Walker. Emery Walker had also worked for William Morris, as his typographical consultant. (The name Doves came from a local inn.)

Unfortunately an initially productive relationship degenerated into bitter quarrels, mainly over Doves, the press's own type, which was based on a Jenson type of 1476. Both partners had worked on Doves and each claimed authorship for himself. In 1912 as a result of this dispute, Cobden Sanderson smashed the matrices and dropped the type into the River Thames over Hammersmith Bridge.

François-Ambroise Didot, 1730-1804
Pierre-François Didot, 1732-95
and Firmin Didot, 1766-1836
Didot, 156

The Didot family of Paris dominated the French book world in the late eighteenth and early nineteenth centuries. Its members were involved in printing, publishing, type-founding, punchcutting and paper manufacture. Among their contributions were what is generally agreed to be the first modern face and a reform of the point system of type measurement.
Its most notable members are François-Ambroise, Pierre-François and François-Ambroise's younger son Firmin. Didot's roman types were the standard book types used in France during the nineteenth century and are still in general use today.

F-A Didot initially printed with Garamond types but began to produce his own in about 1775. In 1784 the first modern face appeared in an edition of Tasso's *Gerusalemme Liberata*. It is characterised by thin serifs, vertical stress and abrupt shading from thick strokes to thin. By this time the Didots were using wove paper and an improved printing press which allowed the fine details of such type to be reproduced. This important type was cut in 1783 by F. A. Didot's son Firmin, then 19. Firmin took over from his father's previous punchcutter Pierre Louis Wafflard. François-Ambroise was also the Director of the *Imprimerie National* and in this capacity he revised Fournier's point system. His name survives in the Continental didot point.

William Addison Dwiggins, 1880-1956
Caledonia, 174
Electra, 148
Metro, 263

Dwiggins had a varied career that took in illustration, printing, advertising and book design. He began designing types when he was 44 at the invitation of Mergenthaler Linotype. His first type was a sans serif, Metro. His best known face is Caledonia which fuses aspects of the Scotch Romans and the types cut for Bulmer by William Martin.

He wrote widely on design matters; Mergenthaler Linotype's idea for a Dwiggins sans serif came from reading him on sans serif faces in one of his books *Layout in Advertising* (Harper, 1928). In 1929 he was awarded the American Institute of Graphic Arts Gold Medal.

Dr. John Fell, 1625-86

Dr Fell was Bishop of Oxford, Dean of Christ Church and Vice Chancellor of Oxford University. With three others (and for an annual payment of £200) he took over the management of the University Press in 1671. Between 1667 and 1672 he imported types, punches and matrices which were bought in Holland on his behalf by Thomas Marshall. These included some Granjon types and some supplied by Van Dijck. In 1676 he set up a type foundry attached to the press and employed a Dutch typecutter, Peter Walpergen. A specimen sheet was issued by the press in 1693, and the types became known as the Fell Types.

Pierre Simon Fournier, 1712-1768
Barbou, 89
Fournier, 90

Pierre Simon Fournier, also known as Fournier le jeune, made several important contributions to the field of type design. He set up his own foundry in Paris where he cut and founded all the types himself, pioneered the concept of the type family and is said to have cut 60,000 punches for 147 alphabets of his own design. He created new printers flowers and ornaments that caught the mood of his age. He invented a point system for standardising type sizes and published it in its first version when he was only 25. (The Didot system used on the Continent today was developed from Fournier's and retained the name of his unit, the point, while fractionally increasing its size). Not surprisingly perhaps Fournier's death at 56 was attributed to overwork. He is probably best remembered as the designer of one of the earliest transitional faces. His St. Augustine Ordinair served as the model for Monotype's Fournier of 1925. Another, version, Barbou, was issued in 1968, the bicentenary of his death.

Adrian Frutiger, b.1928
Apollo, 133
Brueghel, 113
Egyptienne, 210
Frutiger, 266/489
Icone, 223
Iridium, 149
OCR-B, 304
Ondine, 336
Serifa, 198/518
Univers, 267/481/498

Adrian Frutiger is one of the most important type designers to emerge since World War II. Now living just outside Paris, he was born near Interlaken in Switzerland. He was apprenticed as a compositor and later studied wood-cutting and calligraphy before coming to the attention of Charles Peignot of Deberny and Peignot who asked him to adapt Futura.

Finding Futura too geometric, and wanting to design a sans serif with a large, matched, family of weights, Frutiger designed the twenty-one weights of Univers which was issued in 1955. Many founders and designers have followed this idea and have since produced large sans serif families of their own.

Frutiger's other designs do not confine themselves to sans serifs. Apollo is new transitional, Serifa is a slab serif, and OCR-B could be termed experimental.

The face, named after him, Frutiger, was developed from a design he used at Roissy Airport near Paris. While its weights follow the numbered form of Univers, it is much more humanistic in feel.

Aside from type design, Frutiger also designs books and periodicals, and lectures. Among his writings is *Type, Sign, Symbol* (ABE Editions, Zurich).

In 1986 he received the Gutenberg Prize for technical and aesthetic achievement in type.

Joseph Fry; 1728-1787, and Isaac Moore
Fry's Baskerville, 54

Joseph Fry was a Birmingham man by birth who, like Baskerville, came to typefounding relatively late in his career and was also successful in other fields (among his numerous business ventures he started Fry's chocolates).

In 1764, while living in Bristol, Fry decided to go into partnership with a local printer, William Pine, and set up a foundry attached to Pine's print works. Isaac Moore, previously a whitesmith (that is, a metal finisher) was taken on to cut types for them and later became a partner. Moore cut his types after Baskerville's (though they're not close copies) and the foundry's early types are all of this kind.

In 1770 they published their second specimen sheet which shows a much more extensive selection of type sizes than their first and a number of ornaments. In 1776 Moore retired and the foundry produced Caslon style types in preference to Baskerville's.

Claude Garamond, c1480-1561
Garamond, 91-94
Garamont, 96

Claude Garamond was the first person to specialise in the design and cutting of type on a large scale. The roman letters he designed at his Paris foundry took the Aldine (see Aldus Manutius, and the introduction to category 2, p24) roman as their model, but improved upon it; the 'fit' of the letters together was better and the capitals, lower case and italic were better balanced to give a comprehensive and harmonious fount of type.

These types were much copied; by the end of the sixteenth century they had become the standard European type and they were still in use in the eighteenth century. Garamond cut the Grecs du roi letters for Francois I of France but other printers could use them with the King's permission. He is credited with the roman types used by the publishers Estienne from 1532 onwards. Three other French publishers also used related founts around this time. The *caractères de l'université* at the *Imprimerie Royale* were attributed to him until Beatrice Warde proved them to be a later type in the Garamond style cut by Jean Jannon.

In 1545 Garamond began publishing on his own account using types of his own design including a new italic cut in two sizes. His first book was the *Pia et religiosa meditatio* of David Chambellan. After Garamond's death in 1561 his stock was sold off. Among those buying type from the foundry was Christopher Plantin of Antwerp.

Arthur Eric Rownton Gill, 1882-1940
Bunyan/Pilgrim, 183
Floriated Capitals, 538
Gill Sans, 259/425/427-8/476/482
Joanna, 111
Perpetua, 116/438

Gill was born in Brighton, the son of a nonconformist minister. He studied at Chichester School of Art before being apprenticed to the ecclesiastical architect W. D. Caröe in London. While in London he attended classes taught by the calligrapher Edward Johnston at the Central School of Arts and Crafts. Gill was greatly inspired by Johnston's work and the two men became good friends. Gill cut inscriptions for Caröe but also fulfilled commissions from members of the Art Workers Guild and eventually ended his apprenticeship to pursue this work. During his career he also created woodcuts and engravings for Harry Kessler's Cranach Press in Weimar, the St Dominic's Press, owned by Hilary Peplar, and Robert and Moira Gibbins's Golden Cockerel Press.

Gill left London in 1907 to live in Ditchling, Sussex; later he moved to Capel-y-Ffin in the Welsh mountains and finally Piggotts near High Wycombe.

He designed his first typeface at the invitation of Stanley Morison of the Monotype Corporation. The drawings for this type, Perpetua, were begun in 1925. Morison had made the request because he felt Gill's background in cutting stone inscriptions would give him an understanding of serifs. Charles Malin, punchcutter of the French foundry Deberny and Peignot converted Gill's drawings into type.

Gill Sans was influenced by Edward Johnston's Railway Type though Gill distinguished the two faces by saying that his own was designed to be read as a text face whereas Johnston's was intended purely for signs. Gill had used sans serif lettering for signs at Capel-y-Ffin and for the lettering on a Bristol bookshop owned by Douglas Cleverdon, which Gill painted in 1927. It was this bookshop sign which suggested the idea of a Gill sans serif to Morison.

Joanna, a much praised face, was named after his daughter Joan and designed for Hague and Gill, the printing partnership formed by Gill himself and Joan's husband René Hague. It was first used in 1931. In 1938 J. M. Dent bought the exclusive rights to Joanna and the face was not issued to the trade until 1958.

Bunyan, 1934, was Gill's last roman face. An adaptation by American Linotype was issued in 1953 and called Pilgrim.

In 1935 Gill was made an Associate of the Institute of British Architects. Two years later he was made an Associate of the Royal Academy. In 1939 he was among the first group to be given the title Royal Designer for Industry. He died at home the following year after a lung operation.

Frederick W. Goudy, 1865-1947
Goudy Catalogue, 49
Goudy Fancy, 547
Goudy Handtooled, 394
Goudy Modern, 132
Goudy Old Style, 37
Goudy Text, 368
Kennerly Old Style, 6

Frederick Goudy, one of the best known and most prolific of type designers, was born in Bloomington, Illinois in 1865. He became interested in type through the work of the English private presses.

His Kennerly Old Style, produced for New York publishers Mitchell Kennerly in 1911 and a set of titling, Forum, produced at the same time established his reputation and were particularly popular in England. American Type Founders commissioned him to design a face for them and the result was Goudy Old Style. In 1920 Lanston Monotype appointed Goudy as Art Advisor and it was in this capacity that he worked on the revival Garamond.

Goudy had a particular interest in blackletter. His best known such type is Goudy Text. He designed over 100 faces, by his own reckoning (though he counts each italic as a separate face), and perhaps as a result his output was uneven in quality. One of his favourite faces was his last major one; California Old Style (now Berkley Old Style). Goudy died at his home, a water-mill on the Hudson River, in 1947.

Phillippe Grandjean, 1666-1714

Philippe Grandjean de Fouchy was born of an old Mâcon family, and became interested in type design after a chance visit to a Parisian printers. He was recommended to Louis XIV and began working for the Royal Printing Office, the *Imprimerie Royal*, under its director Jean Anisson.

In 1792 Louis XIV appointed a committee from the *Acadêmie des Sciences* to draw up plans for a new typeface which would be the exclusive property of the *Imprimerie Royal*. The committee studied types then in current use, historical manuscripts and principles of geometry. The letter designs it then drew up were based on divisions of the circle. The type was to be called the Romains du Roi (the King's roman). Philippe Grandjean was assigned as punch-cutter and created types which were based on the drawings but did not follow them rigidly.

The Romains du Roi is a significant development in the history of typography because it was the first real departure from the old style faces in use in Europe at the time of its creation. It is thus the first transitional face.

Robert Granjon, 1513-1589

Robert Granjon was the son of Jean Granjon, a Paris printer. His principal work was the design and supply of type but he also printed, going into partnership with Michael Fezendat in 1549.

Granjon began supplying types while in Paris in the 1540s; moved to Lyon in 1557; later to Antwerp and finally to Rome where his clients included the New Vatican Press.

Many of Granjon's types were adopted enthusiastically by European printers, most notably Christopher Plantin. In recent times they have provided the model for Monotype's Plantin 1913 and Times New Roman 1932 as well as Matthew Carter's Galliard, however Granjon, the face that was named after him in a 1924 Linotype revival, is based on a Garamond type.

Chauncey H. Griffiths, 1879-1956

Bell Gothic, 285
Corona, 120
Excelsior, 115
Paragon, 144

In his position as Vice-President of Typographic Development for the Mergenthaler Company of New York, Chauncey H. Griffith was responsible for instigating many new designs. He is best known for the Legibility Group: Ionic, Excelsior, Paragon, Opticon and Corona, all newspaper types. Ionic, designed in 1922, was the first of the series and in 1930 it was adopted by the restyled *Daily Herald*. Excelsior has been described as one of the most influential newspaper faces of all time.

Two designers who worked under his direction were W. A. Dwiggins and Rudolph Ruzicka.

During his time with the company it issued revivals of Granjon, Baskerville, and Janson, and Griffiths also helped prepare Bell Gothic for the Bell Telephone Company. He retired in 1949 but continued to work for Linotype as a consultant.

Francesco Griffo, see Aldus Manutius

Johann Gutenberg, c 1394-1468

Johann Gutenberg of Mainz in Germany is generally believed to be the first European printer, though there are those who credit the invention to Laurents Coster of Haarlem. The invention, which probably took place around 1450, would have involved bringing together several existing techniques: the screw press, oil based pigments, the metal working skills of punch-cutting, and casting.

The principal work produced by Gutenberg's Mainz press was the *Forty-two-line Bible* in 1455, a Latin Bible which gets its name from the number of lines to a page.

The Textura typeface used in the Forty-two-line Bible was later the inspiration for Goudy's Goudy Text.

Jean Jannon, 1580-1658

Jean Jannon was a printer and punchcutter who worked in Sedan and Paris in the seventeenth century. He was the cutter of the *Imprimerie Nationale* Caractères de l'université which were once attributed to Garamond.

Nicholas Jenson, 1420-1480

Jenson, 16

Nicholas Jenson was one of the first printers to use type based on the model of traditional roman letter rather than the dark gothic type used in earlier German printed books.

Although known for his work in Venice, Nicholas Jenson was a Frenchman, born in Sommevoire in the district of Champagne around 1420. He served an apprenticeship in the Paris Mint and was promoted to be Master of the Mint at Tours. Apparently Charles VII sent Jenson to Mainz in 1458 in order that he should discover more about the new invention of printing. From his return to France in 1461 and his first publications in Venice in 1470, nothing is known of him.

In his first year of publishing, Jenson published Eusebius' *De evangelica praeparatione*, Justinus *Epitomata*, Cicero *Epistole ad atticum* and Cicero *Rheorica & De Inventione*. He continued to publish regularly until his death in September 1480. Around 155 editions exist known to be printed by Jenson or attributed to his press.

Jenson's faces had a great influence when a revival of interest in printing and typography took place in the late nineteenth and early twentieth centuries. Among the faces that took his as a model were Morris's Golden, Doves (of the Doves Press), Centaur, Cloister Old Style, Eusebius and Italian Old Style.

Edward Johnston, 1872-1944

Imprint, 67

Edward Johnston came to type designing from a background in calligraphy. He became interested in calligraphy as a young man, rapidly became a central figure in the Arts and Craft movement at the turn of the century and was instrumental in the revival of calligraphy. Among his notable designs are the initial capitals for the Doves Press Folio Bible.

In 1899 he began teaching writing and illuminating at the Central School of Arts and Crafts in London. Among his pupils were type designers Ernst F. Detterer and Eric Gill.

In 1915 Johnston was commissioned by Pick to design what has become his best known face: Johnston's Railway Type, for the exclusive use of London Underground. It is a sans serif face based on classical Roman forms rather than on the nineteenth century grotesques. This face was later to provide the inspiration for Gill's Gill Sans.

George W. Jones, 1860-1942

Granjon, 66

English Linotype made G.W. Jones their printing advisor in 1921 to help them plan a series of type revivals. They were the first British foundry to create such a position (Monotype were to follow with the appointment of Stanley Morison). Jones designed Granjon (1924) as a rival to Monotype Garamond, and named it in honour of Robert Granjon, the sixteenth century punchcutter. He also designed Venezia in 1928 and Estienne in 1930.

Jones lectured on letterpress in Britain and the United States. He was a founder of the British Typographia – an association for printing education, and helped found the journal, *British Printer*.

Jock Kinneir, b.1917, and Margaret Calvert, b.1936

Transport, 282

Jock Kinneir worked for the Design Research Unit and was involved with the Festival of Britain. In 1956 he began working alone and took on one of his students, Margaret Calvert, who became a partner in 1964.

They designed the sign system and lettering at Gatwick Airport in the mid 1950's using a highly legible sans serif face which they refined and used on the motorway and road networks, British Rail and the British Airports Authority.

Margaret Calvert designed the typeface that bears her name in the late 1970's, a slab-serif, it developed from lettering designed for the Tyne and Wear Metro.

Gunter Gerhard Lange, b.1921
Concorde, 100
Concorde Nova, 64
Imago, 274

Gunter Gerhard Lange, born in 1921, is artistic director of the foundry of H. Berthold AG. Under his direction the company has issued original typefaces at a rate as high as one new face a month. Many of those designs are by Lange himself and those he does not design he still corrects by hand. Lange has also adapted classic typefaces such as Baskerville, Caslon, Walbaum, Bodoni and Garamond for film setting.

Aldus Manutius; 1450-1515, and Francesco Griffo; d.1519
Bembo, 35
Poliphilus, 40

Aldus Manutius, the great Renaissance printer and publisher, was born in 1450 in the Duchy of Sermoneta. He spent the early part of his career working under the patronage of the Count Alberto Pio, Prince of Carpi, but left Carpi for Venice in 1489 to further his ambition of publishing Greek classics in the original. While the market for Latin editions in Italy was overcrowded the opposite was true of Greek works and in Venice he had access to collections of fine manuscripts. His types were cut and (it is now generally believed) designed for him by Francesco Griffo. His first publications came out in 1484: an edition of the *Galyeomyomachia* and Musaeus' *De Herone et Leandro*.

The first Aldine roman is the type used in Cardinal Bembo's *De Aetna*, published in 1495. Stanley Morison demonstrated that Claude Garamond used it as the basis for his types, and this makes it the first of the old face types. Monotype have produced two faces based on Manutius' designs. Poliphilus (1923) is a facsimile revival of the type used in the *Hypnerotomachia Poliphili* of 1499 whilst Bembo (1929) is based on the *De Aetna* type.

Aldus published on a large scale (a letter of his refers to a thousand or more volumes a month) and amassed a considerable fortune, aided by a number of copyrights and monopolies which the College of Venice had granted him. He helped to popularise many works by using an octavo format which made his books cheaper and more portable. Francesco Griffo had a dispute with Aldus, whom he claimed had not given him sufficient credit for the types and this dispute over authorship of the so-called Aldine types was later taken up by type scholars.

Aldus died at 65 in his house in the Venetian printing quarter of San Paternian and his body lay in state there surrounded by copies of his books. Francesco Griffo died some time around 1518/19. The cause and exact date of his death are not known but it seems likely that he was hanged as a punishment for killing his brother-in-law, which he did with an iron bar in May 1518 during a fight.

Dr. Hans (also Giovanni) Mardersteig, 1892-1977
Dante, 102
Fontana, 65

Hans Mardersteig was both a scholar and a printer. He researched in Renaissance printing, focusing particularly on the work of Francesco Griffo. He is best known for the work of the private press which he founded, the *Officina Bodoni*, but after World War II he added a commercial press, the *Stamparia Valdonega*.

Many of the types used at the Officina were of Mardersteig's design. They were cut for him by the Paris punchcutter Charles Malin, a productive collaboration, and although Mardersteig continued working until he was 86 his type designing ceased with Malin's death in 1955. Mardersteig's best known type are Fontana and Dante. The first was designed not for the Officina but for the publishers William Collins of Glasgow.

William Martin, d.1815
Bulmer, 58

William Martin was the brother of Robert Martin, Baskerville's punchcutter. William too trained under Baskerville, whose types clearly influenced his own. William Martin's types are cut more sharply than his teacher's and more closely approach the modern face. He is said to have cut the last of the transitionals.

Martin's types were cut for the printer William Bulmer (1757-1830), and being sharply cut were a good choice, since they combined well with engravings and appeared to advantage in the large formats he favoured.

M. F. Benton cut a replica of a Martin type cut for the Shakespeare Press around 1790. This replica, Bulmer, was cut for A.T.F. in 1928.

Max Miedinger,
Neu Haas Grotesque/Helvetica, 279/422/477/493-4/529-530/620/624

Max Miedinger of Zurich was an in-house designer with the Haas Foundry in Munchenstein, Switzerland. In 1956 he was asked to adapt the existing Haas Grotesk and bring it up to date, but the type which was produced from his china ink drawings seemed like a new design. Originally New Haas Grotesque, it became known as Helvetica when released by Stempel A.G. in 1961. It is the most widely available sans serif.

Isaac Moore, see Joseph Fry

Stanley Morison, 1889-1967
Times New Roman, 52/53

Morison was the typographical consultant to the Monotype Corporation and directed its programme of revivals. Monotype was not alone among foundries in reviving historic types and it had already begun to do so before Morison joined the Corporation. Nonetheless Morison, a largely self-taught scholar of printing and typographic history, brought an informed enthusiasm to the work. His interest in types also embraced contemporary designs and he was responsible for commissioning original faces from Eric Gill (whom he introduced to type design) and Jan Van Krimpen.

Stanley Morison designed only one type but that face, which he called Times New Roman, is more commonly used today than any other. It rose rapidly to this position after its launch in the redesigned *Times* newspaper which first appeared on 3rd October 1932.

William Morris, 1834-1896

William Morris was a key figure in the Arts and Crafts movement of the late nineteenth century but did not involve himself in printing and typography until he was approaching the end of his career. In 1890 Morris founded the Kelmscott Press and in 1891 it became established in its own premises. It was always intended as a small private press; he used type which was cut by a hand punchcutter and hand set; hand presses, and he also printed on dampened handmade paper.

Morris designed two types for the press. Golden was the result of his early drawings of Venetian types and it was the more influential. He planned to use it for an edition of *The Golden Legend*, hence the name. Golden sparked off the interest in Jenson revivals.

His other face is a Fere-humanisticas (an informal blackletter) for the Kelmscott Chaucer. This face came in two sizes known as Troy and Chaucer. Morris's punchcutter for the types was E. P. Prince, and Emery Walker, later of the Doves Press, worked as Morris's typographic consultant.

Robin Nicholas, b.1947
Nimrod, 122

Robin Nicholas has been the manager of the Monotype Corporation's type drawing office since 1982. Between 1978 and 1980 he designed Nimrod, a group of related roman faces designed for newspaper text, headlines and small ads. Nimrod has been widely praised for its legibility and is used by *The Guardian*, *Daily Telegraph* and *Today*. He has also supervised the redesign of many Monotype faces such as Bell, Centaur and Janson for the Lasercomp system.

Aldo Novarese, b.1920
Augustea, 171/409/416
Eurostile, 291-2
Microgramma, 294
Novarese, 226/264

Aldo Novarese has designed most of his types for the Nebolio Art Studio in Turin which he joined at 16. Augustea and Microgramma are among those he designed in partnership with Alessandro Butti (1893-1959), while the type that bears his name, Novarese, was designed for Haas. In Italy he is also known as a writer on type and he contributes to a number of design and graphics publications.

George Peignot, d.1914, and Charles Peignot, 1897-1983

George and Charles Peignot were father and son. George took over the Paris type foundry Deberny and Peignot from his father Gustave, and Charles took over in his turn when George and his brothers died in World War I. Both men had a policy of commissioning types from contemporary graphic artists. The Swiss designer Adrian Frutiger worked for Charles Peignot. The type that bears their name, Peignot (1936), was designed for the foundry by the poster artist A.M. Cassandre.

Charles Peignot was extremely active in the cause of typeface copyright and to this end he helped found the *Association Typographique International.*

Charles' son Remy is a type designer. He designed Cristal, a titling face, in 1957.

Frank Hinman Pierpont, 1860-1937
Plantin, 39

Although American, Frank Hinman Pierpont spent most of his career working for English Monotype as the manager of their Salford works in Surrey. He adapted existing type designs to suit Monotype machines, aided by the German Fritz Steltzer. In 1913 they designed Plantin which is based on a face from the Plantin Moretus Museum (although this face was never used by the great Antwerp printer of that name). Pierpont and Steltzer wanted a large-bodied face and they designed Plantin with ink-spread in mind so that it would print well on smooth and coated papers.

Pierpont, a founder executive of Monotype, had reservations about the Corporation's revivals programme. After Morison's appointment by Monotype as their advisor there was a certain amount of friction between the two men. Pierpont regarded the Salford works as his domain and he resented what he saw as Morison's interference.

Christopher Plantin, 1514/20-1589
Plantin, 39

Although Christopher Plantin was born in France it is his work in the Netherlands that made him famous. He began his working life as a bookbinder, first in Caen and then in Paris. It was probably during his time in Paris that he learnt how to print.

In 1548/9 he settled in Antwerp and was soon established as one of the foremost North European publishers and printers.

Although Plantin himself did not design type he was very interested in its selection. He collected type, punches and matrices, buying from, among others, Robert Granjon and Claude Garamond. He has given his name to Plantin, a face designed for Monotype by F. H. Pierpont.

Friedrich Poppl, 1923-1982
Poppl Laudatio, 227
Poppl Pontifex, 85

Friedrich Poppl became known as a calligrapher in the 1960's, when his work was shown in several important exhibitions, but not until the release of Poppl-Pontifex in 1976-9 did he achieve recognition as a type designer. His types were commissioned by Berthold at the instigation of its artistic director Gunter Gerhard Lange.

Paul Renner, 1878-1956
Futura, 254/502/526
Futura Black, 636
Topic, 614

Paul Renner was the designer of Futura: issued by the Bauer foundry in Frankfurt. It was the leading sans serif face for 25 years and still remains popular. Futura was conceived on geometrical principles which Renner modified as the design developed. It was originally cut with a number of experimental forms for some letters which were cut as alternative sorts. Their unfamiliar shapes were not taken up by the trade and were abandoned in later cuttings although Futura retains a single-bowled a.

Bruce Rodgers, 1870-1957
Centaur, 19

Born in Lafayette, Indiana, Bruce Rodgers was a book designer who occasionally designed type. His early work was influenced by William Morris's Kelmscott Press style, although he then developed his own.

At the Riverside Press, Boston, he designed his first type, the Jenson-based Montaigne, for a three-volume edition of the essays of Montaigne, published by the Press 1902-4. He is best known for Centaur which takes as its model the Jenson type used in Eusebius *De evangelica praeparatione* (1470).

A critical reportt Rodgers prepared for Cambridge University on the use of type in the University Press led to their eventual appointment of a type consultant – Stanley Morison.

Sumner Stone, b. 1945

Sumner Stone is Director of Typography at Adobe Systems Incorporated in California. At college he studied mathematics and calligraphy (learning the latter from the calligrapher Lloyd Reynolds in Oregon). He has worked as lettering artist for Hallmark Cards but joined Adobe in 1984. Adobe are the originators of the computer page description language Postscript and it was for Adobe he designed Stone, a family consisting of a roman, a sans serif and an informal.

George Trump, 1896-1985
City, 192
Codex, 334
Schadow Antigua, 203
Trump Mediaeval, 44

George Trump was a teacher of graphics and a type designer with a particular interest in script types. He taught at the Advanced School of Book Printing in Berlin and just before World War II began designing type for the Weber Foundry in Stuttgart. He retired from teaching in 1953 but continued to design type. His most important typeface, Trump Mediaeval dates from this period.

Jan Tschichold, 1902-1974
Sabon, 88

The son of a sign writer, Jan Tschichold spent his teenage years studying calligraphy, typography and engraving. His work at this time was influenced by the types of the Italian Renaissance and blackletter but in 1923 he saw the Bauhaus Exhibition at Weimar. He became the best known publicist and practitioner of the 'new typography' that developed in Europe between the wars. He advocated assymmetric layouts and sans serif typefaces and rejected revivals of historic styles of type as 'fancy dress'.

Later in his career he was to revise such pronouncements, finding them too doctrinaire. Tschichold designed only one widely used type, Sabon. His views were popularised by his writings, particularly *Die neue Typographie* (The New Typography) and *Typographische Gestaltung* (Assymmetric Typography).

Later in his career he was to revise such pronouncements, finding them too doctrinaire. He worked for Penguin Books in London between 1947 and 1949 and was responsible for establishing design guidelines and series styles. In the 1960's he designed the Garamond-derived Sabon.

In 1958 he was awarded the Institute of Graphic Arts Gold Medal and was made an Honorary Royal Designer for Industry by the Royal Society of Arts in 1965.

Cristoffel Van Dijck, 1601-1672
Van Dijck, 107

Cristoffel Van Dijck (also Dyck) was a celebrated Dutch type founder whose work is associated with the golden age of Dutch printing. His type foundry was established in 1648. In 1937 Stanley Morison and Van Krimpen designed a face called Van Dijck for Monotype. This is based on a type used in a 1671 Ovid attributed to his foundry.

Jan Van Krimpen, 1892-1958
Cancelleresca Bastarda, 381
Lutetia, 25
Romulus, 105
Spectrum, 97

After studying at the Academy of Art in the Hague Jan Van Krimpen worked as a freelance designer and illustrator. At 31 his work was spotted by Dr Johannes Enschedé of the Joh. Enschedé en Zohen in Haarlem, Holland. Enschedé asked him to design a new type for his company, and was so pleased with the result he invited Van Krimpen to join them as one of their house designers. He was to stay with the company until his retirement.

Van Krimpen was a skilled calligrapher but believed calligraphy and type design to be essentially different and his types show little calligraphic influence. His letter forms have been described as 'austerely restrained'. Although beautiful and influential they are not widely used.

Van Krimpen did not confine himself to type design but was also a notable book designer, working for Enschedé and fulfilling commissions from other presses.

Justus Erich Walbaum, 1768-1839

Walbaum, 161/167/168/187

Justus Erich Walbaum had his own letter foundry, first based in Goslar and later in Weimar. His faces were neo-classical, derived from the Didot roman.

The founders Berthold still own his original matrices which they bought (from F.H. Brockhaus) in 1918. Berthold's Walbaum was cast from these. Walbaum's types became available in Britain through the Curwen Press in 1925 and some Continental sizes of Monotype Walbaum were available after 1930.

Frederic Warde, 1894-1939

Arrighi, 379

Frederic Warde was the husband of Beatrice Warde, the type publicist and (as Paul Beaujon) type scholar.

In 1926 he published *The Calligraphic Models of Ludovico Degli Arrighi* a complete facsimile of a book by the sixteenth century writing master. The introduction to this book, by Stanley Morison, was set in a new italic modelled on Arrighi's and cut by Georges Plumet. The design of this italic, Arrighi, is generally attributed to Warde although James Moran, in his book on Morison, disputes this. He adapted this first Arrighi italic for Monotype to use with Bruce Rodger's Centaur in 1929, this version is called Centaur Italic.

Emery Walker, see Thomas J. Cobden Sanderson, p.269

Emil Rudolf Weiss, 1875-1943

Weiss, 98

Professor Emil Rudolf Weiss was interested in many aspects of art and design and had already established himself in other areas before the Bauer foundry encouraged him to turn his attention to typefaces. Bauer had a policy of commissioning types from graphic artists and all three of Weiss's types (plus a number of ornaments) were designed for them. The best known, Weiss Antiqua, evolved very slowly. It can be identified by its distinctive 'upside-down' S.

Alexander Wilson, 1714-1784

In 1742 Alexander Wilson set up a type foundry in St Andrews. This foundry, which later moved to Glasgow, ended the dependence of Scottish printers on types brought in from London and the Netherlands, indeed it was to become a serious rival to London foundries. While Alexander Wilson ran the foundry (originally with a partner) it produced types which were influenced by the work of Caslon and Baskerville.

Notable cutters to work for the Wilson foundry include Richard Austin, who cut a modern face for them, and Johann Bauer who was later to start his own foundry in Frankfurt. The Miller Foundry in Edinburgh was started by an ex-manager of Wilson's, and The Wilson Foundry itself was to open an Edinburgh branch (Bauer trained here and Alexander's grandson kept this branch open when he transferred the foundry's main operation to London in 1834).

In this century English Roman No. 1, a Wilson Foundry type though possibly not designed by Alexander Wilson himself, served as the model for Hans Mardersteig's Fontana, designed for Collins of Glasgow in 1936.

Berthold Wolpe, 1905-1989

Albertus, 218
Pegasus, 235

Berthold Wolpe, born in Offenbach near Frankfurt in 1905, spent the greater part of his working life in England. From 1941-1975 he designed book-jackets for the publishers Faber & Faber, creating as many as 1500 designs. His best known type is Albertus which was commissioned by Stanley Morison of the Monotype Corporation. He taught lettering to students at Camberwell College of Art and the Royal College of Art, London. A retrospective exhibition of his work was held at the Victoria and Albert Museum in London in 1980 to mark his 75th birthday.

Hermann Zapf, b.1918

Aldus, 75
Comenius, 125
Kompact, 451
Melior, 138
Optima, 268
Orion, 139
Palatino, 84
Sapphire, 546
Zapf Book, 169/443
Zapf Chancery, 316
Zapf International, 150

Hermann Zapf is a prolific type designer and a notable writer on type. He spent the early part of his career working for the Stempel foundry in Germany and his work helped to fill the shortage of designs for roman typefaces that existed in West Germany after the war (the main source of such types, Leipzig, having gone to the East).

Although he was to resign this post in 1956 to spend more time on other work this was to be a particularly productive time for him. Zapf faces of this period include Palantino, a design based on Renaissance forms which was much admired and quickly taken up by other foundries.

In 1958 Zapf designed Optima, at that time an unclassifiable face but one which Zapf himself called a serifless roman. It was inspired by inscriptional lettering he had seen in Florence, and is probably his best known typeface.

Since leaving Stempel Zapf has created typefaces for a number of other companies including Berthold, Hell Digiset, Mergenthaler Linotype, Hallmark Cards, and ITC. He has designed new faces for filmsetting and digitisation as well as overseeing the transfer of many of his older designs to the new systems. In 1977 he was made Professor of Typographic Computer Programming at Rochester Institute of Technology in New York.

Bibliography/Further Reading

Apicella, Pomeranz & Wiatt. *The Concise Guide to Type Identification*. New York: Design Press, 1990.

Biggs, John R. *An Approach to Type*. London: Blandford Press, 1949.

British Standards Institution, *Typeface Nomenclature and Classification*. (BS 2961), 1967.

Carter, Sebastian. *Twentieth Century Type Designers*. New York: Taplinger, 1987.

Dowding, Geoffrey. *An Introduction to the History of Printing Types*. London: Wace & Company Limited, 1961.

Gates, John. *Type*. New York: Watson-Guptill Publications, 1973.

Gottschall, Edward M. *Typographic Communications Today*. Cambridge, MA: MIT Press, 1989.

Haley, Allan. *A Guide to In-House Typography & Design*. London: Robert Hale Limited, 1981.

Haley, Allan. *Phototypography*. New York: Charles Scribner's Sons, 1980.

Jaspert, Berry & Johnson. *Encyclopaedia of Typefaces*. New York: Sterling, 1962, 1970 and 1983 editions.

Jongejans. *Typefaces*. Wolters-Noordhoff/steen drukkerij de Jong & Co. Hilversum. c. 1980.

Karch, Robert R. *How to Recognise Typefaces*. London: McKnight & McKnight, 1959.

Lieberman. *Types of Typefaces and How to Recognise Them*. New York: Sterling, 1967.

McClean, Ruari. *Typography*. New York: Thames and Hudson, 1980.

Merriman, Frank. *Type Comparison Book*. The Advertising Typographers Association of America, Inc., 1965.

Monotype Corporation, Student's type study leaflets

Rosen, Benjamin. *Type and Typography*. New York: Van Nostrand Reinhold, 1976.

Sutton, James & Bartram, Alan. *An Atlas of Typeforms*. New York: Hastings, 1968.

Wheatley, W.F. *Typeface Analogue*. Arlington, VA: National Composition Association, 1988.

Catalogues & typeface information of the following companies were also referred to:

Alphatype Systems Limited
American Type Foundry
AM International Inc.
Amsterdam Foundry
Association Typographique Internationale (A. Typ.I)
H. Berthold AG
Bobst SA (Bobstgraphic Division)
Compugraphic Corporation
Harris Communications
International Typeface Corporation (ITC)
ITEK Corporation
Linotype-Paul Limited
Letraset UK Limited
Mecanorma
Mergenthaler, Linotype, Stempel, Haas
The Monotype Corportion
Mouldtype Foundry Limited
Stephenson, Blake & Company Limited
Tetterode-Nederland (Lettertypen)
Yendall & Company Limited (Riscatype)

TYPEFOUNDRY NAMES

Foundry	Abbreviation
AM International	AM
American Type Founders	ATF
Alphatype Corp.	Alpha
Apple Computers, Inc.	Apple
Autologic, Inc.	Auto
Baltimore Type Foundry	Baltimore
Bauersche Giesserie (Germany)	Bauer
H. Berthold AG (Germany)	Berthold
Bitstream, Inc.	Bitstream
H.W. Caslon (England)	Caslon
Compugraphic Corp.	CG
Deberney & Peignot (France)	D&P
Dearborn Foundry	Dearborn
Fonts/Ingrama SA (Spain)	Fonts
Haas'sche Schriftgiesserei AG (Germany)	Haas
Harris Graphics Corp.	Harris
International Business Machines Corp.	IBM
Information International Inc.	III
International Typeface Corp.	ITC
Intertype Company	Intertype
ITEK Composition System	Itek
Klingspor	Klingspor
Ludwig & Meyer GmbH (Germany)	L&M
Lanston Monotype	Lanston
Letraset Ltd. (England)	Letraset
Linotype AG (Germany)	Lino
Ludlow Typography Company	Ludlow
Merganthaler Linotype Co.	Merg
Monotype Corporation, Ltd. (England)	Mono
Societa Nebiolo (Italy)	Nebiolo
Neufville, SA (Spain)	Neufville
Olive	Olive
Photon, Inc.	Photon
Quality Micro Systems, Inc.	QMS
Scangraphic Dr. Boger GmbH (Germany)	Scan
Simoncini (Italy)	Simoncini
D. Stempel AG (Germany)	Stempel
Stephenson & Blake (England)	Stephenson
TypeSpectra	Typespectra
Typoart (Germany)	Typoart
J. Wagner (Germany)	Wagner
Wang Graphic Systems, Inc.	Wang
C.E. Weber (Germany)	Weber
Xerox Corp.	Xerox

INDEX

INDEX

D

E

F

G

H

INDEX

I

J

K

L

M

N

O

P

Q

R

S

INDEX

Z